Schomburg Studies on the Black Experience

Schomburg Studies on the Black Experience

Howard Dodson, *Managing Editor*
Colin Palmer, *Series Editor*

Ideology, Identity, and Assumptions
Cultural Life
Origins

SSBE Schomburg Studies on the Black Experience

Origins

Edited by Howard Dodson *and* Colin Palmer

 The New York Public Library

 SCHOMBURG CENTER FOR RESEARCH
IN BLACK CULTURE

 Michigan State University Press • *East Lansing*

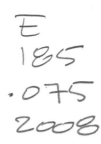
Copyright © 2008 by ProQuest LLC

♾ The paper used in this publication meets the minimum requirements of ANSI/NISO Z39.48-1992 (R 1997) (Permanence of Paper).

 Michigan State University Press
East Lansing, Michigan 48823-5245

Printed and bound in the United States of America.

14 13 12 11 10 09 08   1 2 3 4 5 6 7 8 9 10

LIBRARY OF CONGRESS CATALOGING-IN-PUBLICATION DATA
Origins / edited by Howard Dodson and Colin A. Palmer.
p. cm. — (Schomburg studies on the Black experience)
Includes bibliographical references.
ISBN 978-0-87013-817-1 (pbk. : alk. paper)
1. African Americans—History. 2. Africans—America—History. 3. Blacks—America—History. 4. African diaspora. 5. United States—Race relations. 6. America—Race relations. 7. African Americans—Historiography. 8. Africans—America—Historiography. 9. Blacks—America—Historiography. 10. African Americans—Study and teaching.
I. Dodson, Howard. II. Palmer, Colin A., 1942–
E185.O75 2008
973'.0496073—dc22
2008014988

Cover and book design by Sharp Des!gns, Inc., Lansing, MI

Visit Michigan State University Press on the World Wide Web at www.msupress.msu.edu

Contents

Introduction

Howard Dodson

The Schomburg Center for Research in Black Culture, the ProQuest Company, and Michigan State University Press are pleased to present this unique research, study, and teaching resource. In the more than thirty-five years since the field of black studies established its presence in American higher education, the volume of research, writing, and publications on the global black experience has increased exponentially. Scholars in African American and African Diasporan studies have contributed in significant ways to the development of this new knowledge. So have scholars in mainstream disciplines in the United States and Europe, as well as scholars and intellectuals in Africa and throughout the Americas. When added to the extraordinary volume of research resources on the black experience that existed before the coming of Black Studies, the challenge of selecting appropriate materials for research, for study, and for teaching has become extremely difficult. Schomburg Studies on the Black Experience is a resource designed to assist users in making such choices.

This project had its origins some fifteen years ago. In the course of a conversation with a publisher about what kinds of reference works would be of greatest use to students and scholars in the developing field of African American Studies, I proposed that we jointly publish a judiciously curated collection of 25 to 30 volumes on major themes in African American Studies.

At the time, I envisioned a process by which leading authorities on major themes in the field would write critical reviews of the scholarship, as well as select articles and book chapters that were essential to grounding oneself on the subject matter. I also envisioned the author/editor of each thematic volume projecting an agenda for future research on the topic.

The late Dr. Ruth Simms Hamilton and her African Diasporan Studies Program at Michigan State University collaborated with the Schomburg Center in identifying themes, selecting contributing editors, and commissioning volumes. Well into this ambitious project, the publisher became overextended and was obliged to cancel it. When the staff at ProQuest came to the Schomburg Center looking for an intellectual framework in which to develop an on-line resource on African American Studies, I proposed to revisit the project conceived more than a decade earlier. The resulting website is an on-line realization of my initial vision, which has now come full circle and is finally being published in book form.

Both the electronic and the printed editions of Schomburg Studies on the Black Experience contain a critical review essay for each theme, recommendations for essential readings, and research questions for the future. Extensive bibliographies, lists of primary research materials, timelines, and other resources are also included. Included in the online edition are many full-text recommended readings, as well as a multimedia library.

An ideal resource for faculty curriculum preparation and research, the online version of the Schomburg Studies on the Black Experience offers a dynamic online teaching and learning environment. Easily searchable across all of the diverse content, the electronic version allows users to select and store their search results, full-text key resources, bibliographic records, and multimedia records in their personal MyArchive section of the database, for retrieval at any time. Users may also add their annotations and create a reading list in their MyArchive space. Over 2,000 images and 200 video clips add a rich dimension to each topic. More information about the database may be found at: *http://ssbe.chadwyck.com.*

Schomburg Studies on the Black Experience offers users a way to understand the evolution of scholarship on the selected themes and to access the essential literature that supports it. Schomburg Studies affirms both the quantity and the quality of the intellectual underpinnings of Black Studies

Substantive academic programs are measured by the quality of intellectual/scholarly content that undergirds them. Of course, administrative structures are necessary and trained faculty are essential. But without a solid, well-researched, authenticated body of knowledge about their subject matter, academic programs are doomed to fail.

· · · · · · · · ·

The field of African American or Black Studies emerged out of the political and cultural renaissance among African Americans that exploded on the American national scene in the wake of the assassination of Dr. Martin Luther King, Jr., in April 1968. Stokely Carmichael and Willie Ricks of the Student Nonviolent Coordinating Committee had announced the emergence of this new black consciousness movement in 1966 when they had asserted the need for Black Power at the Meredith March Against Fear in Mississippi. King's death transformed their plea into a demand. Eventually, every sector of American society was faced with the challenge of accommodating an assertive, newly conscious, critically thinking African American presence in all spheres of human endeavor. The urban rebellions that started in the mid 1960s and intensified after King's death were the catalyst for the emergence of Black Studies in the American academy.

The political context out of which Black Studies came into existence led many of its critics to question the intellectual viability of the field. What the critics implied by raising this question was that there was not sufficient content—intellectual/scholarly resources—to support sustained study of the history and cultural legacy of people of African descent. What they obviously did not know was that the Schomburg Center for Research in Black Culture and the Moorland/Spingarn Research Center were repositories of thousands of books and millions of pages of documents on the black experience worldwide. Central to the development of the Schomburg and Moorland/Spingarn collections was a nascent body of scholarship by African American and African descended scholars. That material, dating back to the nineteenth century, provides the foundations of the black intellectual tradition. Most of the work by these intellectuals took place outside of the academy.

One of the pioneering organized efforts to promote scholarship on the black experience among African Americans was the American Negro

Academy (ANA), founded in 1897 by Episcopalian minister and intellectual Rev. Alexander Crummell. The ANA was "an organization of Colored authors, scholars and artists" that included among its objectives: "to promote the publication of literary and scholarly works"; "to aid, by publications, vindication of the race from vicious assaults in all the lines of learning and truth"; and "to publish, if possible, at least once a year an 'Annual' of original articles upon various Literary, Historical and Philosophical topics, of a racial nature, by selected members, and by these and diverse other means, to raise the standard of intellectual endeavor among American Negroes."[1] The Academy eventually counted among its members eminent African American intellectual luminaries such as Carter G. Woodson, W. E. B. Du Bois, and Arturo Alfonso Schomburg, all of whom would become major catalysts in the development of a black (American) intellectual tradition.

Schomburg, the renowned bibliophile and self-taught historian, had teamed up with New York–based journalist and sponsor of his membership in the Academy John E. Bruce, to found the Negro Society for Historical Research in 1911. The Society became a global network of black nationalists, largely lay historians, and counted among its membership Edward Wilmot Blyden of Sierra Leone, J. E. Casely Hayford of the Gold Coast (Ghana), General Evaristo Estenoz of Cuba, and journalist Pedro C. Timothee of San Juan, Puerto Rico.[2] With Bruce as president and Schomburg as secretary, the Society collected and loaned books, sponsored lectures, and published occasional papers on black-related themes. Schomburg's larger contribution to promoting scholarship on the global black experience, however, was as a bibliophile. His personal collection of more than 10,000 items became the foundation on which today's Schomburg Center rests. Over the years, the Schomburg Center has become the most comprehensive public research library in the world devoted exclusively to documenting and interpreting the black experience worldwide.

Both Du Bois and Woodson were Harvard University trained historians. Together, they pioneered the development of twentieth-century scholarship on the black experience. Following his graduation from Harvard in 1895 with a PhD, Du Bois organized and developed a major program of research on the black condition at Atlanta University. His Atlanta University Conferences, which started in 1895 and continued through 1910, summarized research and public policy regarding the black condition, the proceedings of which were published. In addition, over the course of his 95 years, he founded and edited the NAACP's *Crisis*, founded and edited Atlanta University's scholarly journal *Phylon*, and published some of the classic works in African American and African Diasporan scholarship.

Woodson earned his PhD from Harvard in 1912. Three years later he organized the Association for the Study of Negro Life and History, and a year later (1916) he began to publish the *Journal of Negro History*, the first significant scholarly journal devoted to the study of black life. Woodson published the quarterly journal until his death in 1950 without ever missing an issue. *The Journal of Negro History* provided scholars (black and white) a vehicle through which to publish research findings on the black experience. Woodson's Associated Publishers offered scholars a vehicle through which to publish book-length monographs. As founder of Negro History Week (now Black History Month), Woodson promoted the study of the black experience in schools, churches and other public settings and inspired new generations to pursue scholarly careers devoted to research and study of the black experience. His pioneering contributions earned him the title of "father of black history."

By the 1960s, the tradition of black intellectuals—lay and academic—working to rescue and reconstruct the true history and cultural legacy of people of African descent had been well established. Except in a few historically black colleges and universities, however, teaching based on this knowledge had not been institutionalized. Even in the historically black colleges and universities, the course offerings were random—more a reflection of individual teachers' interests than part of a formal African American Studies curriculum. The Black Studies Movement, a by-product of the Black Power Movement of the late 1960s, brought the black intellectual tradition into the academy.

Black students were recruited to enroll in mainstream universities in the wake of King's assassination and the attendant urban uprisings. What students found on these campuses was not very inviting—no black faculty members, no black administrators, few if any courses on the black experience, and research by mainstream scholars that affirmed and reinforced negative characterizations of people of African descent. Conspicuously absent was any acknowledgement of the existence of a black intellectual tradition.

Shortly after King's assassination, Columbia University in conjunction with WCBS-TV launched a project to produce 108 half-hour programs on African American history. Billed as an eighteen-week college-level course, *Black Heritage: A History of Afro-Americans* was the largest single undertaking by a commercial television station to present the history of African Americans to a broad, general public. Vincent Harding, chairman of the History and Sociology Departments at Spelman College in Atlanta, Georgia, served as chair of the project's advisory board, and John Henrik Clarke as the project consultant. These two scholars—Harding, a Columbia PhD in history who was teaching at an historically black college, and Clarke, a widely respected lay historian—assembled a faculty of some thirty scholars, artists, and intellectuals to deliver the content of this televised course. Lecturers included leading scholars from historically black colleges, lay historians, activists/intellectuals from the civil rights movement, artists and art critics within and outside of the mainstream academy, and a few black and white scholars from mainstream institutions who specialized in black history. Significantly, the quality of the lectures demonstrated to the viewing public as well as to the academy that there was, indeed, sufficient intellectual content to offer substantive courses, programs, and departments in African American Studies.

On college and university campuses across the country, black students demanded change in their respective academic environments—changes in the ratio of black students to white students; changes in the number of black faculty and administrators employed on the campuses; changes in the college and university curriculums to more adequately reflect the presence and roles of people of African descent in world affairs; and, yes, the establishment of Black Studies programs and departments to better organize and coordinate research and teaching on the black experience.

College and university administrators responded in uneven ways. San Francisco State College in California yielded to organized student pressures, demonstrations, and a strike by establishing a Black Studies program in 1968. Yale University, through black student prodding and leadership, organized a national symposium on Black Studies, Black Studies in the University, in

1968. Riding on the momentum of the symposium, a student-faculty committee put together a proposal to establish an Afro-American Studies Program at Yale. On December 12, 1968, the Yale College faculty approved the first degree-granting Afro-American Studies program at a major university in the United States. In time, more than three hundred colleges and universities established Black Studies programs or departments. The major challenge facing most of them was not the intellectual foundations on which such programs and departments would rest, but who would teach courses in African American Studies. Whereas San Francisco State students had demanded all black faculty members, Yale, from the inception of the Black Studies program idea, had included white scholars who specialized in African American–related themes in their faculty ranks. In the furious competition for qualified faculty members that ensued, new opportunities opened on mainstream university campuses for African American, Caribbean, and African scholars.

Recruiters for Black Studies programs at mainstream universities first turned to historically black colleges. Hundreds of black college faculty members were enticed to take positions in Black Studies programs and departments. Advanced African American graduate students were also targeted. African and Caribbean scholars who specialized in African, African American, or Caribbean subjects were also recruited as universities and Black Studies program directors tried to strengthen the intellectual credibility of their faculties.

At the same time, colleges and universities collaborated with foundations to offer graduate study opportunities for individuals interested in African American and African Diasporan themes. Given the fact that there were no graduate study programs in African American Studies, students enrolled in traditional disciplines with major or minor emphasis in African American and African Diasporan related themes. The Ford Foundation and the Andrew W. Mellon Foundation were among those most active in promoting graduate study in the field.

Black student activism led black scholars and intellectuals to launch their own organizing efforts. Sometimes, groups of black scholars within mainstream professional and academic organizations formed themselves into black caucuses within the organization to increase black membership and promote advancement opportunities in the discipline. They also used these formations to create opportunities for members to present papers on African American themes. The Caucus of Black Economists (1969) and the Caucus of Black Sociologists (1969) were among those that chose to work within their respective mainstream professional organizations. Others chose to form their own independent professional organizations. The National Association of Black Psychologists (1968), the National Conference of Black Political Scientists (1969), and the African Heritage Studies Association (1967) are among the associations of scholars that chose to take the independent route.

Research centers and institutes were also established to organize and coordinate the research activities of scholars and intellectuals related to the field. Many of those who participated in the CBS Black Heritage Series became affiliated with the Institute of the Black World, founded by Vincent Harding in 1969 as the research arm of the Martin Luther King, Jr. Center in Atlanta, Georgia. The Institute and Harding broke with the King Center a year later and established an independent think tank of black intellectuals that included on its agenda promoting the development of black studies and scholarship on the black experience.

The Black Economic Research Center was also founded in 1969. Black economist Robert Brown spearheaded the founding of the Center as well as the Center's scholarly journal, *The Review of Black Political Economy*. The Center also sponsored and supported research on the black economic condition, including a major study and initiative to prevent the loss of black-owned land in the American South. *The Review of Black Political Economy*, a quarterly, provided a forum in which black economists and others could carry on sustained, critical dialogues on themes affecting the economic well-being of blacks. The Black World Foundation, a nonprofit organization, was founded in the San Francisco Bay area in 1969 by Nathan Hare and Robert Chrisman to "provide analysis, research and symposium on all the basic issues that concern Black America." The Foundation published a monthly journal, *The Black Scholar*, which became one of the major organs for black intellectuals seeking to present research and analysis on themes affecting black people worldwide. A year later, Molefi Asante (aka Arthur L. Smith) founded the *Journal of Black Studies*, sponsored by the UCLA Center for the Study of Afro-American History and Culture (1970). Observing that "sustained intellectual development in this area [Afro-American Studies] . . . cannot be based upon awakening rhetoric," Smith/Asante contended that the purpose of the journal was to "nurture the expanding community of scholars whose interests are in adding to the factual, analytical and evaluative bases upon which Black Studies must be established." Johnson Publication's *Negro Digest/Black World*, under the editorship of Hoyt Fuller, served a similar function, as did the longstanding movement journal *Freedomways*, based in New York. At the same time, most of the major scholarly journals of mainstream professional disciplinary associations made space for more frequent articles and occasional special issues on black-related themes.

Publishers, acknowledging the emergence of this new field of study in the academy, rushed to supply content to support these new academic programs. Publishing houses "discovered" places like the Schomburg Center and the Moorland-Spingarn Research Center, where they could go to package major reprint series in the field. Significant works by black scholars that had received little or no attention by the academy when they were originally published were reprinted along with historic texts that had long since been out of print. *The Dictionary Catalogs* of the Schomburg Center and the Moorland-Spingarn Collections were published and distributed to college and university librarians across the country to serve as guides for building research collections in the field. Microfilm and fiche publishers also created reprint collections. African American and African intellectuals established their own publishing houses to give voice to authors to whom mainstream publishers had turned a deaf ear. In addition to Johnson Publications, Haki Madhubuti (Don L. Lee) and Dudley Randall, among others, established their own presses to publish and disseminate works by black writers.

In the three decades since those formative years, Black Studies programs and departments have proliferated throughout the country. Most are based in part on the Yale University model in which faculty members hold joint appointments in a traditional disciplinary department and the African American Studies program. But there are also departments that award degrees in African American Studies, whose faculty members are only accountable to their department. Finally, in recent years, masters- and doctoral-degree programs in African American Studies have begun to make their presence felt in American universities.

Graduate study in the field was nurtured throughout the 1970s and 1980s through graduate fellowships in African American and African Diasporan Studies funded by the Ford, Mellon, and other foundations. While this support tapered off in the 1990s, the overall decline in humanities PhDs has sparked new interest in the foundation community in supporting graduate level education and faculty development efforts. The National Endowment for the Humanities, through its summer seminars and fellowships programs, has also been supporting the development of scholars and scholarship in the field. Finally, each of the traditional academic disciplines, especially in the humanities and social sciences, has been obliged to explore more fully than ever before, the African American (as well as the Hispanic, Asian, and Native American) experience in their research, publications, and pedagogy.

As a consequence, the last three decades have witnessed the publication of more research and scholarship on the global black experience than all the previous decades/centuries combined. The existence of such an expansive intellectual basis for the development of black studies is what makes a project like Schomburg Studies on the Black Experience necessary. We thank Colin Palmer, managing editor, and all of the contributing editors for making Schomburg Studies possible. And we thank the thousands of scholars and intellectuals who have taken the African American and African Diasporan experience seriously and have contributed to the development of the intellectual foundations of the field. Thanks to their work, the intellectual validity of Black Studies is no longer a question.

• •

NOTES

1. William M. Banks, *Black Intellectuals: Race and Responsibility in American Life* (New York: Norton, 1996), 58.
2. Elinor Des Verney Sinnette, *Arthur Alfonso Schomburg, Black Bibliophile and Collector: A Biography* (New York: New York Public Library, Distributed by Wayne State University Press 1989), 42–43.

Slavery in the Americas: A Survey of the Scholarship

Michael A. Gomez

Abstract

The historiography of slavery throughout the Americas, from its inception to its abolition, is discussed. Given the hemispheric-wide focus, the vast literature will be used to identify principal articles and book chapters that simultaneously represent the examination of both a particular phenomenon and a specific region or site. Stated differently, the essay employs articles/chapters written in English, French, Spanish, and Portuguese that address the primary thematic concerns of slavery studies—the economics of slavery, the treatment of the enslaved, the cultures of Africans and their descendants in the Americas within servile contexts, their communities and social relations, and various manifestations of resistance. There is also a discussion of the question of mediation, and the various recovery mechanisms by which the voices and perspectives of the enslaved are conveyed.

To this end, each theme is introduced by reference to a lead article/chapter that also provides insight into a particular geographic location, and that responds to preceding literatures in ways that both sum up the major debates and indicate the probable trajectories. Secondary and tertiary references are made to materials that relate to the lead document. This allows for the development of a "conversation" among the various materials that will effectively serve as a historiographic exercise, as it also opens up spaces for an intra-hemispheric dialogue too often inhibited by the artificial constraints of nation-state preoccupations.

The Economics of Slavery and the Treatment of Slaves

A discussion of slavery in the Americas is too complex and wide-ranging to be adequately encapsulated in the space available here. The limited objective here, therefore, is to examine aspects of slavery that will allow for a consideration of important literature on slavery in such a way as to provide some coverage of various sites within the western hemisphere. Essential materials are mentioned in the key resources section; however, references are made to additional sources both in the text and in the accompanying bibliography.

To summarize briefly, enslaved Africans began arriving in the Americas within ten years of Columbus's 1492 voyage. European dependency upon enslaved African labor was the consequence of several factors, including the growth of sugar cane cultivation in the Mediterranean world since the twelfth century; the end of Muslim-Christian conflicts in the Black Sea region (1453) and Iberia (1492), from which had come most of the servile labor used for sugar cane cultivation; and seafaring improvements that allowed Europeans to navigate the Atlantic coast of Africa. David Brion Davis's *Slavery and Human Progress*; and John Thornton's *Africa and Africans in the Making of the Atlantic World, 1400–1800* both contain very useful chapters describing this process, while A. J. R. Russell-Wood's *A World on the Move* discusses Iberian developments in relation to the slave trade.

Early destinations for African slaves included Hispaniola, Cuba, and other territories claimed by the Spanish. Brazil also emerged as an important receptor in the sixteenth century, accounting for some 42 percent of all captive Africans in the Americas for the whole of the eighteenth century. By 1867, nearly 90 percent of the conservatively estimated 11 to 13 million Africans exported through the transatlantic slave trade were deposited in Brazil and the Caribbean, while North America brought in 7 percent or fewer.

Certainly one of the most important and contentious issues flowing out of a recognition of the African presence in the Americas has been the nature of their contribution. Stated in the form of a question, what were the contributions of enslaved Africans and their descendants, not only to the economies of territories in the Americas, but also to those of Europe? Especially with respect to the Caribbean, there can be little doubt that the seminal response to this question was the publication of Eric Williams's classic *Capitalism and Slavery*. In it, Williams promotes the thesis that beyond the New World, the metropolitan economies themselves received enormous benefits from both the slave trade and the ensuing servile economies in the colonies, such that European port cities, as well as European international commerce, were greatly stimulated. To be more precise, the Industrial Revolution itself was substantially financed by the export and labor of the enslaved. Williams turns the British imperialist school of historical writing on its head, inverting the cone by emphasizing in particular the Caribbean contribution to British economic success, rather than the reverse. He further argues that capitalism's development, rather than European moralism, led to the demise of slavery. The extraordinary appeal of the Williams thesis continues to reverberate some sixty years after its publication and serves as the basis for scholarly contestation. Volumes have been devoted to the debate itself, and Barry Higman's work, *Slave Populations of the British Caribbean, 1807–1834*, serves as a useful corrective.[1] Even so, Williams's influence can still be discerned in the most recent scholarship related to the topic.[2]

The Williams thesis, which was originally framed within a western-hemispheric context, can obviously be extended to other American sectors. As for the Caribbean itself, the production of staples, in particular sugar, accounted for most of the value of exports from such islands as Haiti and Cuba, whereas indigo, tobacco, coffee, and cocoa were produced in significant quantities and represented a substantial proportion of island revenue. Regarding what later became the United States, the fact that the American South was producing 60 percent of the world's cotton by 1840, representing over 50 percent of the value of all U.S. exports, meant that its production and export was not only critical to manufacturing and shipping in the North, but was also the basis for the textile industry in western Europe—so much so that there were many who believed England and France would find it in their economic interests to support the South's secession and fight for independence.

There are a vast number of studies devoted to the assorted agricultural components of slavery—rice, indigo, tobacco, coffee, cacao, cocoa, etc. As sugar cane production constituted the economic enterprise around which the labor of most of the enslaved was centered, however, there are several publications that together form the basis of subsequent trajectories of studies of sugar and its impact upon the Americas, especially the Caribbean. Eric Williams's *From Columbus to Castro* provides an introduction to the sugar industry in the Caribbean, as does Moreno Fraginals's article on the Spanish-speaking Caribbean, "Plantations in the Caribbean: Cuba, Puerto Rico and the Dominican Republic in the late nineteenth century." Regarding Brazil, Schwartz's *Sugar Plantations* is an important contribution, while Mintz's chapter, "Production," in *Sweetness and Power* is also useful.

A theme closely related to the question of the economic contributions of the enslaved concerns their treatment, by which is meant here the quotidian experiences of their condition. (The clearly related matter of family constitutes a separate discussion in this essay.) The literature has evolved over the last sixty years from a static profile of slavery in which treatment was differentiated according to regime—English, French, Spanish, Portuguese, Dutch—and the cultural values associated with the enslaving and colonizing power. Based upon the early work of Stanley Elkins's *Slavery: A Problem in American Institutional and Intellectual Life*; Frank Tannenbaum's *Slave and Citizen*; and Gilberto Freyre's *Casa-grande e senzala*, the enslaved experience in Spanish- and Portuguese-claimed territories was previously understood to be more "benign" than that of the English counterpart, and very much influenced by the policies of the Catholic Church. While there is some factual basis for such distinctions, especially with regard to the maintenance of slave families (when ecclesiastical law was in fact enforced), more recent research has underscored just how brutish and cruel slavery in Spanish- and Portuguese-speaking lands could be, offering a much more nuanced approach to the inquiry.

Literature addressing the treatment of the enslaved by slaveholders and slaveholding societies is extensive; perhaps one of the more electric moments of the historiographical progression came out of the rise of considerations of econometrics within the history of economics, known as "cliometrics." This facilitated reliance upon data that could be quantified, and was at some distance from such "impressionistic" and therefore less reliable sources as the narratives of former slaves and abolitionist publications. Robert Fogel and Stanley Engerman's *Time on the Cross* challenged just about every established notion regarding the enslaved experience in North America, arguing that slaves were in fact relatively well fed, that punishment was infrequent, as were family separations, etc. The work directly challenged Kenneth Stampp's *Peculiar Institution*, which argued that coercion (read, "the whip") was necessary for the maintenance of slavery.

The thrust of Fogel and Engerman's work was in the general direction of another influential publication on North American slavery, Eugene Genovese's *Roll, Jordan, Roll*, in which the enslaved community was seen as somewhat participatory in their own predicament by virtue of their subscription to the role of the slaveholder as paterfamilias, from whom their personhoods could be (qualifiably) affirmed. In this way, Genovese's scholarship is not unrelated to an older, apologist school led by U. B. Phillips—see, for example, *American Negro Slavery: A Survey of the Supply, Employment, and Control of Negro Labor as Determined by the Plantation Regime.* The most immediate response to Fogel and Engerman came from Herbert Gutman in his *Slavery and the Numbers Game,* and *The Black Family in Slavery and Freedom,* effectively responding to several points raised by the cliometricians. At least one consequence of the debate was to encourage historians of slavery to weigh their sources more carefully, and to approach them more critically. John Blassingame's *Slave Community,* and Nathan Huggins's *Black Odyssey,* on the other hand, began to re-envision and emphasize the social and cultural autonomy of the enslaved in ways that will be discussed subsequently in this essay.

Perhaps the subject of the enslaved's treatment in the Caribbean is best represented by Franklin Knight's *Slave Society in Cuba*; and Rebecca Scott's *Slave Emancipation in Cuba,* the latter of which represents the culmination of a process whereby earlier arguments regarding metropolitan moralism and economic determinism as competing explanatory strategies for slavery's end are engaged and a new synthesis is achieved, one that embraces a complex set of interrelated factors whose pace was influenced by the agitation of the enslaved themselves. Scott also builds upon Manuel Moreno Fraginals's magisterial three-volume *El ingenio*, examining such questions as the relationship between mechanization and slave labor. As for Brazil, an important work remains Kátia M. de Queirós Mattoso's *To Be a Slave in Brazil*. Equally important for the English- and French-speaking Caribbean are Gabriel Debien's *Les esclaves aux Antilles*; Richard Dunn's *Sugar and Slaves*; and James Millette's *Society and Politics in Colonial Trinidad*. With respect to health and disease, the Kiples's work on the Caribbean, "Deficiency Diseases in the Caribbean," set standards for the kind of work that would follow.

Working Conditions, Women, and Family Life

Of course, the treatment of the enslaved was very much a function of their working conditions. Slavery in the Caribbean tended to be characterized both by large plantations of at least one hundred slaves and by routine planter absence; in contrast, convention required only twenty enslaved workers for a plantation to officially qualify as such in North America. Sugar cane production, largely confined to the Caribbean and Latin America (with exceptions such as the Mississippi basin) required women and men organized into groups to work eighteen hours a day on average, with the grinding season just as arduous as the planting and harvest periods. Those working on coffee plantations experienced a different seasonal system, while the cotton fields of North America required "sunup-to-sundown" labor during the harvest. Reference to varying agricultural schemes directs attention to the growth of studies that complicate slavery as a differentiated experience along lines of gender, region, and age, but also within the various economies. The enslaved were engaged in a variety of activities, from cultivating staples to raising livestock to diving for pearls to mining for gold and silver, and were skilled as coopers, carpenters, boilermen, wheelwrights, and so forth. Literature on slave experiences in urban areas can be examined in Mary Karasch's *Slave Life in Rio de Janeiro*; and John Blassingame's *Black New Orleans*.

Slaves work on a cotton plantation somewhere in the South around 1800. Cotton underpinned the southern economy, earning it the nickname of "King Cotton." As Great Britain became the first country in the world to industrialize, the insatiable demands of the great mills in England were met by the cotton fields of South Carolina, Georgia, and other Southern states. But cotton growing was a labor-intensive process, needing an almost limitless supply of cheap manpower to tend the plants, gather in the crop, separate seeds from the raw cotton, bale it, and move it out to the ports and harbors. White plantation owners relied on slavery, and it is thought that around 20,000 slaves were brought to Georgia and South Carolina in 1803 alone.

The slavery experience was also differentiated by gender. Of course, women and girls worked just as hard and at many of the same tasks as men and boys, especially on large plantations. In fact, sugar cane plantations required more female labor than did coffee because males were disproportionately used in subsequently processing the cane. Women and girls were susceptible to sexual exploitation in ways that males were not, and intimacies with white males could both carry consequences and create options otherwise closed, depending on the status of the male and the peculiarities of the circumstances and society in question. Markets were also often a female preserve wherever they were allowed to participate, and this was especially true in the

Caribbean. The contributions to this category of analysis stress the plight of women; such studies have increased considerably over the last forty years, and include works that focus on specific regions as well as those attempting a transnational, western-hemispheric approach that is often comparative in structure. With respect to the Caribbean, Rhoda Reddock's "Women and Slavery in the Caribbean: A Feminist Perspective," and "Women and the Slave Plantation Economy in the Caribbean" are forerunners to her important *Women, Labour, and Politics in Trinidad and Tobago: A History*. The historiography of the region includes such critical works as Hilary Beckles's *Natural Rebels: A Social History of Enslaved Black Women in Barbados*; Marietta Morrissey's *Slave Women in the New World: Gender Stratification in the Caribbean*; Barbara Bush's *Slave Women in Caribbean Society*; Lorna Simmonds's "Slave Higglering in Jamaica, 1780–1834"; Bernard Moitt's "Gender and Slavery: Women and the Plantation Experience in the Caribbean before 1848"; and a volume edited by Verene Shepherd et al., *Engendering History*. Perhaps much of this work was anticipated by Lucille Mathurin-Mair's *The Rebel Woman in the British West Indies during Slavery*, in which she demonstrated the leadership of women in the resistance to slavery.

Joseph C. Dorsey's "Women Without History: Slavery and the International Politics of Partus Sequitur Ventrem in the Spanish Caribbean" is a very useful source for Latin America. Regarding the United States, Deborah G. White's *Ar'n't I a Woman*; Jacqueline Jones's *Labor of Love, Labor of Sorrow*; and Elizabeth Fox-Genovese's *Within the Plantation Household* have received critical acclaim. In addition, there are several publications that place the experience of enslaved women in a transnational framework, the most useful of which is David Gaspar and Darlene Clark Hine's *More Than Chattel: Black Women and Slavery in the Americas* — see Hilary Beckles's contribution, "Black Female Slaves and White Households in Barbados." Earlier publications focusing on women (but not limited to slavery) include the trail-blazing compilation of Filomina Steady and Kenneth Bilby, *The Black Woman Cross-Culturally*; and Rosalyn Terborg-Penn and Andrea Rushing's *Women in Africa and the African Diaspora*.

Of course, closely related to the issues of women and gender in slavery is the matter of the slave family. Notwithstanding spatial considerations, the

A family of slaves gathers outside their homestead in South Carolina in 1862. Although the working lives of many slaves were hard, it was in the interest of slaveowners to ensure that slaves were fed, clothed, and provided with rudimentary living accommodation. Demand for cheap labor was such that slaves were encouraged to settle and raise families. The abolition of slavery denied white plantation owners the source of their cheap labor, but it also freed them of the obligation to provide for their workers.

literature often attempts to locate the "African family" as a beginning point, and then proceed with a discussion that follows trajectories of change in various American settings and periods. In the process, data often taken uncritically from anthropological sources on Africa are extrapolated onto New World landscapes, and by historians who may or may not be in a position to translate the material across methodological, disciplinary, cultural, and geographical boundaries, often resulting in unhelpful generalizations and misconceptions. As a consequence, issues surrounding the protocols of adult sexual relations, marriage and the question of polygamy, proscribed and nuclear families, "matriarchy" and "matriarchal societies," and so forth, all require further and much more careful research as they relate to African antecedents. In any event, correlations between African and American formulations must first consider new familial relations developed in the Middle Passage itself, as fictive kinship ties were established on the basis of common suffering, ties so strong that those who survived lived out their lives as relatives, even observing rules of exogamy.

Slaveholding in French and Spanish sectors of the Americas was ostensibly subject to the *Code Noir* and the *Siete Partidas,* laws that addressed various aspects of slavery as well as other matters. Such prescriptions also covered enslaved families, and this, with the support of the Catholic Church, generally encouraged the maintenance of nuclear families while discouraging their fracturing through individual sales. The theoretical often diverged from the lived experience, and slaveholders were not necessarily even aware of legalisms pertaining to slavery. Economic factors, however, were quite determinant in planter policies towards enslaved families, such that by 1790 the pressures to abolish the transatlantic slave trade forced slaveholders to embrace such pronatalist measures as alleviating work loads for near-term pregnant women and providing them with special houses or plantation hospitals. North American planters had long pursued policies that enhanced the ability of the enslaved to replicate themselves, but the mother-child bond was the only one of true significance. Slave marriages certainly had no legal standing.

For North America, alongside Gutman's work on the family, another important work is Brenda Stevenson's *Life in Black and White,* in which the author demonstrates attempts on the part of the enslaved in Virginia to achieve some degree of stability against tremendous odds. What emerges is a picture in which marriage is a shared aspiration among the enslaved, so that partners sold far from each other often remarried, and "abroad" marriages (between partners belonging to neighboring plantations and farms) were widespread. The unavoidable reality was that the male presence in the lives of wives and children was variable, while enslaved women often had little choice except to live as abroad wives and single mothers.

In addition to materials concerning women and gender in the Caribbean and Latin America cited above, there are several publications that merit consideration here. Barry Higman has written extensively on the question of family in specific Caribbean sites as well as the region in general: "African and Creole Slave Family Patterns in Trinidad"; "Household Structure and Fertility on Jamaican Slave Plantations: A Nineteenth-Century Example"; and "The Slave Family and Household in the British West Indies, 1800–1834." There is also Marietta Morrissey's instructive "Women's Work, Family Formation, and Reproduction among Caribbean Slaves." For the United States, Ann Malone's *Sweet Chariot: Slave Family and Household Structure in Nineteenth Century Louisiana* is a significant contribution. Those interested in more quantified discussions of such matters as fertility rates and related phenomena should begin with Herbert Klein and Stanley Engerman, "Fertility Differentials between Slaves in the United States and the British West Indies: A Note on Lactation Practices and Their Possible Implications"; and Jerome Handler and Robert Corruccini, "Weaning among West Indian Slaves: Historical and Bioanthropological Evidence from Barbados." Finally, Humphrey Lamur's work on Suriname—"Fertility Differentials on Three Slave Plantations in Suriname," and "The Slave Family in Colonial Nineteenth Century Suriname"—demonstrates the linkages in these topics.

Of course, several of these works do not address simply the enslaved family, but also the broader social context in which enslaved families were embedded. Stratifications within slaveholding societies, as they related to the enslaved, were multiple and inter-informative, with significant permutations per slaveholding society. Among the enslaved were the African-born and American-born (Creoles), and although acculturative experiences varied between the two groups, slaves born into that condition in the Americas had greater familiarity with European-derived cultural expressions, as a general rule, than did those who were captured in Africa and transported to the Americas. Greater facility with European languages, for example, could serve as one basis for labor differentiations among the enslaved. Those perceived as more intelligent or better disposed for certain kinds of nonagricultural labor could be chosen for tasks resulting in the acquisition of vocational skills, which, in turn, could lead to relatively "easier" lives as domestic servants, or to more opportunities to achieve personal freedom (through the accumulation of means to purchase individual liberty), or to both. Slaveholders based their decisions on labor distinctions on a variety of criteria, but perhaps the two most important were the reputations of certain ethnolinguistic African groups for certain types of labor (usually agricultural), and the extent to which the somatic representations of the enslaved approximated that of Europeans. The higher the intimacy of the work involved, the more European slaveholders preferred servants who looked like them. From North America through the Caribbean to Brazil, slaveholders consistently exhibited partialities of this nature. In many instances, the relative privileging of slaves does not always have its origins in miscegenation, but was often based upon phenotypic differences among Africans as perceived by whites.

So, there emerged a kaleidoscopic array of categories into which Africans and their descendants could be placed. They were enslaved and free, rural and urban, African and Creole, male and female. The classification "African" was by no means uncomplicated; individuals usually saw themselves as members of a group or community that could be defined lineally, territorially, religiously (especially with regard to Islam), and culturally (including but extending beyond religion), but they did not necessarily see themselves as "Africans." Creole-born individuals, therefore, were in many instances very aware of the specific cultural heritage of their African-born forbears, and this helped shape the development of Creole communities in a number of sites, especially in the Caribbean (in English-, French-, and Spanish-speaking isles). In other locations, such as what later became the United States, ethnolinguistic allegiances that were important in the eighteenth century began to give way in the nineteenth century to the rise of a new socioeconomic marker of status, "race."

Race and Culture

The concept of race significantly antedates the nineteenth century, and it can be argued that essentialist divisions of the human family go back at least to eighth- and ninth-century writings in Arabic about sub-Saharan Africa. Winthrop Jordan's *White over Black* remains a classic study of the shock northern Europeans experienced in their initial encounters with sub-Saharan Africans. In his autobiography, *The Interesting Narrative of Olaudah Equiano*, Equiano registered no less a surprise (trauma would be a better word) upon seeing whites for the first time. Within slaveholding societies in the Americas, race became a principal mechanism by which privileged whites maintained that power—that is, by reserving proscribed privilege and opportunity for those of appropriate race, and by restricting more significant arrogations of power through the artifice of racial privilege, such that disempowered whites would focus not on their lack of prerogative, but on their superior status vis-à-vis "blacks." Nonetheless, the African-descended also began to embrace race as a theory of mobilization. This is apparent, for example, in the United States in the Denmark Vesey conspiracy (1822), and in the Paul Bogle–led Morant Bay Rebellion in Jamaica (1865), in which the revolt was clearly organized on the basis of race rather than African ethnicity, which had previously characterized revolt in Jamaica (where uprisings were often described as Akan or Coromantee affairs).

Where races lived in close proximity to one another, it inevitably led to the creation of intermediate groups of varying mixtures of indigenous or Native American, African, and European ancestry. Depending upon the society, the number of categories for these middling groups could be considerable. In some places (such as Brazil), a myriad of distinctions crystallized into stable units within the social pantheon, whereas in others (such as the United States), various possible genetic combinations were consistently (though not always successfully) lumped into a single "mixed race" category. Notwithstanding the variety of site-specific configurations, these groups tended to serve as buffers between white privilege and black enslavement.

Related to the question of the modalities by which enslaved families and slave societies eked out their existence is the problematic of culture. Enslaved families necessarily moved through life in ways that involved religious, linguistic, and artistic expression. Standards of social engagement, as well as a range of values, connected to every aspect of life. Another way to state the matter is that the regime of slavery and its attendant extractions of labor, though demanding and extraordinarily intrusive, could not achieve the ultimate deprivation, the divestment of individuals of their humanity. So the question becomes, how did the enslaved choose to interpret and lead those aspects of their lives over which they exercised any modicum of control?

This has to be one of the more contentious issues among scholars of slavery, engendering lively and strenuous debate. The essence of the various disagreements concerns a series of tensions flowing from the interaction of the African antecedent with the American subsequent. The controversy begins in Africa itself: just how "African" were captives of the slave trade; that is, to what extent had significant numbers already been exposed to European cultural influences? Do we really understand the extent to which the process of slaving within Africa disrupted the normal mechanisms by which culture was communicated and maintained? And what of the effect of the Middle Passage, the quintessential severing of ancestral ties?

Scholars who accentuate such disruptive forces over the ongoing significance of African cultural influences tend to argue a variant of the creolization thesis that posits the origins of the process in Africa itself. There are multiple uses of the term "creolization," each with meanings that can differ to greater or lesser degrees. In this context, "creolization" refers to the emergence of cultural forms and identities that are unique to the Americas, as they were forged there as a result of the interaction of African, European, and indigenous elements. As such, creolization flows out of the study of linguistics and was adapted for application to broader cultural issues, and is more prominent as a constituent element of analysis among Caribbeanists. What one makes of the African past therefore has direct implications for the interpretation of cultural dynamics in the Americas. Unfortunately, some of the scholarship has developed in just the opposite direction; arguments fully or substantially based upon interpretations of phenomena in the New World are often established first, with the question of ongoing African influences answered subsequently and in ways that comport with the New

World interpretation. On the other hand, scholarship emphasizing an ongoing relevance of African-based culture in American settings is at times guilty of creating static models that do not sufficiently take into account changes that were only logical and inevitable. Whatever the tendency or orientation, the scholarship has largely suffered from a lack of adequate grounding in African history and related studies, such that certain perspectives are entirely predictable if not unavoidable. Earlier scholarship was at a disadvantage in that Western study of Africa was in embryonic form. At this more mature stage of scholarly inquiry, however, failure to view Africa as fully participatory in the creation of American cultures can only be interpreted as willful and, by extension, inexcusable.

Just a few publications will be cited here to demonstrate the broader theoretical principles at stake. Sidney Mintz and Richard Price's *Anthropological Approach to the Afro-American Past* is a short treatise succinctly laying out the position that cultural transformations in the New World were so thoroughgoing that antecedent African cultural influences were ultimately of far less importance than what developed in America. In fact, the document calls into question the utility of making assumptions about African cultures and ethnolinguistic communities, taking the view that the disruption of slaving was such that Africans arrived in "crowds" as opposed to identifiably viable groupings. John Thornton's *Africa and Africans,* also controversial but for other reasons, takes the Mintz and Price position to task, arguing for African cultural zones that were of ongoing significance for African captives and their progeny in the Americas. Thornton's findings move the debate beyond the pioneering work of Melville Herskovits, who created a framework of analysis whereby "retentions" and "survivals" could be catalogued according to a cultural morphology and then comparatively viewed (and ranked) throughout the Americas—see *The Myth of the Negro Past.* So remarkable was Herskovits's contribution that scholars who undertake analyses of phenomena in the Americas and who find it unavoidable to privilege African influences are invariably categorized within a Herskovitsian paradigm, notwithstanding the originality of their work or the degree to which their arguments are painstakingly nuanced. As such, work that actually represents significant advances is relegated to the bin of the familiar and unimaginative.

Regarding the Caribbean, Orlando Patterson's *Sociology of Slavery* stands as an important inquiry into the ways in which Jamaican society was stratified. Patterson promotes what has been called the "plantation society" model, a structural approach emphasizing slavery as an all-encompassing, violent institution within which the agency of the enslaved is highly proscribed. Patterson's characterization of slave society stands in contrast to M. G. Smith's *Plural Society in the British West Indies*. Smith envisions a complex "cultural pluralism" among the various populations in the Caribbean, for whom there was no agreement regarding the prioritizing of cultural elements. Initially responding to Patterson, the contribution of Kamau Brathwaite to the formation of Jamaican society during slavery remains a foundational publication. In *The Development of Creole Society in Jamaica*, he argues for a creolization that was significantly grounded in African cultural antecedents. As such, Brathwaite creates an alternative interpretative space to both the plantation society and the culturally pluralistic model. The degree to which Brathwaite's analysis is applicable to more "complex" Caribbean societies such as Trinidad and Tobago (with increased complexity a function of a partly Indian population) can be debated. However, even for Trinidad the argument for a strong and ongoing African cultural presence is persuasively made in *Guinea's Other Suns: The African Dynamic in Trinidad Culture*. Looking at West African (largely Yoruba) and West Central African influences that arrived on the island through both the slave trade and the later advent of "emancipated" Africans, Warner-Lewis has marshaled an impressive catalog of evidence that leaves no doubt that in Trinidad, the African cultural influence was (and is) decisive. The most celebrated response to the African thesis comes not from the work of historians or anthropologists, but from such literary figures as Derek Walcott (for example, in his *Dream on Monkey Mountain*); and Edouard Glissant (*Caribbean Discourse*), who insist upon Caribbean identities that are, for all practical purposes, regionally novel, unique, and contingent.

Interesting aspects have developed in the scholarship for North America. There is a growing body of research that argues that the enslaved population was far more Africanized culturally than has been previously understood (or accepted). In addition to Herskovits, forerunners to this tradition include Lorenzo Turner's *Africanisms in the Gullah Dialect*. Turner carried out extensive linguistic recoveries along the Georgia–South Carolina littoral. Sterling Stuckey's "Through the Prism of Folklore" certainly establishes the premise that much of what is known about the cultural can be retrieved through the memories of the enslaved themselves—memories that invariably link to an African past. The more recent historiography includes Gwendolyn Midlo Hall's *Africans in Colonial Louisiana;* Margaret Washington Creel's *A "Peculiar People": Slave Religion and Community-Culture among the Gullahs;* and especially Sterling Stuckey's *Slave Culture: Nationalist Theory and the Foundations of Black America,* with his pathbreaking elaboration of the ring-shout religious ritual as derivative of West and West Central African practices and foundational to African American culture. Meanwhile, Michael Gomez, in *Exchanging Our Country Marks,* expands consideration of African influences to include those from what is now southeastern Nigeria and from Islam, and interrogates the processes through which cultural transformations take place. Judith Carney's *Black Rice: The African Origins of Rice Cultivation in the Americas* takes the discussion of African contributions to the New World far beyond the cultural and to the realm of the technological, as she explores the transfer of West African agricultural expertise to North America with respect to rice cultivation. Given West African knowledge in a variety of planting techniques and for an assortment of crops, this is a relatively undeveloped area of inquiry.

In contrast to the interest in the African cultural and technological presence, Philip Morgan's *Slave Counterpoint: Black Culture in the Eighteenth-Century Chesapeake and Lowcountry* weakens the African thesis, insofar as it applies to the Carolina-Georgia Lowcountry, in a manner reminiscent of Mintz and Price, arguing that such African antecedents are of far less consequence than what emerged subsequently on American soil. Ira Berlin, in his *Many Thousands Gone: The First Two Centuries of Slavery in North America,* employs a variant approach. Rather than taking sides with either the African thesis or the Mintz-Price rebuttal in an explicit fashion, he instead narrows the inquiry to a specific period, in which he argues for a "charter" generation of slaves who often had exposure to European cultural influences before coming to the Americas, but who nonetheless underwent significant acculturation once in the New World. The cultural forms of this generation were therefore Creole, and constituted the foundation for the subsequent and much larger numbers of captive Africans arriving in the Americas in the eighteenth and nineteenth centuries.

Turning to Latin America, although not necessarily an exhaustive discussion of culture, Gonzalo Aguirre Beltrán's *La población negra de México, 1519–1810: Estudio etnohistórico,* which looks at early Mexico, clearly establishes a significant and ethnolinguistically differentiated African servile population in that territory. Colin Palmer's intervention, *Slaves of the White God,* builds upon this work in innovative ways that, in striking fashion, address cultural issues, establishing an enduring and vital African presence and cultural practice in early Mexico. Additional works, indeed foundational works supporting the African thesis in Latin America, are often not confined to considerations of slavery, but nonetheless should be cited. They include Fernando Ortiz's *Hampa afro-cubana: Los negros brujos;* Raymundo Nina Rodrigues's *Os africanos no Brasil;* and Arthur Ramos's *O negro brasileiro: Ethnographia, religiosa, e psychanalyse.* The extent to which some of this early literature coming out of the Spanish-speaking and Lusophone worlds embraces the African thesis is dubious, however, in that some held African cultural continuities to be the basis for social and economic disparities found among communities of the African-descended. Supplementing this literature is Mieko Nishida's *Slavery and Identity: Ethnicity, Gender and Race in Salvador, Brazil,* an inquiry into the ways in which race and gender intersected in Bahia, along with materials on other parts of Latin America that would include Winthrop Wright's *Café con leche: Race, Class and National Image in Venezuela;* Peter Wade's *Blackness and Race Mixture,* and *Race and Ethnicity in Latin America;* and Richard Graham's *The Idea of Race in Latin America.*

Resistance to Slavery: Maroon Communities

Whatever the position on culture among the enslaved in the Americas is, it is often not far from the related question of resistance to slavery. Indeed, culture itself is often presented as a form of resistance to slavery, but this is by no means universally held. To the extent to which slaveholders sought to suppress or even eradicate African cultural practices among the enslaved, the latter's insistence upon retaining those practices was clearly a manifestation of resistance. On the other hand, the enslaved necessarily fell back upon established patterns of familial bonding, child-rearing, horticultural skills, masonry and architecture, and so forth, just to live, and repetition of African-informed patterns in the Americas did not, by itself, constitute a political statement.

One of the earliest and clearly incontestable expressions of resistance to slavery was the "maroon" society. As early as 1503, enslaved Africans were colluding with the Taíno population of Hispaniola and fleeing to the mountains to establish maroons, and by 1556 the maroon threat in Panama had fully surfaced. In Cuba, maroon communities were also formed in mountain fastnesses and were known as *palenques* or *cumbes*. Life was supported by a combination of agriculture, confiscations from neighboring estates, and trade (often through enslaved third parties) of such products as honey and virgin wax, which were sold to outsiders in exchange for weapons, gunpowder, tools, sugar, and clothing. There were hundreds of *palenques* throughout Cuba.

The success of a maroon society depended upon a number of factors, including the reception of the native population. An accommodation with the latter could involve adjacent but independent settlements, or it could mean integration into those communities, including intermarriage. There was also the issue of constant pressures from colonial and slaveholding interests. Maroons sometimes had to return runaway slaves in exchange for continuing noninterference.

Perhaps the greatest example of the maroon community was "Palmares" in Pernambuco, Brazil, established in 1605 and lasting until 1694. One of the earliest and still important studies on Palmares (along with other maroon formations) is R. K. Kent's article "Palmares: An African State in Brazil," published in Richard Price's *Maroon Societies: Rebel Slave Communities in the Americas*. It is perhaps more accurate to think of Palmares as an independent state, the first created by non-native peoples in the New World. In the parlance of the Brazilian context, Palmares was one of ten major *quilombos* or *mocambos* (both are African terms) in colonial Brazil, and of the ten, it was by far the most significant. They were initially founded by African-born runaways. Distinctions between those from Africa and those born in Brazil, the *crioulos*, became less significant over time. Friction between the Portuguese and Palmares intensified as individuals increasingly fled the surrounding *engenhos* (sugar mills and adjacent lands) for the *quilombo*. The final destruction of Palmares came after a siege of forty-four days, after which the Palmares ruler was captured and decapitated, his head publicly displayed to dispel belief in his immortality.

The maroons of Jamaica have also attracted scholarly interest, though much more work remains to be done. Mavis Campbell's *The Maroons of Jamaica* is one such example. With the instability of the transition to British rule in 1655, some 1,500 of the enslaved formed independent settlements informed by African cultures (especially Akan, or the so-called Coromantee or Kromanti from the Gold Coast) in the mountains, and eventually formed the Windward and Leeward groups. Nanny Town was the former's center, named after a woman skilled in war and *obeah* (the practice of manipulating spiritual forces to inflict harm). Works on Nanny include Alan Tuelon's "Nanny: Maroon Chieftainess"; and Lucille Mathurin-Mair's aforementioned *The Rebel Woman in the British West Indies during Slavery*. Around 1720 the First Maroon War broke out between the maroons and the British. Cudjoe led the Leeward group, while the Windward sector, initially under Nanny's control, was marshaled by Cuffee following Nanny's planter-instigated murder around 1733. The war ended after both groups signed a series of treaties with the British in 1738–1739.

Jean Fouchard's *Les marrons de la liberté* brings the discussion to the islands controlled by the French, where maroons were divided into *petit* and *grand marronage*. The former involved small groups who abandoned the plantation for several days, only to return. *Grand marronage* could also involve small numbers, but was characterized by the fairly permanent nature of the stay and was therefore of greater concern. In Saint Domingue, the most famous maroon society was le Maniel, which owed much of its success to its location on the border with the Spanish-held eastern part of the island, from which it received support against the French. François Makandal is probably the most famous of Saint Domingue's maroon leaders. An eloquent man with extensive knowledge of both medicinal and injurious properties of plants and herbs, he developed a following of undetermined size. He was arrested in early 1758, and after a brief but sensational escape, he was recaptured and burned at the stake.

In various places throughout the Caribbean, Africans and indigenous populations engaged in a complex set of relations. Some merged communities reportedly began with seventeenth-century shipwrecks, such as the "Black Caribs" of St. Vincent, whose descendants were later taken to Belize, Guatemala, and Honduras, where they became the Garifuna nation (or Garinagu, as they prefer to name themselves); and the "Zambos Mosquitos" of Nicaragua's Mosquito Coast.

There were also maroons in what would become the United States, scattered throughout the swamps, forests, and mountains of Florida, Louisiana, Mississippi, Alabama, Georgia, Virginia, and the Carolinas between 1672 and 1864. Relative to maroons elsewhere in the Americas, they were often ephemeral and numerically smaller. In Florida, however, Africans and Seminoles became culturally fused, establishing a fortified position called Fort Blount. The number of runaways among the Seminoles rose so dramatically that the United States government mounted a military campaign in 1816 that evolved into the so-called Seminole Wars, which lasted until 1858. Works on African–Native American relations include Jack Forbes, *Black Africans and Native Americans*, and William Katz, *Black Indians: A Hidden Heritage*.

Perhaps the ultimate maroon formation developed in the Guyanas. Maroons in French and British Guyana were eradicated by the end of the eighteenth century, but those in Suriname continue to the present, representing a legacy of more than three hundred years. Formerly called "Bush Negroes," these people escaped the littoral plantations of Suriname in the late seventeenth and early eighteenth centuries and moved into the interior. Principally informed by African cultures, they comprised various groups, with the Juka (Djuka) and the Saramaka being the most prominent. An interesting article that examines women in maroon societies is de Groot's "Maroon Women as Ancestors, Priests and Mediums in Surinam."

Resistance to Slavery: Rebellion and Revolution

The formation of maroon communities was but one expression of resistance to slavery. Open revolt was another, concerning which there is a rich literature. In *From Rebellion to Revolution: Afro-American Slave Revolts in the Making of the Modern World,* Eugene Genovese places slave revolts within successive categories that begin with attempts to recreate "Africa" in the early phases of slavery in the Americas and end with more mature insurrections that are much more informed by Enlightenment principles in the latter stages. Slave revolts do not always fall neatly into these categorizations, but some do. The maroon societies of sixteenth-century Hispaniola, for example, were often the consequence of revolt, and were probably heavily influenced by Senegambian cultural patterns. The 1736 conspiracy in Antigua also demonstrates the African influence, and is the subject of David Gaspar's *Bondsmen and Rebels: A Case Study of Master-Slave Relations in Antigua.* Led by Court (or Tackey) and Tomboy, an Akan speaker and a Creole, respectively, and by Obbah (Aba) and Queen, both Akan women, preparation for the revolt included a "Damnation Oath," an Akan-derived ceremony that involved drinking rooster blood, cemetery dirt, and rum; and Court's coronation as "king of the Coromantees," which in turn was based upon an Akan *ikem* ceremony that traditionally preceded war.

Decades later, the insurgency in Antigua was followed by conspiracies and revolts throughout the circum-Caribbean: Bermuda and Nevis in 1761; Suriname in 1762, 1763, and 1768–1772; British Honduras in 1765, 1768, and 1773; Grenada in 1765; Montserrat in 1768; St. Vincent in 1769–1773; Tobago in 1770, 1771, and 1774; St. Croix and St. Thomas in 1770; and St. Kitts in 1778. In Jamaica in 1760, another Tackey, accompanied by Akan queen-mother Abena, led a six-month revolt involving over one thousand slaves. Again, the revolt was Akan-based and saw participants take an oath similar to the 1736 Antiguan "Damnation Oath." Ironically, it was the Leeward and Windward maroons who, in compliance with the 1739 treaty, fought alongside the planters to end the revolt. They would do the same in the revolts of 1761, 1765, and 1766, all Akan-led conspiracies betrayed by informants. Michael Craton's *Testing the Chains: Resistance to Slavery in the British West*

Indies discusses some of these, whereas Stella Dadzie's "Searching for the Invisible Woman: Slavery and Resistance in Jamaica" addresses the role of women in Jamaica. A broader perspective regarding women and resistance can be found in Rosalyn Terborg-Penn's "Black Women in Resistance: A Cross-Cultural Perspective."

The end of the eighteenth century saw an important development in Jamaican insurrectionary activity. Although led by Cuffy, yet another Akan-speaker, the revolt this time saw significant involvement by several ethnolinguistic groups, perhaps suggesting a heightened awareness of similarities among the enslaved, and movement away from specific African groups to a broader sense of African-derived identity. In 1831–1832, some 20,000 slaves from all ethnolinguistic backgrounds, together with the Jamaican-born or Creoles, waged a widespread war against their slavery, representing the culmination of these developments. The best organized of all Jamaica's slave revolts, it proved to be the most costly to repress, and was a critical factor in the eventual collapse of slavery in the British Caribbean, as were major uprisings in Barbados in 1816 and Demerara (present-day Guyana) in 1823, the subject of Emília Viotti da Costa's *Crowns of Glory, Tears of Blood: The Demerara Slave Rebellion of 1823.*

In eighteenth-century New York City, similar forms of resistance were taking place, and again the Akan were prominent. Between 1700 and 1774, an estimated 41.2 percent of the enslaved imported into the city were African-born. Before 1742, some 70 percent came from the Caribbean and other areas in the Western Hemisphere, with thousands arriving from Barbados and Jamaica. After 1742, however, 70 percent came directly from Africa, the result of the revocation of the *asiento* after 1750, when Spanish markets were closed to English slavers and traders flooded New York and other English colonies with captives. Those from Jamaica and other Caribbean locations would have been aware of slave revolts and unrest in the islands; some had in fact been shipped to New York because of their participation. It is not surprising, then, that the Akan played prominent roles in the New York City rebellion of 1712. The conspiracy of 1741 involved similar participation from the Akan and other ethnolinguistic groups, when it was believed (partially informed by white paranoia) that some 2,000 slaves were poised to torch the city.

João José Reis's discussion of slave revolt in Brazil, *Slave Rebellion in Brazil*, also features African actors and culture as important components. It represents a disruption of the Genovese thesis, however, in that although it was primarily Africa-oriented, it took place in the nineteenth century as opposed to much earlier. As in Jamaica, revolt in Brazil tended to be organized along ethnolinguistic lines. In particular, the northeastern province of Bahia was notorious for slave revolts in the first half of the nineteenth century, and it is there that a multiplicity of identities arising from the intersection of a variety of elements, including racial intermixing, free versus slave statuses, urban versus rural settings, and religious adherence, can be discerned. The Hausa, Muslims from what is now northern Nigeria, had been implicated in revolts for many years, and in 1807 the Hausa near the city of Salvador were again accused of a conspiracy to capture ships and sail to West Africa. Revolts continued from 1809 to 1835, involving Hausa and "Nagôs" (or Yoruba) from what are now northern and southwestern Nigeria, respectively.

It was in 1835 that the insurrection of the so-called "Malês" took place, Malês being African Muslims who were by then mostly Nagôs rather than Hausa. Islam had become an important religion in Bahia, though not the dominant religion among blacks, nor were all Nagôs Muslim. In January of 1835, up to five hundred Africans, enslaved and free, mostly Muslim, took to the streets of Salvador under Muslim leadership. Betrayal forced the conspirators to the premature launch of a plan that envisioned recruitment from surrounding plantations. The revolt was brutally repressed.

Concerning Saint Domingue (the French colony on Hispaniola; the Spanish-controlled area of the island was called Santo Domingo), site of the single most far-reaching revolt in the New World, the literature both supports and contradicts the Genovese thesis. C. L. R. James's *Black Jacobins*, the classic work on the Haitian Revolution, which incorporates a Marxist reading into the analysis, emphasizes the influence of the French Revolution upon the leadership of Haiti's insurrection. In contrast, Carolyn Fick's *Making of Haiti* focuses on an approach referred to as "history from below," and features the activities of the masses, for whom African cultural factors and sensibilities contributed very heavily to the decision to revolt. Whatever the specific analytical lens, the Haitian Revolution stands apart as the only revolt to defeat militarily the slaveocracy and colonialism, and is the only revolt that ended slavery directly. News of the revolution sent shock waves all over the Americas, alarming slaveholders throughout.

The revolution began in 1791 and was led by Dutty Boukman, a voodoo priest; Jean-François; and Georges Biassou. The first two apparently had some maroon experience. Toussaint L'Ouverture, the eventual leader of the revolution, was a black *affranchi* (a category consisting of free blacks and persons of "color") and a coachman. Women played important roles as well, the most prominent being Cécile Fatiman, a voodoo high priestess who, along with Boukman, officiated at a solemn voodoo ceremony for the conspirators in the dense forest of Bois-Caïman, a ceremony not unlike the "Damnation Oath" in Antigua and Jamaica, again demonstrating the centrality of African religions.

The Haitian Revolution would take many unpredictable turns and shifts. The conflict assumed different forms in the south and west where, in contrast with the north, the enslaved were not as organized or cohesive, and were overshadowed by the politics of the free blacks and *gens de couleur* (free people of "color"). The latter two groups teamed up to fight white planters in the south, while the enslaved were enlisted to fight on both sides. The combination of insurrection and conflicts between Britain, France, and Spain led the French to abolish slavery throughout Saint Domingue on October 31, 1793. For the most part, however, little changed for the ex-slaves.

In the meantime, Toussaint had emerged as leader of the forces in the north, and under him served Dessalines, Henri-Christophe, his brother Paul, and his adopted nephew Moïse. By 1798, Toussaint had forced the evacuation of the British; by the next year, he had defeated Rigaud, leader of the mixed-race elite. In 1801, he invaded Spanish Santo Domingo and freed the slaves there; he now controlled the entire island. Lured to France, where he would be arrested and die of consumption in 1803, Toussaint was succeeded by Dessalines, who went on to defeat the French and declare independence on January 1, 1804.

There were also slave revolts on the North American mainland. A striking example is the 1739 Stono Rebellion, when a contingent took up arms twenty miles west of Charleston, South Carolina, and marched through the countryside spreading havoc. Another is the response of the African-descended to the

American War of Independence. Blacks fought on both sides of the war with the hope of ensuring their freedom, so it is not inaccurate to characterize their participation as a slave revolt coinciding with, or taking advantage of, an anticolonial struggle. As a result of Virginia governor Lord Dunmore's 1775 declaration, freeing all slaves and indentured servants who bore arms on the side of the British, it is estimated that Georgia lost 75 percent of its enslaved population (of 15,000), while Virginia and South Carolina combined may have lost some 55,000 slaves.

The August 1800 revolt of Gabriel Prosser and Jack Bowler saw over 1,000 of the enslaved march on Richmond, Virginia, only to be thwarted by weather and betrayals. The Denmark Vesey conspiracy of 1822 also developed in an urban setting, Charleston, and demonstrates the interconnectedness of the African Diaspora by the early nineteenth century. Vesey, born either in the Caribbean or Africa, was a fifty-five-year-old seafarer who had purchased his freedom in 1800. Organizing a revolt by forming columns of distinct groups, such as the Igbo and Gullah (West Central Africans and/or Gola from West Africa), Vesey invoked the Haitian Revolution, maintaining that help would arrive from that island and from Africa itself, if only those in and around Charleston would take the initiative. Made aware of the conspiracy by informants, white authorities preempted the revolt; suspects were either hanged or deported. There is a discussion on the use of source materials regarding the Vesey conspiracy in "Forum: The Making of a Slave Conspiracy" in the *William and Mary Quarterly*.

David Walker may have been in Charleston at the time of the Vesey conspiracy; in any event, his 1829 antislavery *Appeal . . . to the Colored Citizens of the World . . .* called for a general uprising. Walker died in Boston under very suspicious circumstances the following year, but Nat Turner would eventually answer his summons, launching a large-scale revolt in August of 1831 in Southampton, Virginia. Captured on October 30, Turner was executed on November 11. In October 1859 John Brown and around fifty men, including several blacks, raided the federal arsenal at Harpers Ferry, Virginia. This example underscores that whites were involved in several of these uprisings, usually in supportive roles. John Brown's small force was defeated, and he was hanged on December 2, 1859.

HORRID MASSACRE IN VIRGINIA.

The Scenes which the above Plate is designed to represent are—Fig 1, a Mother intreating for the lives of her children.—2. Mr. Travis, cruelly murdered by his own Slaves.—3. Mr. Barrow, who bravely defended himself until his wife escaped.—4. A comp. of mounted Dragoons in pursuit of the Blacks.

A newspaper print graphically details the murder of white plantation owners, and the hunting down of the perpetrators by dragoons, during Nat Turner's rebellion in Virginia in 1831. Turner, a 31-year-old preacher and slave, claimed he had received visions urging him to rise up. Turner and seven of his fellow slaves stole into his master's house on the night of August 21, and killed the entire family. When they had finished, the gang moved on to the next house, their numbers eventually growing to around seventy-five. Some sixty white people were killed before Turner and his associates were hunted down by militia. Many people in authority blamed the killings on the spread of seditious ideas from outside of the Southern states, and introduced strict laws forbidding slaves from receiving any form of education, including teaching them to read or write. Turner himself was hanged on November 11, 1831.

Other Forms of Resistance to Slavery

Beyond revolt and maroons, there were other forms of resistance. Planters and overseers were sometimes killed, often poisoned, or seriously injured and maimed. There were work slowdowns and stoppages, the sabotage of equipment and torching of fields, and the confiscation of food and provisions.

There are also accounts of mothers allegedly killing their young infants, or even choosing not to have children (or sex)—demonstrating that not all slaves saw survival as resistance, while underscoring the relative and mutable nature of opposition. While infanticide remains an open question, less open to debate is the use of birth control, often accomplished by prolonging lactation through breast-feeding, and abortion, practiced throughout the Americas and especially in the Caribbean, where knowledge of it was largely derived from African procedures and involved the use of herbs, shrubs, plant roots, and so forth. Slaveholders in the Caribbean believed enslaved women induced miscarriages, turning to older women and *obeah* practitioners for assistance. Use of abortifactants may have been a deliberate strategy to deny the slaveocracy the labor it needed.

Perhaps the most fundamental expression of resistance was absconding, widespread throughout the Americas and the first step to marronage. While many headed for such communities, others made their way to towns and cities, where they could possibly achieve anonymity and ply their trades. Some of the more striking cases involved newly arrived Africans heading for the coast, or towards some body of water, apparently intending to return to Africa or some other place. And yet there was another, far more drastic choice: suicide was common throughout the Americas, among men as well as women, African-born as well as Creole. Reference in the folklore to "flying Africans" is often a euphemism for suicide.

Various abolitionist efforts in the Americas and Europe combined with slave resistance to bring slavery to an end. Throughout the Americas there were those who opposed the slave trade and/or slavery and fought for their destruction by way of publications (pamphlets, newspapers, novels, slave narratives) and government petitions, seeking legislative means to this end. In North America, manumission and antislavery societies, first organized by the

Quakers in 1775, were in every state from Massachusetts to Virginia by 1792, in tandem with similar forces in Britain. In 1808 the United States outlawed the transatlantic slave trade. Though the trade continued illegally in parts of the United States, Britain gradually committed its naval capabilities to interdicting the trade, with some success. The real effect of the ban in the United States was the acceleration of the domestic slave trade via westward expansion.

Antislavery literature includes the important publication of Olaudah Equiano's *The Interesting Narrative of the Life of Olaudah Equiano*; such newspapers as William Lloyd Garrison's *Liberator*, first appearing in January 1831; and religious treatises such as James G. Birney's *Letter to the Churches: To the Ministers and Elders of the Presbyterian Church in Kentucky on the Sin of Holding Slaves and the Duty of Immediate Emancipation*, and in 1937 Theodore Weld's *The Bible Against Slavery*. Black abolitionists had their own newspapers, including the first black newspaper, *Freedom's Journal*, published in 1827 by John Russwurm and Samuèl Cornish. Others included the *National Watchman*, published by Henry Highland Garnet and William G. Allen in 1842, and the *North Star*, begun by Frederick Douglass in 1847. Important slave narratives included Douglass's own story, first published in 1845 and subsequently revised, while the most prominent antislavery novel was Harriet Beecher Stowe's *Uncle Tom's Cabin*.

There was also an abolitionist movement in Brazil, which before 1850 included the activities of independence leader José Bonifácio de Andrada e Silva. Some antislavery societies were created in the late 1860s, led by such men as the poet Antônio Frederico de Castro Alves. In 1880, José do Patrocínio of Rio de Janeiro was instrumental in the creation of the Abolitionist Confederation, while the more elite Brazilian Anti-Slavery Society was founded by Joaquim Nabuco and intellectual André Pinto Rebouças in the same year. Luís Anselmo da Fonseca, a medical professor, was also a force in the abolitionist movement. These activities are discussed in Kim Butler's *Freedoms Given, Freedoms Won*.

Efforts to repatriate the African-descended to Africa also grew out of abolitionism. While the African-descended may have viewed such efforts as an opportunity to reconnect with Africa, there were those in Britain who

This poster advertises Harriet Beecher Stowe's novel *Uncle Tom's Cabin*, published in 1852. Stowe was an abolitionist writer who was inspired to actively oppose slavery after hearing a speech by the antislavery campaigner Theodore Weld. *Uncle Tom's Cabin* was first serialized in the abolitionist newspaper *National Era*.

were often interested in using returnees as commercial agents, while many in the United States saw repatriation as a means of strengthening slavery by exporting free blacks.

Whatever the motivation, repatriation to Africa from Britain and Canada began in 1787 and centered on the British settlement at Sierra Leone. These initial groups would be joined, beginning in the nineteenth century, by captives taken from slavers bound for the Americas, the result of the British effort to outlaw the trade. Sierra Leone received thousands of such recaptives, reaching a peak in the 1840s. In the United States, the American Colonization Society was founded in 1817, and in 1822 began a colony in Monrovia, Liberia. Not more than 15,000 blacks participated in this return, to whom can be added captives liberated from slavers by the American navy.

While many Africans and their descendants returned to the continent by way of the American and British governments and private assistance, others financed their own way. In North America, Paul Cuffe, possibly of Akan (but more clearly of Native American) descent, carried blacks back to Africa in 1811 and 1815, financing the entire enterprise himself. There were also those who returned from Brazil and Cuba to West Africa, particularly to what is now southwestern Nigeria and Benin. Those not sent back as conspirators were usually members of *cabildos* (in Cuba) and *irmandades* (Brazil), fraternal organizations based upon purported membership in ethnolinguistic groups. These brotherhoods pooled their resources to pay for such return voyages, among other things. Pierre Verger's *Trade Relations between the Bight of Benin and Bahia* remains an important source on such developments.

The end of legal slavery in the Americas took place over a long stretch of time, territory by territory. Haiti freed itself in 1793, followed by the colonies under Spanish control, where wars of independence were organized as early as 1808 and to which black soldiers contributed heavily. Slavery was officially abolished in Chile, the countries of Central America, and Mexico in 1823, 1824, and 1829, respectively, but not until 1852 in Colombia. Ecuador followed suit that year, then Argentina and Uruguay (1853), Peru and Venezuela (1854), Bolivia (1861), and Paraguay (1869).

For the British Caribbean, Parliament passed the Emancipation Act of 1833, ratified the following year, which ushered in the Apprenticeship period.

Under these provisions, children under six years of age became free, while all others were to work for their former slaveholders for another four years, after which all would be emancipated in 1838. Slavery in Canada, a modest institution in Nova Scotia, New Brunswick, and Lower Canada, was also destroyed by Parliament's 1833 Act, following its demise in Upper Canada (now Ontario) in 1793. Slavery in what remained of the French- and Danish-held Caribbean was abolished in 1848, while the Dutch afforded abolition to their colonies in 1863. It would take a major civil war, however, for the institution to be abolished in the United States. Lincoln's Emancipation Proclamation, effective January 1, 1863, applied only to those in the Confederacy, and did not emancipate the enslaved in states loyal to the Union or in territory under Union occupation. It was not until the war's end and the ratification of the Thirteenth Amendment on December 18, 1865, that the formerly enslaved were freed.

In the remaining Spanish-held territories of Puerto Rico and Cuba, slavery was abolished in the former in 1873, and in the latter in 1886 after considerable participation of Cuban blacks in anticolonial wars against Spain. Excellent works on the Cuban experience include Rebecca Scott's *Slave Emancipation in Cuba*; and Ada Ferrer's *Insurgent Cuba: Race, Nation, and Revolution, 1868–1898*. Brazil was the last to abolish slavery, with passage of the Golden Law in 1888.

There are many stories and multiple narratives associated with the history of the Americas after Columbus. Certainly the notion of progress, the extension of Enlightenment ideals, the ongoing experiment with democracy, the spread of capitalism, and the triumph of science have constituted the most celebrated elements of the narrative associated with the rise of the United States. Undergirding that particular narrative were other, far less celebrated accounts, all of which were inextricably connected. These concern the decrease of the autochthonous populations, the massive immigration and exploitation of millions of working-class Europeans and Asians in the nineteenth and twentieth centuries, the subversion of democracy and working-class aspirations throughout the Americas, and the constriction of privilege and opportunity throughout the western hemisphere. Central to many, if not most, of these closely related stories, and certainly foundational to Western powers in both North America and Europe, was the institution of slavery. Given its importance, modern scholars have not yet achieved a satisfactory examination of its history, nor have they arrived at a mature comprehension of its far-reaching consequences.

. . . .

NOTES

1. Barbara L. Solow and Stanley L. Engerman, eds., *British Capitalism and Caribbean Slavery: The Legacy of Eric Williams* (Cambridge, England: Cambridge University Press, 1987); Heather Cateau and Selwyn H. H. Carrington, eds., *Capitalism and Slavery Fifty Years Later: Eric Eustace Williams—A Reassessment of the Man and His Work* (New York: Peter Lang, 2000); Barry W. Higman, *Slave Populations of the British Caribbean, 1807–1834* (Baltimore, Md.: Johns Hopkins University Press, 1984).
2. Selwyn H. H. Carrington, *The Sugar Industry and the Abolition of the Slave Trade, 1775–1810* (Gainesville: University Press of Florida, 2002); Joseph E. Inikori, *Africans and the Industrial Revolution in England: A Study in International Trade and Economic Development* (Cambridge, England: Cambridge University Press, 2002).

BIBLIOGRAPHY

Armstrong, Erica R. "Negro Wenches, Washer Women, and Literate Ladies: The Transforming Identities of African American Women in Philadelphia, 1780–1854." Ph.D. dissertation, Columbia University, 2000.

Beckles, Hilary. "Black Female Slaves and White Households in Barbados." In *More Than Chattel: Black Women and Slavery in the Americas*, edited by David Barry Gaspar and Darlene Clark Hine. Bloomington: Indiana University Press, 1996.

———. *Natural Rebels: A Social History of Enslaved Black Women in Barbados*. New Brunswick, N.J.: Rutgers University Press, 1989.

Beltrán, Gonzalo Aguirre. *La población negra de México, 1519–1810: Estudio etnohistórico*. Mexico City: Ediciones Fuente Cultural, 1946.

———. "Tribal Origins of Slaves in Mexico." *Journal of Negro History* 31 (1946): 276–77.

Berlin, Ira. *Many Thousands Gone: The First Two Centuries of Slavery in North America*. Cambridge, Mass: Belknap Press of Harvard University Press, 1998.

Birney, James G. *Mr. Birney's Letter to the Churches: to the Ministers and Elders of the Presbyterian Church in Kentucky on the Sin of Holding Slaves and the Duty of Immediate Emancipation*. Mercer County, Ky.: N.p., 1834.

Blassingame, John W. *Black New Orleans, 1860–1880*. Chicago: University of Chicago Press, 1973.

———. "The Slave Family." *The Slave Community: Plantation Life in the Antebellum South*. Oxford: Oxford University Press, 1972.

Brathwaite, Kamau. "The 'Folk' Culture of the Slaves." *The Development of Creole Society in Jamaica, 1770–1820.* Oxford: Clarendon Press, 1971.

Bush, Barbara. *Slave Women in Caribbean Society, 1650–1838.* Bloomington: Indiana University Press, 1990.

Butler, Kim. *Freedoms Given, Freedoms Won: Afro-Brazilians in Post-Abolition São Paulo and Salvador.* New Brunswick, N.J.: Rutgers University Press, 1998.

Campbell, Mavis. *The Maroons of Jamaica, 1655–1796: A History of Resistance, Collaboration, and Betrayal.* South Hadley, Mass.: Bergin and Garvey, 1988.

Carney, Judith. *Black Rice: The African Origins of Rice Cultivation in the Americas.* Cambridge, Mass.: Harvard University Press, 2001.

Carrington, Selwyn H. H. *The Sugar Industry and the Abolition of the Slave Trade, 1775–1810.* Gainesville: University Press of Florida, 2002.

Cateau, Heather, and Selwyn H. H. Carrington, eds. *Capitalism and Slavery Fifty Years Later: Eric Eustace Williams—A Reassessment of the Man and His Work.* New York: Peter Lang, 2000.

da Costa, Emília Viotti. *Crowns of Glory, Tears of Blood: The Demerara Slave Rebellion of 1823.* Oxford: Oxford University Press, 1994.

Craton, Michael. *Testing the Chains: Resistance to Slavery in the British West Indies.* Ithaca, N.Y.: Cornell University Press, 1982.

Creel, Margaret Washington. *A "Peculiar People": Slave Religion and Community-Culture among the Gullahs.* New York: New York University Press, 1988.

Dadzie, Stella. "Searching for the Invisible Woman: Slavery and Resistance in Jamaica." *Race and Class* 32 (1990): 21–38.

Davis, David Brion. *Slavery and Human Progress.* Oxford: Oxford University Press, 1984.

Debien, Gabriel. *Les esclaves aux Antilles françaises, XVIIe–XVIIIe siècles.* Basse Terre: Société d'histoire de la Guadeloupe, 1974.

Dorsey, Joseph C. "Women without History: Slavery and the International Politics of Partus Sequitur Ventrem in the Spanish Caribbean." *Journal of Caribbean History* 28 (1994): 165–207.

Dunn, Richard S. *Sugar and Slaves: The Rise of the Planter Class in the English West Indies, 1624–1713.* Chapel Hill: University of North Carolina Press, 1972.

Elkins, Stanley M. *Slavery: A Problem in American Institutional and Intellectual Life.* Chicago: University of Chicago, 1959.

Equiano, Olaudah. "The Author's Birth . . ." and "The Author is Carried to Virginia . . ." *The Interesting Narrative of the Life of Olaudah Equiano, Written by Himself.* Edited by Robert Allison. London: Printed for and sold by T. Wilkins et al., 1789; Boston: St. Martin's Press, 1995.

Ferrer, Ada. *Insurgent Cuba: Race, Nation, and Revolution, 1868–1898.* Chapel Hill: University of North Carolina Press, 1999.

Fett, Sharla. "Body and Soul: African-American Healing in Southern Antebellum Plantation Communities, 1800–1860." Ph.D. dissertation, Rutgers University, 1995.

Fick, Carolyn E. *The Making of Haiti: The Saint Domingue Revolution from Below.* Knoxville: University of Tennessee Press, 1990.

Fogel, Robert William, and Stanley L. Engerman. *Time on the Cross: The Economics of American Negro Slavery.* Boston: Little, Brown, 1974.

Forbes, Jack D. *Black Africans and Native Americans: Color, Race, and Caste in the Evolution of Red-Black Peoples.* Oxford: Blackwell Publishers, 1988.

"Forum: The Making of a Slave Conspiracy." *William and Mary Quarterly* 58 (2001), and 59 (2002).

Fouchard, Jean. *Les marrons de la liberté,* reprinted as *The Haitian Maroons: Liberty or Death.* Translated by A. Faulkner Watts. Paris: Éditions de L'École, 1972; New York: E. W. Blyden Press, 1981.

Fox-Genovese, Elizabeth. *Within the Plantation Household: Black and White Women of the Old South.* Chapel Hill: University of North Carolina Press, 1988.

Fraginals, Manuel Moreno. *El ingenio: Complejo económico social cubano del azúcar.* 3 vols. Havana, Cuba: Editorial de Ciencias Sociales, 1978; Barcelona, Spain: Crítica, 2001.

——. "Plantations in the Caribbean: Cuba, Puerto Rico and the Dominican Republic in the Late Nineteenth Century." In *Between Slavery and Free Labor: The Spanish-Speaking Caribbean in the Nineteenth Century,* edited by Manuel Moreno Fraginals, Frank Moya Pons, and Stanley L. Engerman. Baltimore, Md.: Johns Hopkins University Press, 1985.

Freyre, Gilberto. *The Masters and the Slaves (Casa-grande e senzala): A Study in the Development of Brazilian Civilization.* Translated by Samuel Putnam. New York: Alfred A. Knopf, 1946.

Gaspar, David Barry. "Daring Spirits to Lead Them On." *Bondsmen and Rebels: A Case Study of Master–Slave Relations in Antigua, with Implications for Colonial British America.* Baltimore, Md.: Johns Hopkins University Press, 1985.

Gaspar, David Barry, and Darlene Clark Hine, eds. *More Than Chattel: Black Women and Slavery in the Americas.* Bloomington: Indiana University Press, 1996.

Genovese, Eugene D. *Roll, Jordan, Roll: The World the Slaves Made.* New York: Pantheon Books, 1974.

——. "Slave Revolts in Hemispheric Perspective." *From Rebellion to Revolution: Afro-American Slave Revolts in the Making of the Modern World.* Baton Rouge: Louisiana State University Press, 1979.

Glissant, Edouard. *Caribbean Discourse.* Translated by Michael Dash. Charlottesville: University Press of Virginia, 1989.

Gomez, Michael A. *Exchanging Our Country Marks: The Transformation of African Identities in the Colonial and Antebellum South.* Chapel Hill: University of North Carolina Press, 1998.

Graham, Richard, ed. *The Idea of Race in Latin America, 1870–1940.* Austin: University of Texas Press, 1990.

de Groot, Silvia W. "Maroon Women as Ancestors, Priests and Mediums in Surinam." *Slavery and Abolition* 7 (1986): 160–74.

Gutman, Herbert G. *The Black Family in Slavery and Freedom, 1750–1925.* New York: Pantheon Books, 1976.

———. *Slavery and the Numbers Game: A Critique of "Time on the Cross."* Urbana: University of Illinois Press, 1975.

Hall, Gwendolyn Midlo. *Africans in Colonial Louisiana: The Development of Afro-Creole Culture in the Eighteenth Century.* Baton Rouge: Louisiana State University Press, 1992.

———. *Social Control in Slave Plantation Societies: A Comparison of St. Domingue and Cuba.* Baltimore, Md.: Johns Hopkins University Press, 1971.

Hall, Rebecca. "Not Killing Me Softly: African American Women, Slave Revolts, and Historical Constructions of Racialized Gender." Ph.D. dissertation, University of California, Santa Cruz, 2004.

Handler, Jerome S., and Robert S. Corruccini. "Weaning among West Indian Slaves: Historical and Bioanthropological Evidence from Barbados." *William and Mary Quarterly* 43 (1986): 1, 111–17.

Herskovits, Melville. *The Myth of the Negro Past.* London, England: Harper and Brothers, 1941; Boston: Beacon Press, 1990.

Higman, Barry W. "African and Creole Slave Family Patterns in Trinidad." *Journal of Family History* 3 (1978): 163–80.

———. "Household Structure and Fertility on Jamaican Slave Plantations: A Nineteenth-Century Example." *Population Studies* 27 (1973): 527–50.

———. "The Slave Family and Household in the British West Indies, 1800–1834." *Journal of Interdisciplinary History* 6 (1975): 261–87.

Higman, Barry W. *Slave Populations of the British Caribbean, 1807–1834.* Baltimore, Md.: Johns Hopkins University Press, 1984.

Huggins, Nathan I. *Black Odyssey: The Afro-American Ordeal in Slavery.* New York: Pantheon Books, 1977.

Hull, Gloria T., Patricia Bell Scott, and Barbara Smith. *All the Women Are White, All the Blacks Are Men, but Some of Us Are Brave: Black Women's Studies.* Old Westbury, N.Y.: Feminist Press, 1981.

Inikori, Joseph E. *Africans and the Industrial Revolution in England: A Study in International Trade and Economic Development.* Cambridge, England: Cambridge University Press, 2002.

James, C. L. R. "The San Domingo Masses Begin." *The Black Jacobins: Toussaint L'Ouverture and the San Domingo Revolution.* New York: Dial Press, 1938.

Jones, Jacqueline. "'My Mother Was Much of a Woman': Slavery." *Labor of Love, Labor of Sorrow: Black Women, Work, and the Family from Slavery to the Present.* New York: Basic Books, 1985.

Jordan, Winthrop D. "Fruits of Passion: The Dynamics of Interracial Sex." *White over Black: American Attitudes toward the Negro, 1550–1812.* Chapel Hill: University of North Carolina Press, 1968.

Karasch, Mary C. "Samba and Song: Afro-Cariocan Slave Culture." *Slave Life in Rio de Janeiro, 1808–1850.* Princeton, N.J.: Princeton University Press, 1987.

Katz, William Loren. *Black Indians: A Hidden Heritage.* New York: Atheneum, 1986.

Kent, R. K. "Palmares: An African State in Brazil." In *Maroon Societies: Rebel Slave Communities in the Americas,* edited by Richard Price. Baltimore, Md.: Johns Hopkins University Press, 1973/1979.

Kiple, Virginia H., and Kenneth F. Kiple. "Deficiency Diseases in the Caribbean." *Journal of Interdisciplinary History* 11 (1980): 197–215.

Klein, Herbert S., and Stanley L. Engerman. "Fertility Differentials between Slaves in the United States and the British West Indies: A Note on Lactation Practices and Their Possible Implications." *William and Mary Quarterly* 35 (1978): 357–74.

Knight, Franklin W. "Slavery in a Plantation Society." *Slave Society in Cuba during the Nineteenth Century.* Madison: University of Wisconsin Press, 1970.

Lamur, Humphrey E. "Fertility Differentials on Three Slave Plantations in Suriname." *Slavery and Abolition* 8 (1987): 313–35.

——. "The Slave Family in Colonial Nineteenth Century Suriname." *Journal of Black Studies* 23 (1992): 344–57.

Long, Margaret Geneva. "Doctoring Freedom: The Politics of African-American Medical Care, 1840–1910." Ph.D. dissertation, University of Chicago, 2004.

Malone, Ann Patton. *Sweet Chariot: Slave Family and Household Structure in Nineteenth Century Louisiana.* Chapel Hill: University of North Carolina Press, 1992.

Mathurin-Mair, Lucille. "Guerilla Women." *The Rebel Woman in the British West Indies during Slavery.* Kingston, Jamaica: African-Caribbean Institute of Jamaica, 1975.

Mattoso, Kátia M. de Queirós. *To Be a Slave in Brazil, 1550–1888.* Translated by Arthur Goldhammer. New Brunswick, N.J.: Rutgers University Press, 1986.

Millette, James. *Society and Politics in Colonial Trinidad.* Curepe, Trinidad: Omega, 1970.

Mintz, Sidney W. *Sweetness and Power: The Place of Sugar in Modern History.* New York: Penguin, 1985.

Mintz, Sidney W., and Richard Price. *An Anthropological Approach to the Afro-American Past: A Caribbean Perspective.* Philadelphia: Institute for the Study of Human Issues, 1976.

Moitt, Bernard. "Gender and Slavery: Women and the Plantation Experience in the Caribbean before 1848." In *Born out of Resistance: On Caribbean Cultural Creativity,* edited by Wim Hoogbergen. Utrecht, Holland: ISOR-Publications, 1995.

Morgan, Philip D. *Slave Counterpoint: Black Culture in the Eighteenth-Century Chesapeake and Lowcountry.* Chapel Hill: University of North Carolina Press, 1998.

Morrissey, Marietta. *Slave Women in the New World: Gender Stratification in the Caribbean.* Lawrence: University Press of Kansas, 1989.

——. "Women's Work, Family Formation, and Reproduction among Caribbean Slaves." *Review: A Journal of the Braudel Center* 9 (1986): 339–67.

Nishida, Mieko. *Slavery and Identity: Ethnicity, Gender and Race in Salvador, Brazil, 1808–1888.* Bloomington: Indiana University Press, 2003.

Ortiz, Fernando. *Hampa afro-cubana: Los negros brujos.* Madrid: Editorial America, 1906.

Palmer, Colin. "Church, State, and Slavery." *Slaves of the White God: Blacks in Mexico, 1570–1650.* Cambridge, Mass.: Harvard University Press, 1976.

Patterson, Orlando. "Authority, Alienation, and Social Death." *The Sociology of Slavery: An Analysis of the Origins, Development, and Structure of Negro Slave Society in Jamaica.* London: MacGibbon and Kee, 1967.

Phillips, Ulrich B. *American Negro Slavery: A Survey of the Supply, Employment, and Control of Negro Labor as Determined by the Plantation Regime.* New York: D. Appleton & Co., 1918; Baton Rouge: Louisiana State University Press, 1966.

Price, Richard, ed. *Maroon Societies: Rebel Slave Communities in the Americas.* Baltimore, Md.: Johns Hopkins University Press, 1979.

Ramos, Arthur. *O negro brasileiro: Ethnographia, religiosa, e psychanalyse.* Rio de Janeiro, Brazil: Civilização Brasileira, 1934; Recife, Brazil: Fundação Joaquim Nabuco, Editora Massangana, 1988.

Reddock, Rhoda. "Women and Slavery in the Caribbean: A Feminist Perspective." *Latin American Perspectives* 12 (1985): 63–80.

——. "Women and the Slave Plantation Economy in the Caribbean." In *Retrieving Women's History: Changing Perceptions of the Role of Women in Politics and Society,* edited by Jay S. Kleinberg. Boston: St. Martin's Press, 1988.

——. *Women, Labour, and Politics in Trinidad and Tobago: A History.* London: Zed Books, 1994.

Reis, João José. "The Sons of Allah in Bahia." *Slave Rebellion in Brazil: The Muslim Uprising of 1835 in Bahia.* Translated by Arthur Brakel. Baltimore, Md.: Johns Hopkins University Press, 1993.

Rodrigues, Raymundo Nina. *Os africanos no Brasil.* São Paulo, Brazil: Companhia Editora Nacional, 1932.

Russell-Wood, A. J. R. *A World on the Move: The Portuguese in Africa, Asia, and the Americas, 1415–1808.* Manchester, England: Carcanet Press, 1992.

Schwartz, Stuart B. *Sugar Plantations in the Formation of Brazilian Society: Bahia, 1550–1835.* Cambridge, England: Cambridge University Press, 1985.

Scott, Rebecca. "Sugar and Slavery." *Slave Emancipation in Cuba: The Transition to Free Labor, 1860–1899.* Princeton, N.J.: Princeton University Press, 1985.

Shepherd, Verene, Bridget Brereton, and Barbara Bailey, eds. *Engendering History: Caribbean Women in Historical Perspective.* Boston: St. Martin's Press, 1995.

Simmonds, Lorna. "Slave Higglering in Jamaica, 1780–1834." *Jamaica Journal* 20 (1987): 31–38.

Smith, M. G. *The Plural Society in the British West Indies.* Berkeley: University of California Press, 1965.

Solow, Barbara L., and Stanley L. Engerman, eds. *British Capitalism and Caribbean Slavery: The Legacy of Eric Williams.* Cambridge, England: Cambridge University Press, 1987.

Stampp, Kenneth M. "To Make Them Stand in Fear." *The Peculiar Institution: Slavery in the Ante-Bellum South.* New York: Alfred A. Knopf, 1956.

Steady, Filomina Chioma, and Kenneth Bilby. *The Black Woman Cross-Culturally.* Cambridge, Mass.: Schenkman Publishing Company, 1981.

Stevenson, Brenda E. "Slave Marriage and Family Relations." *Life in Black and White: Family and Community in the Slave South.* Oxford: Oxford University Press, 1996.

Stowe, Harriet Beecher. *Uncle Tom's Cabin.* Boston: J. P. Jewett, 1852; Oxford: Oxford University Press, 2002.

Stuckey, Sterling. *Slave Culture: Nationalist Theory and the Foundations of Black America.* Oxford: Oxford University Press, 1987.

———. "Through the Prism of Folklore: The Black Ethos in Slavery." *Massachusetts Review* 9 (1968): 417–37.

Tannenbaum, Frank. *Slave and Citizen: The Negro in the Americas.* New York: Vintage Books, 1946.

Terborg-Penn, Rosalyn. "Black Women in Resistance: A Cross-Cultural Perspective." In *Resistance: Studies in African, Caribbean and Afro-American History,* edited by Gary Y. Okihiro. Amherst: University of Massachusetts Press, 1986.

Terborg-Penn, Rosalyn, and Andrea Benton Rushing. *Women in Africa and the African Diaspora.* Washington, D.C.: Howard University Press, 1989.

Thornton, John K. *Africa and Africans in the Making of the Atlantic World, 1400–1800.* Cambridge, England: Cambridge University Press, 1998.

Tuelon, Alan. "Nanny: Maroon Chieftainess." *Caribbean Quarterly* 19 (1973): 20–27.

Turner, Lorenzo Dow. *Africanisms in the Gullah Dialect.* Chicago: University of Chicago Press, 1949.

Verger, Pierre. *Trade Relations between the Bight of Benin and Bahia from the 17th to 19th Century.* Translated by Evelyn Crawford. Ibadan, Nigeria: Ibadan University Press, 1976.

Wade, Peter. *Blackness and Race Mixture: The Dynamics of Racial Identity in Colombia.* Baltimore, Md.: Johns Hopkins University Press, 1993.

———. *Race and Ethnicity in Latin America.* London: Pluto Press, 1997.

Walcott, Derek. *Dream on Monkey Mountain, and Other Plays.* New York: Farrar, Straus, and Giroux, 1970.

Walker, David. *Walker's Appeal, in Four Articles: Together with a Preamble to the Colored Citizens of the World, but in Particular, and Very Expressly to Those in the United States of America. Written in Boston, in the State of Massachusetts, Sept 28th, 1829.* Boston: The Author, 1829; New York: Hill & Wang, 1995.

Warner-Lewis, Maureen. "Africans in Nineteenth-Century Trinidad." *Guinea's Other Suns: The African Dynamic in Trinidad Culture.* Dover, Mass.: Majority Press, 1991.

———, ed. *Central Africa in the Caribbean: Transcending Time, Transforming Cultures.* Kingston, Jamaica: University of the West Indies Press, 2003.

Weld, Theodore. *The Bible Against Slavery. An Inquiry into the Patriarchal and Mosaic Systems on the Subject of Human Rights.* Detroit: Negro History Press, 1837/1970.

White, Deborah Gray. "Jezebel and Mammy: The Mythology of Female Slavery." *Ar'n't I a Woman: Female Slaves in the Plantation South.* New York: W. W. Norton, 1985.

Williams, Eric. "British Commerce and the Triangular Trade." *Capitalism and Slavery.* 1944; Chapel Hill: University of North Carolina, 1994.

———. *From Columbus to Castro: The History of the Caribbean, 1492–1969*. London: André Deutsch, 1970.

Wright, Winthrop R. *Café con leche: Race, Class and National Image in Venezuela*. Austin: University of Texas Press, 1990.

CHRONOLOGY

1736	Conspiracy in Antigua.
1739	Stono Rebellion (South Carolina).
1791	Haitian Revolution begins.
1800	Revolt of Gabriel Prosser and Jack Bowler.
1804	Haiti frees itself after thirteen years of revolt.
1822	Denmark Vesey conspiracy in Charleston.
1829	Publication of David Walker's *Appeal*.
1830	Founding of Ilê Iyá Nassô or Engenho Velho (*terreiro* in Brazil).
1831	Nat Turner's revolt in Virginia.
1835	Malê revolt (Brazil).
1859	John Brown's raid on Harpers Ferry.
1863	Lincoln's Emancipation Proclamation frees slaves in Confederate-controlled territory, but does not apply to slaves held in the rest of the United States.
1865	The Morant Bay Rebellion led by Paul Bogle starts in Jamaica.
1865	The Thirteenth Amendment abolishes slavery in the United States.
1873	Slavery is abolished in Puerto Rico.
1886	Cuba makes slavery illegal.
1888	With the passage of the Golden Law, Brazil becomes the last country to abolish slavery.

GLOSSARY

Affranchi. Free blacks and persons of color on St. Domingue.

Asiento. Slave traders or nations paid the Spanish Crown a fee for monopoly rights to supply African slaves to the Spanish colonies in the Americas for a stipulated period of time.

Black Caribs. People of mixed Spanish, African, and indigenous descent.

Code Noir. Codes that regulated slaveholding in the French American colonies.

"Emancipated" Africans. Set free from the bonds of slavery.

Garifuna. A person of mixed Carib and African ancestry.

gens de couleur. Free people of color.

Malê. African Muslims in Brazil, specifically Bahia.

Maroons. Fugitive black slaves (and descendants) who formed their own communities in the West Indies.

Nagô. Term in Brazil for the Yoruba from southwestern Nigeria.

Nanny Town. A town that was the center of the Windward maroon community, named after "Nanny," its chieftainess.

palenque (cumbe). Term used in Spanish-speaking lands for a maroon community.

Palmares. One of the largest maroon communities. Established c.1605 and lasting until 1695 in Pernambuco, northwestern Brazil.

quilombo. Term used in Brazil for a maroon community.

Siete Partidas. Spanish laws which regulated various aspects of slavery in the Spanish Americas.

The "Middle Passage": The Enforced Migration of Africans across the Atlantic

Paul E. Lovejoy

Abstract

The enforced migration of Africans to the Americas in conditions of slavery lasted from the middle of the sixteenth century until the 1860s and constituted the largest movement of people across the Atlantic until the middle of the nineteenth century. Referred to as the notorious "Middle Passage" because of the terrible conditions on board slave ships, this migration involved at least 12 million people and was a major factor in the economic and demographic development of the colonies in the Americas, including the Caribbean region and Latin America as well as North America. Merchants from Europe and the Americas were responsible for transporting and otherwise subjugating the enslaved Africans, who came from many parts of Africa, but mostly from the coastal regions of Sierra Leone and Guinea, modern Ghana, Nigeria, Angola and Congo—regions known as the upper Guinea coast, the Gold Coast, the Bights of Benin and Biafra, and west central Africa. The enslaved population included large numbers of specific ethnic groups, especially Akan, Gbe, Yoruba, Igbo, Ibibio, Kongo, and other Bantu-speaking people from west central Africa. Because of this concentration, many features of African culture, including religion, cuisine, and music, were transferred to the Americas and had a profound impact on the cultural amalgamation and transformation that occurred in the Americas, at least until the middle of the nineteenth century, when the transatlantic trade in slaves came to an end as a result of international pressure and the eventual emancipation of the enslaved population.

A Defining Migration

The transatlantic movement of enslaved Africans to the different parts of the Americas was the defining migration of the western hemisphere after 1492, influencing all parts of the Atlantic world, from western Europe to the Pacific shores of the Americas. The resulting migration created the African Diaspora, as it has become known. The settlement of Africans and the history of their descendants included many people who were in fact of mixed racial background, incorporating people of European and Amerindian background, and more recently people of Asian background as well. Between 1500 and 1860, about 12 million people are known to have left the shores of Africa destined for the Americas, and to a much lesser extent to Europe, although not everyone made it alive, and some died soon after arrival. Despite heavy loss of life during what has been called the "Middle Passage," many more Africans crossed the Atlantic than Europeans. The transportation of enslaved Africans constituted the largest single migration of people before the middle of the nineteenth century. From the sixteenth to the nineteenth centuries, the great majority of people moving from the Old World to the New World were black people. When gender is taken into consideration, then it can be said that far more black girls and women were forcibly taken to the Americas than the number of European girls and women who migrated, at least before the middle of the nineteenth century. It follows, therefore, that the immigrant women who mothered America were disproportionately of African descent, and that they came under conditions of slavery and not voluntary migration.

While there is considerable debate over attempts to estimate the number of enslaved Africans who crossed the Atlantic, the broad parameters of this

Table 1. Slave Exports from Africa, 1450–1867

PERIOD	ENSLAVED AFRICANS IDENTIFIED	
	NUMBER	PERCENT
1450–1600	409,000	3.6
1601–1700	1,348,000	11.9
1701–1800	6,090,000	53.8
1801–1867	3,466,000	30.6
Total known population	11,313,000	

Source: Paul E. Lovejoy, *Transformations in Slavery: A History of Slavery in Africa* (Cambridge, England: Cambridge University Press, 2000), 19.

massive demographic movement are well understood, in large part because of a concerted effort of scholars to track every voyage that took Africans to the Americas.[1] W. E. B. Du Bois recognized the basic problem of estimating the number of people in his pioneering Harvard dissertation of 1895.[2] Subsequently, Philip Curtin reviewed the stereotypes and guesses that had characterized the study of the slave migration, demonstrating the possibilities of reasonably accurate estimates, despite warnings by David Henige of the inevitable difficulties of using incomplete and often inaccurate information.[3] The trade lasted about four hundred years, from the late fifteenth century until the middle of the nineteenth century. As shown in table 1, which charts the movement of 11.3 million people of the estimated 12 million who left Africa, it can be seen that the demographic movement was largely confined to the period 1700–1860, with over half (53.8 percent) of all Africans transported across the Atlantic in the eighteenth century, and another 30.6 percent transported in the nineteenth century.

That is, the number of people in the first two hundred years or so of this migration was relatively small, with less than 4 percent of the total number of people moved before 1600, and about 12 percent moved in the seventeenth century, and much of this number transported in the late seventeenth century. The vast majority of enslaved Africans crossed the Atlantic from the last two decades of the seventeenth century through the middle of the nineteenth century, a period of 170 years. Undoubtedly these estimates will be revised, but it is unlikely that the revisions will alter the conclusion that the overwhelming majority of Africans came to the Americas after 1700.

In the context of the transatlantic migration of enslaved Africans, the size and significance of immigration to North America has to be kept in perspective. For the transatlantic trade as a whole, for an estimated 11.8 million people who were sent into slavery from Africa, less than one twentieth (or 5 percent) of the total reaching the Americas came to what is now the United States. Ten times as many went to Brazil alone, with the Caribbean islands receiving about the same numbers. Nonetheless, the number of people today who trace African ancestry in the United States is so large that it can seem as if the size of the initial migration was much larger than was actually the case.

In order to understand the movement of such a large population across the Atlantic, it is essential to recognize that it was initiated by European countries, although the migration could not have taken place without the cooperation and full involvement of African countries. Otherwise there would not have been a migration in which there were many more Africans than Europeans in the early centuries of the colonization of the Americas, including North America. Moreover, how else can it be explained that many more African females arrived in the Americas than European women than by looking for African reasons as well as European designs, for it is African women who were most crucial in the demographic growth of the Americas. Among immigrants, African women more likely mothered the generations born in the Americas before the end of the nineteenth century than European women, because there were more African women than European women before the large-scale migration of Europeans after the middle of the nineteenth century.

As table 2 demonstrates, there were many more African males taken to the Americas than females, whether women or girls. Slave traders generally tried to get twice as many males as females, but their ability to attain these quotas varied over time and over geographical regions of the African coast. In the earliest periods, when the numbers of Africans crossing the Atlantic were relatively few, the proportion of females was very high, between 41 and 45 percent, but for the first two-thirds of the eighteenth century the proportion was about one-third, and in the nineteenth century it was even less, perhaps 31 percent. In the last quarter of the eighteenth century, when the slave trade

Table 2. Proportion of Females among Enslaved Africans Crossing the Atlantic (percent), 1651–1867

REGION	1651–1675	1676–1700	1701–1725	1726–1750	1751–1775	1776–1800	1801–1825	1826–1850	1851–1867
Senegambia	—	27.0	31.0	21.3	37.8	31.6	46.8	32.6	—
Sierra Leone	—	23.2	31.9	—	41.4	34.8	32.0	28.1	—
Windward Coast	—	—	—	39.7	38.4	33.0	26.3	25.7	—
Gold Coast	42.7	46.8	32.9	32.2	37.9	34.2	28.1	28.7	—
Bight of Benin	41.3	41.0	36.0	40.8	46.2	34.3	24.3	34.9	27.7
Bight of Biafra	50.3	41.1	48.3	24.6	39.9	42.6	35.0	34.3	—
West Central	—	40.1	26.2	32.8	32.5	35.2	29.1	26.8	24.7
South East Africa	—	—	—	47.3	—	28.5	30.5	19.4	13.2
Origin unknown	38.5	40.6	34.5	33.6	43.4	30.1	31.3	24.8	27.3
Average	45.0	41.3	33.9	33.8	38.5	45.1	31.2	31.7	24.5

Data derived from: David Eltis, Stephen Behrendt, David Richardson, and Herbert Klein, T*he Atlantic Slave Trade: A Database on CD-Rom* (Cambridge, England: Cambridge University Press, 1999).

was at its height, the proportion of females was about 45 percent, as in the early period.[4] Moreover, an analysis of where girls and women came from overwhelmingly shows that they were from areas close to the Atlantic coast, especially in the cases of the Bight of Biafra, the Bight of Benin before about 1800, the region of Sierra Leone, and the Angola and Congo regions of west central Africa. Hence the mothers of the generations of blacks born in the Americas usually came from coastal areas of Atlantic Africa rather than from the interior.

Regional Origins of the Migration

The regional origins of the enslaved population in Africa are outlined in table 3. The enslaved population came from all parts of the Atlantic coast of Africa, from Senegambia to southern Angola, and some enslaved people came from southeastern Africa, especially in the nineteenth century.

Table 3. Regional Origins of Enslaved Africans Destined for the Americas, 1601–1867

REGION	1601–1650	1651–1700	1701–1750	1751–1800	1801–1850	1851–1867
Senegambia	536	17,836	54,714	139,977	30,440	—
Sierra Leone	—	2,834	4,962	132,378	66,076	898
Windward Coast	—	180	9,092	135,653	16,454	—
Gold Coast	82	35,478	155,631	345,886	80,597	—
Bight of Benin	519	134,219	374,509	399,630	209,612	12,795
Bight of Biafra	488	48,897	92,854	581,187	217,488	295
West Central	51,775	45,343	310,203	696,868	898,272	54,665
South East Africa	244	7,289	8,991	38,032	225,947	10,557
Origin unknown	16,917	106,959	771,812	557,010	691,281	117,747
Total sample	70,561	399,242	1,781,305	3,027,302	2,436,321	196,957

Data derived from: David Eltis, Stephen Behrendt, David Richardson, and Herbert Klein, *The Atlantic Slave Trade: A Database on CD-Rom* (Cambridge, England: Cambridge University Press, 1999).

Based on records for about eight million people, there are some clear patterns that help to explain the probable cultural and ethnic backgrounds of the displaced population.[5] The most important feature of the demographic structure is the central role played by the west-central African regions of Angola and the Kingdom of Kongo. This region was important very early in the trade, when the numbers of Africans were relatively small by comparison with the period after the late seventeenth century, and west central Africa remained an important source of people until the end of the trade in the nineteenth century. Together, perhaps as many as 40–45 percent of all enslaved Africans came from this region, and since people in this area spoke one or another of the closely related Bantu languages, they shared many cultural features.

The second most important source of slaves was the region of the Bight of Benin (the "Slave Coast" of European accounts, but often referred to as the "Mina" coast), stretching westward as far as the Gold Coast. But this area, unlike west central Africa, only became important at the end of the seventeenth century and was associated with the political history of various states in the interior of the Gold Coast and the Bight of Benin, including the Akan states (Akwamu, Asante, for example) and the Gbe states (Ouidah, Allada, and Dahomey). Moreover, by the end of the eighteenth century, large numbers of Yoruba also came from this region, especially as a result of the consolidation of Oyo in the interior. The Bight of Biafra—the region of the Niger River delta and the Cross River estuary—became important in the 1730s and remained a significant source of immigrants for the slave trade for about one hundred years. Most of the people of this area were Igbo or spoke Igbo as a second language, although a significant minority of the people were Ibibio.

Other areas of the coast—Senegambia, Sierra Leone, the "Windward" Coast between Sierra Leone and the Gold Coast—were important at specific periods, usually relating to political events in the interior and along the coast. However, the total number of enslaved persons from these parts of western Africa was relatively small by comparison with the Bight of Benin, the Bight of Biafra, and west central Africa. Finally, the enslaved population from southeastern Africa was culturally and linguistically similar to other parts of Bantu Africa. It should be noted that the coastal origins of a large percentage of the enslaved population is unknown. However, circumstantial evidence allows for a reasonably accurate understanding of the ethnic and cultural backgrounds of the enslaved population.

As noted above, the proportion of males and females among the deported population is known with some precision, the ratio of two males for every female being the standard aim of many European slaving firms, although the proportions changed over time and by coastal region. Moreover, it is also possible to know the approximate age composition of the enslaved population. There were many children—meaning those below the age of puberty—but very few infants. As shown in table 4, the number of children, and especially boys, increased over time, and many of the enslaved during the last decades of the trade were children.

The proportion of children was relatively small in the early period, before the great expansion in numbers after the end of the seventeenth century, being 5 to 10 percent of the enslaved population for many places in the seventeenth and even the early eighteenth centuries. However, the proportion of children in the nineteenth century from both west central Africa and southeastern

Table 4. Proportion of Children among the Enslaved Africans Crossing the Atlantic (percent), 1651–1867

REGION	1651–1675	1676–1700	1701–1725	1726–1750	1751–1775	1776–1800	1801–1825	1826–1850	1851–1867
Senegambia	—	5.4	9.1	12.0	30.2	16.7	25.7	19.7	—
Sierra Leone	—	7.3	6.5	—	34.3	25.5	41.1	41.9	—
Windward Coast	—	—	—	35.3	42.7	24.9	34.5	29.3	—
Gold Coast	6.4	8.8	17.5	15.1	21.4	19.4	38.0	46.2	—
Bight of Benin	6.5	12.3	19.6	26.1	19.3	14.5	22.5	36.1	18.8
Bight of Biafra	12.8	9.7	23.9	18.4	34.3	19.7	29.7	39.3	—
West Central	—	19.8	24.5	32.1	30.4	18.3	41.0	52.9	41.6
South East Africa	—	—	—	—	—	29.6	ʹ47.0	62.4	—
Origin unknown	9.1	18.1	22.9	23.7	27.1	34.5	46.0	29.6	—
Average	10.5	11.3	19.3	22.6	28.8	22.2	42.6	40.7	35.9

Data derived from: David Eltis, Stephen Behrendt, David Richardson, and Herbert Klein, *The Atlantic Slave Trade: A Database on CD-Rom* (Cambridge, England: Cambridge University Press, 1999).

Africa was over 40 percent, and in the last decades of the trade as high as 60 percent, and the greatest numbers were boys.

The Middle Passage

Many accounts describe the horrors of the notorious "Middle Passage." Conditions onboard ship were usually crowded; sickness was a major problem, killing many of the enslaved and the crews of the slave ships as well; and shortages of food and drinking water were chronic. Misjudgments in rations, weather problems, and slave resistance onboard ships could affect the length of the passage and the conditions of the people onboard. The conditions of the Middle Passage are best described by contemporary accounts, including the testimonies for the British parliamentary enquiry into the conditions of the slave trade in 1789—see the various testimonies in the *House of Commons Sessional Papers of the Eighteenth Century*.[6] Of the surviving memories, those of Olaudah Equiano (who was enslaved when he was eleven and shipped from the Bight of Biafra in 1754) and Mahommah Gardo Baquaqua (who left the Bight of Benin in 1845) are particularly graphic; the fictionalized rendition of the journey by Barry Unsworth in his award-winning novel *Sacred Hunger* is also important here.[7]

Statistics on mortality during the crossing of the Atlantic demonstrate that death rates were very high.

As revealed in table 5, the percentage of slaves onboard ship who died fluctuated considerably, depending upon the fortunes of individual ships, the part of the African coast from which the enslaved came, and the period under consideration. In general, death rates declined over time, as European slaving firms introduced some measures to lower the incidence of death—in the interest of profits, of course, because dead slaves were worth nothing. Death rates declined from approximately 26 percent of the people on the ships in the first half of the seventeenth century to 15 percent or so for much of the eighteenth century, declining to 10 percent or less at the height of the trade in the late eighteenth and early nineteenth centuries. Death rates increased again at the end of the slave trade because of efforts to stop the trade and the extra pressure that put on slave merchants to get their human cargoes to the Americas. The Bight of Biafra and southeastern Africa sustained the highest death rates, in part because of the much longer voyages that were necessary to take slaves from these regions to the Americas. As can be seen from table 6, the length of voyages varied considerably, but again, trips became shorter as time passed, and there were improvements in ship design and construction that made for faster sailing times.

In the second half of the seventeenth century, it took an average of 133 days to cross the Atlantic from Africa, while in the first half of the eighteenth century it usually took 75–80 days, and then only 50–65 days in the last part of the century. In the period 1820–1850, the time was reduced to 40–50 days. The voyages from the Bight of Biafra in the period 1730s–1750s took almost 120 days, while traveling from southeastern Africa in the second half of the eighteenth century could take up to 146 days. The longer individuals were on the slave ships, in the terrible conditions that prevailed, the more likely they would die.[8]

Because many more female Africans crossed the Atlantic than European women, the "new" societies of the Americas, sometimes called "Creole," were largely African in demographic structure. Even when the African component was not dominant, it was usually strong. In North America, the settlement of Europeans and Africans overlapped and were complementary with each other, but even so, the number of African women was still significant in terms of the impact on how they gave birth to the new generations. And it must be remembered that the Native American population, although suffering demographic loss of enormous proportions, nonetheless also contributed to the "new" societies of the Americas. Furthermore, people of African and Native American origins intermingled, generating composite and dynamic

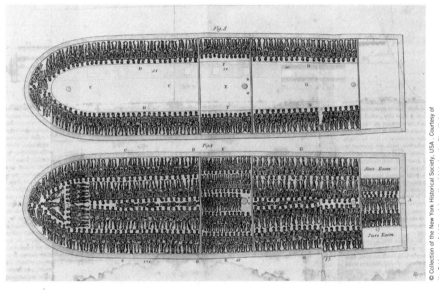

Diagram of the Liverpool slave ship *Brookes*, 1789 (engraving by American School, 18th Century). In the late eighteenth century the British Parliament passed legislation restricting the number of Africans that a slave ship or slaver could carry. The *Brookes* was limited to a cargo of 454 persons, although abolitionists noted that it occasionally carried more than 600. The infamous Middle Passage, the transatlantic voyage from Africa to the Americas, lasted anywhere from twenty-one to ninety days, unless a ship lost its way or insurrections on board ship interfered with the passage. In many cases the slaves were chained to low-lying platforms stacked in tiers, with an average space of 6 feet by 16 inches allotted to each individual.

Table 5. Mortality among the Enslaved Population of the Middle Passage (percent), 1601–1867

REGION	1601–1650	1651–1675	1676–1700	1701–1725	1726–1750	1751–1775	1776–1800	1801–1825	1826–1850	1851–1867
Senegambia	—	—	11.7	10.5	9.6	14.7	12.2	8.4	9.5	—
Sierra Leone	—	—	14.5	10.0	—	15.9	5.7	6.0	6.3	—
Windward Coast	—	—	—	—	6.0	13.0	4.4	2.5	7.1	—
Gold Coast	—	6.0	22.4	14.1	16.0	14.2	8.0	6.1	11.1	—
Bight of Benin	—	22.8	23.4	16.3	15.3	15.3	8.8	5.8	7.3	10.1
Bight of Biafra	—	—	32.9	35.3	42.1	22.8	14.5	16.0	15.8	—
West Central	29.2	—	13.3	13.6	10.7	9.3	7.0	7.6	6.9	13.1
South East Africa	—	—	—	26.0	—	—	27.5	21.0	13.9	30.4
Origin unknown	16.4	17.7	27.2	13.6	18.5	14.1	15.7	16.5	22.8	20.6
Average	26.2	20.3	21.7	15.8	14.5	14.2	9.9	10.0	9.4	16.1

Data derived from: David Eltis, Stephen Behrendt, David Richardson, and Herbert Klein, *The Atlantic Slave Trade: A Database on CD-Rom* (Cambridge, England: Cambridge University Press, 1999).

communities that owed little if anything to European influence. Most important, these migrations and the intermingling of populations involved individuals; they were people whose history, sometimes even on the individual level, can be known. The scale of the migration, and the tremendous suffering and the terrible destruction it entailed, should not disguise the importance of the individual experiences that went into the construction of the African Diaspora, and hence the development of the countries and societies of the Americas.

Enslaved Africans, therefore, were essential in the settling of the Americas after the demographic upheaval caused by the European conquest of the Americas. The movement of people of African descent to the Americas was a central dynamic of the resettlement of the Americas after the disastrous decline in the Native American population. As a slave migration, the African exodus was based on coercion and was not voluntary. The reliance on coercion and the perpetual threat of violence defined the African American experience

Table 6. Length of the Middle Passage (days and half days), 1651–1867

REGION	1651–1675	1676–1700	1701–1725	1726–1750	1751–1775	1776–1800	1801–1825	1826–1850	1851–1867
Senegambia	—	43.5	47.5	41.5	54.5	42.5	52.5	36.5	—
Sierra Leone	—	55.5	45.5	74.5	58	43	45.5	40.5	—
Windward Coast	—	—	54.5	87	65	49.5	44	47	—
Gold Coast	—	82	68.5	94	85	67.5	48.5	30.5	—
Bight of Benin	100.5	91	84	107	120	89	42	36	45
Bight of Biafra	166	89	87	117.5	83.5	66	48	42	—
West Central	165	82	69	70.5	68	58	39	34	46
South East Africa	—	—	—	—	146	121	78.5	62	75
Origin unknown	—	65.5	82	91.5	85	66	52	46	64
Average	133	78	74.5	87	80.5	64	51	39.5	49

Data derived from: David Eltis, Stephen Behrendt, David Richardson, and Herbert Klein, *The Atlantic Slave Trade: A Database on CD-Rom* (Cambridge, England: Cambridge University Press, 1999).

within a colonial, exploitive setting. Africans, and their descendants, were subjected to layers of colonialism and victimization, being forcibly moved from Africa to the Americas and required to remain in the Americas as slaves for generations. Despite this oppression, the enslaved population managed to resist and otherwise survive bondage in numerous ways—from open revolt, to sabotage, to apparent collaboration. Individuals found ways to express themselves, and despite the oppressive conditions, Africans and their descendants reestablished old practices and formulated new communities in which religious expression, music, and folklore had a prominent role, prompting a series of cultural renaissances in Brazil, Cuba, and elsewhere.

Effects of Migration on the Americas

Based on coercion, the slave trade was a dynamic force in the development of colonialism in the Americas. The migration of Europeans, especially from England, France, Spain, and Portugal, and involving Catholics and

Protestants, Christians and Jews, determined who would be sent to the Americas and therefore set the parameters of the African migration. At the time, people of European stock controlled all of the Americas but almost no parts of Africa, except in coastal Angola and Cape Town, South Africa. The principal population movements were across the Atlantic, and the settlement of the colonial territories in the Americas was by immigrants from the Old World, both Europe and Africa. The colonialism that emerged as a result of the international slave trade differed from the later colonial period in Africa. In the era of the international slave trade, European countries did not occupy Africa itself, but instead purchased enslaved individuals and transported them to the Americas. That is, the slave trade enabled Europeans to take foreign peoples and forcibly resettle them as slaves.

The forced migration of Africans across the Atlantic was part of an important historical development that resulted in the consolidation of a single "world" around the Atlantic, including western Europe, western Africa, the Caribbean islands, and mainland North and South America. In its broadest outline, the emergence of this Atlantic world led to the dominance of Europe and the industrialization of northwestern Europe. Africans provided much of the labor for this emerging world order, especially in the production of tropical and cash crops and also in mining gold and silver, and in the transportation associated with producing these commodities. Slave labor was the mechanism by which those in political power and with access to economic resources could further amass wealth and influence. While some African merchants and political officials benefited from their cooperation in this concentration of wealth, in general wealth ultimately flowed into the hands of the political and economic elites of Europe, and the benefits to African merchants and officials were incidental. Hence the overwhelming impact of involvement in the rise of the modern Atlantic world was negative for Africa—a loss of population, particularly the able-bodied, and relatively marginal commercial gains for a small elite.

The movement of enslaved Africans to North America was part of a broader context of African migration in the Atlantic world and the emergence of what has been called "Atlantic Africa" or the "Black Atlantic"—for the initial conception, see Paul Gilroy's *The Black Atlantic*. The experiences of African Americans in North America had similarities and differences from the broader history of the "Black Atlantic," notably in relation to the origins of people and the timing of their arrival, and therefore the nature of the cultural and social impact of Africans on the development of North America. Although the North American experience of Africans and their descendants was unique in time and place, enslaved Africans were also common in the Islamic world, including the Sahara, North Africa, and the Middle East. They were found on the islands of the Indian Ocean, as well as in Persia and Muslim India, and they were known throughout Europe, as far as Russia. These markets for enslaved Africans depended upon commercial networks into Africa that enabled the evacuation of the enslaved and the importation of commodities needed for the exchange. The internal political and social conditions within the continent of Africa allowed the enslavement of people and their sale and exploitation, whether locally or through export to distant lands. That the international slave trade to North America was part of the much larger slave trade, therefore, must be kept in mind in assessing the impact of slavery on Africa and Africans. Moreover, the role of Indian textiles, cowrie shells as a currency, and the relationship between Hispanic America and Asia in the flow of silver raise questions about the extent to which the Atlantic world was part of the whole world.

The first encounters between western Europe and western Africa set the stage for the development of the Atlantic slave trade. We can trace the origins of the Atlantic trade to the fifteenth century and the movement of Portuguese ships down the Atlantic coast of Africa in an effort to bypass Muslim-dominated North Africa and access gold, spices, and other commodities wanted in Europe. Atlantic trade grew out of the confrontation between Christian Europe and Islamic North Africa and the Middle East, which led to maritime discoveries and technological improvements in shipping that made the Atlantic more easily navigable. For the first 100–150 years of European trade on the Atlantic coast of Africa, the slave trade was marginal in terms of the number of enslaved people who were taken to Europe and then, after the middle of the sixteenth century, increasingly to the Americas. Initially, Portuguese shipping was involved in the transport of a variety of trade commodities, and enslaved Africans were only one of these. Other European countries, especially England and the Netherlands, became involved early, but primarily as pirates preying on Portuguese shipping and raiding the mainland of Africa. Early concentration of European activity was confined to Senegambia (in the interior, in the regions of Bure and Bambuhu), and also to the Gold Coast because of the presence of gold. The Portuguese also developed commercial and diplomatic relations with the Kingdom of Benin and the Kingdom of Kongo, initially on the basis of equality, and only after considerable time was this relationship transformed. The Kingdom of Kongo, which became Christian, was tied to and eventually undermined by Portugal and the infectious spread of slave trading, while the Kingdom of Benin moved to restrict Portuguese influence and limited the extent of the slave trade.

Organization of the Slave Trade

The organization of the trade changed over the course of time, but can be divided into three periods: 1450–1650, 1650–1807, and 1807–1867. The first period was formative and dominated by the Portuguese. The second period, from the middle of the seventeenth century until the abolition of the slave trade in 1807 by Britain, and in 1808 by the United States, witnessed the rise of the plantation economies of the Caribbean, and was dominated first by the Dutch and then the French and the British. This was the period of greatest and most extensive exploitation of enslaved African labor. In the final period, after British and American abolition, enslaved Africans went primarily to Cuba, Puerto Rico, and Brazil. The slave trade continued among the islands in the Caribbean, and within the United States, after the ending of the "legal" transatlantic slave trade, and hence the demographic impact of the trade continued well into the nineteenth century, even though direct arrivals of enslaved Africans from Africa were confined almost entirely to Cuba, Puerto Rico, and Brazil.

The Portuguese dominated the first period. Some slaves were moved along the shores of western Africa, for retention and use within Africa, and some were taken to Portugal and Spain. Already by the 1490s, before Columbus reached the Caribbean, one tenth of the population of Lisbon, then one of the largest cities in Europe, was of African origin. Other slaves were taken to islands off the African shore, including the Madeiras, the Cape Verdes, and especially the island of São Thomé, where the Portuguese established sugar plantations using enslaved labor on a scale that foreshadowed the development of plantation slavery in the Americas. Enslaved Africans were already being taken to the Americas; they were part of every expedition into the regions that became the Spanish colonies, and after the 1540s they were taken to Portuguese Brazil to grow sugar, as they had been doing on São Thomé. The Spanish used Africans to grow sugar on Hispaniola and to mine for gold as well, and they were forced to drain the shallow lakes of the Mexican plateau, completing the subjugation of the Aztecs.

Sugarcane was introduced into Hispaniola and then Brazil in the sixteenth century, thereby jumping the Atlantic as part of an exchange of food crops and commodities that increased demand for tropical goods and therefore the need for labor. In all these activities, enslaved Africans were used as a principal source of labor, as well as for occasional military employment. The transfer of sugar cane was the most important development and would lead to the enslavement of millions of Africans, but many other crops, including indigo, rice, tobacco, coffee, cocoa, and cotton were introduced, with varying degrees of success but always with the input of enslaved African labor. However, before the middle of the seventeenth century, the total number of enslaved Africans that were taken away from western Africa was relatively small, especially in comparison with the great expansion in slavery thereafter. Even in this early period, however, the number of enslaved Africans being forced to cross the Atlantic was greater, by far, than the numbers of Europeans voluntarily doing so.

In this early period, before about 1650, the regions in Africa that were affected by the demand for slaves were relatively restricted, and consequently the corresponding impact was limited. Nonetheless, the impact was real, and it was connected with important developments in western Africa. Slaves came from the far-western coast, in the area of the Senegal and Gambia rivers, often referred to as "Senegambia." Culturally and linguistically unified via Islam and Manding culture and language, the region had an ancient and glorious history, centered on the ancient kingdom of Ghana and the medieval empires of Mali and Songhay. The early history of Atlantic Africa is closely tied with the history of these empires in the interior of Senegambia because of the gold trade. West African gold was the principal source of gold for the Islamic lands of North Africa, and also for western Europe, before the exploitation of gold from the Americas after approximately 1500. In West Africa, gold reached the Mediterranean and hence Europe from Songhay, having been obtained at the headwaters of Senegambia, in Bure and Bambuhu, and also in the Volta basin, south of Jenne and Timbuktu. The Portuguese, who arrived on the Gold Coast in the 1470s, tapped these inland sources and gave the coast its name, while the other sources of gold were accessible to the Portuguese along the Senegambian coast. Gold, not slaves, was the quest, but any trade was developed, including malaguetta pepper that would not last long as a delicacy of the European market (it was replaced instead by black pepper from Asia).

By the middle of the seventeenth century, the demand for labor in the Americas was expanding rapidly, and this demand increasingly meant enslaved African labor. The corresponding impact on Africa was intensified as more parts of western Africa were brought into the orbit of transatlantic slavery. This second period lasted until 1807–1808, when the British and Americans abolished the slave trade, thereby beginning a period of contraction in the use of slave labor and the eventual emancipation of those in slavery in the Americas. Inevitably, this demand, and the opportunities provided by attempting to supply that demand, resulted in numerous innovations, encouraged opportunists and entrepreneurs, and resulted in deceptions and barbarities, upon which the slave trade ultimately rested.

There were African collaborators in the slave trade, in addition to the elites and thieves who managed to enslave people in wars and through judicial actions and corruption. Merchants made money from slavery, and they invested in slaves, even marrying or taking as concubines women they had bought or otherwise acquired as gifts. These profiteers were collaborators in the international slave trade, relying on enslavement and its threat as mechanisms of social control in hierarchical regimes dominated by Muslim and non-Muslim men. There were religious brotherhoods in the Islamic lands and in diasporic Muslim communities and other secret societies of the most powerful that were able to interpret their actions and decrees in religious form that related to ancestral rights and the domain of gods. Wherever the transatlantic slave touched western Africa, there were men, and a few women, ready to profit through deception and clever organization. Control of trade was a serious issue, tied to political control.

The final period of the transatlantic trade in humans lasted until the 1860s. In this period, Brazil, Cuba, and Puerto Rico were the principal destinations for enslaved Africans, since slaves could no longer legally be brought into North America, British or French colonies in the Caribbean, or the independent countries of Spanish America. Despite this restricted market, the numbers of enslaved Africans did not decline until the late 1840s. The trade raged on, despite efforts of British anti-slave-trade patrols and the efforts of abolitionists to expose abuses and thereby close the trade down. The dominant issues in Africa related to the jihads of West Africa and the resulting turmoil in the affected coastal regions, as well as the impact of the demand for slaves, on the turbulent polities of Bantu Africa, both inland from Angola and from Mozambique. This later impact affected the distribution of children and youth, with the propulsion of boys into the external trade, largely to Brazil but also to Cuba, and the retention of girls in the rapidly expanding households of specific "ethnic" groups such as the Cokwe and Yao.

As this overview of the three periods of the slave trade suggests, there were distinct national trades, in which specific western European countries dominated or otherwise established a niche. Moreover, within the various European countries one or two ports tended to monopolize the trade, which demonstrates a concentration in insider knowledge about trade, since the principal merchants knew each other. Similarly, on the African side, most slaves were traded in only a few ports. Of these, Luanda in Angola, Ouidah (Whydah) in the Bight of Benin, Bonny in the Bight of Biafra, and the adjacent trade "castles" at Koromatin and Winneba on the Gold Coast stand out as the points of departure for the greatest number of enslaved Africans bound for the Americas; these points probably accounted for at least one-third of all Africans sent to the Americas. Other major ports included Old Calabar in the Bight of Biafra; Benguela in southern Angola; Cabinda, to the north of the Congo River; and Lagos, important in the Bight of Benin in the nineteenth century. These ports of departure accounted for more than half of all the enslaved Africans who were sent to the Americas.

The trade, and the way in which the transport of enslaved Africans to the Americas was funneled through relatively few ports that were controlled by relatively few merchants, whether in Europe, Africa, or the Americas, has important implications. The experiences of individuals, including what they were exposed to, the types of information to which they had access, and the cultural and personal bonds that were established and recognized even before boarding ships for the Americas, must be considered. While enslaved individuals came from widely different backgrounds, and the number of "ethnic groups" and identifying markers were extensive, certain ethnicities and languages, usually in pidgin and creolized forms, as well as religion, were maintained—sometimes exaggerated and manipulated, but always interpreted in the context of adjustments to slave life in the Americas.

Patterns of Cultural Continuity

These patterns of cultural and historical continuity and rupture can be discerned because people reached the Americas as commodities. The records of this trade are extensive and revealing. There were various national companies, sanctioned by royal decree and parliamentary order; there were private companies; and there were merchants who could turn into pirates. A portion of the trade was nominally covered by the Spanish *asiento*, which gave monopoly rights to companies to transport slaves to the Spanish colonies. The trade involved much smuggling, as well as the fulfillment of contracts. The English trade was handled through the Royal African Company, but interlopers undermined the monopoly. Ships from Bristol and, especially, Liverpool came to dominate the British trade in the eighteenth century; they not only challenged the interests of the Royal African Company and London in the establishments on the Gold Coast and in the Gambia, but the new merchants also opened up markets, especially in the Bight of Biafra and the northern Angola coast. Each country, and each port, experimented in an effort to win a share of the trade. Sometimes this competition required the maintenance of trading depots, often called factories or trading castles, which was the case on the Gold Coast and in the Bight of Benin, as well as in the less important ports along the upper Guinea coast and in Senegambia. The rule of thumb seems to have been the availability or accessibility of gold. European establishments were not found in the Niger Delta or the Cross River, both in the Bight of Biafra, where gold was not available.

The credit that ran the trade tended to flow outward from Europe; that is, European merchants came to West Africa, and in order to buy enslaved people, they had to do it by providing credit. This credit was on goods advanced in lieu of payment in slaves. There were considerable risks involved in trade. In the first place, there were risks because the commodity in question was human, and humans had agency that could result in flight, assassination, suicide, or other calamity for the owner. People could disappear with the goods and never produce what was stated in the contract—slaves. There were also risks because trade was across political and cultural frontiers in which recourse to courts and governments in the event of commercial dishonesty and loss was less than perfect. There was no international court or diplomatic system that could handle abuses of trade, let alone the violations of human rights involved in slavery itself.

The trade was important in terms of the development of modern, capitalist institutions and practices, from modern banking to insurance. Lloyd's of London became a major insurance company in the course of doing business with slave traders, as well as anyone else willing to pay/play the rates. One of the best sources for knowledge of the British slave trade is the records kept by Lloyd's. Technical advances and increasingly sophisticated commercial and banking practices were developed in the slave ports of Europe—Lisbon, Amsterdam, London, Nantes, Liverpool, and Bristol. The merchants who were involved were centered at the major European ports, where credit flowed and the commodities of trade were available. These merchants in the European ports came from a variety of backgrounds themselves, featuring upstart entrepreneurs, diasporic Huguenots, Jews, "New Christians" (Jews or Moors recently converted to Christianity), and Scots. Individuals moved into the margins, hoping to survive and make money. There was a fine line between piracy, entrepreneurship, kidnapping, and slave-driving.

In order to guarantee that commercial contracts would be honored, European merchants resorted to a variety of measures, some of them experimental and sometimes tied to African institutions and practices that shaped the commercial exchange in ways that were not recognized in other parts of the Atlantic world. There were local taxes and customs that had to be honored. For example, in some places, such as Old Calabar and in the minor ports of the upper Guinea coast, European ship captains accepted human beings, often relatives of local merchants and officials, as collateral for credit; these were human pawns that could be enslaved if debts were not paid.[9] In other places, such as in Angola and Senegambia, European merchants married or otherwise cohabited with local women, who sometimes amassed considerable fortunes as agents and merchants in their own right. Their offspring, mulatto and sometimes using Portuguese or other European names, became an intermediate class of merchants along the coast, especially concentrated along the upper Guinea coast as far as Senegambia and in Luanda, Benguela, and their commercial outposts in the interior of Angola.

The principal goods of trade sent to Africa in exchange for slaves can be divided into three groups: items used as money, such as cowries, strips of cloth, iron bars, copper bracelets called "manilas," and even silver coins and gold; consumer goods, especially textiles, alcohol, and a great range of items used as jewelry; and military wares. In general, these imports did not replace African production but rather supplemented output. The import of money increased circulation in the market and therefore tended to promote trade in all goods, not just slaves. Since many of the monies were in fact commodities that had other uses as well, their commodity value could also be realized. Hence, cloth strips, imported via Europe from India, were used as currency in Senegambia, along with gold and other mediums, but the cloth could be, and was, made into clothing. Local textile production was not undermined; people just had more cloth. The demand for textiles seems to have been virtually inexhaustible, and the more variety the better. Similarly, iron was fashioned into small hoe-shaped pieces of money in the interior of Sierra Leone, but the money could be combined and used to make real hoes or any other iron implement. Even cowries could be strung into necklaces and used to adorn hair, costumes, and baskets. But their principal use remained as money, which was acquired through the exchange for slaves.

Military wares, especially firearms, were sometimes important, especially in the nineteenth century, and in places such as the Gold Coast in the eighteenth century. However, the importance of the guns in enslavement can be exaggerated. Before the nineteenth century, firearms were not always that effective, especially in tropical areas where the problem of keeping powder dry was serious. Firearms were important on the Gold Coast in the crucial wars of the eighteenth century that enslaved many people and eventually resulted in the political ascendancy of Asante. Firearms were not significant in the rise of Oyo as the dominant slaving power in the interior of the neighboring area inland from the Bight of Benin. Oyo relied on its cavalry and the relative military advantage horses gave in a region in which horses had to be imported from further inland via Oyo's commercial partners. The export of slaves enabled the import of money, in the form of cowries, and consumer goods, especially textiles, for re-export inland for horses. Imported textiles did not replace or otherwise undermine local production of textiles, which was a major industry throughout the interior and often used imported fabrics as a source of thread for embroidery on locally produced cloth.

Alcohol was an important item of trade in Angola, and it was a luxury almost everywhere. Although Muslims were not a significant market, and indeed shunned alcohol, the coastal elites wanted Brazilian rum and French brandies. These were even sent into the interior, but usually diluted with distance. Nonetheless, as with many textiles, alcohol was an imported item for conspicuous consumption. There were local alternatives, but the issue was not one of substitution, only cumulative effect. As with textiles, where people wore more clothing if they could afford it, other people drank more if they could afford it.

The slave trade was demand-driven; people who could afford it wanted labor and did not care how the labor was obtained. The trade was also greed-driven. Individuals became involved because they could benefit—from theft, plunder, kidnapping, ransoming, and the sale of humans as commodities. Such an approach to acquisition means that people took advantage of political misfortune, religious differences, legal technicalities, economic crisis, and outright callousness to exploit individuals who were helpless. Such a realization returns us to the specific circumstances of enslavement, the events and places where the reduction to slavery was achieved.

The specific events in Africa that resulted in the transportation of Africans to the Americas and the corresponding methods of enslavement fall into different categories. One category involves war, slave raiding, and political struggle, which probably accounted for the great majority of those who were enslaved and taken to the Americas. Among the most important wars that resulted in massive enslavement, including the export of war prisoners to the Americas, the ransoming of prisoners, and the use of captives as slaves within Africa itself, were the Akan wars of the late seventeenth and first half of the eighteenth centuries that grew out of a power struggle among various states in the hinterland of the Gold Coast, including Akwamu, Akyem, Denkyira, Fante, and Asante—with Asante emerging as the dominant state. Similarly, the consolidation of Oyo as an imperial power after 1650 involved wars with the Bariba and Nupe to the north and other Yoruba states to the south.[10] War also affected the balance of power among the various Gbe groups, leading to the emergence of Allada as a small kingdom on the lagoons behind the coast, and the rise of Dahomey in the early eighteenth century. Dahomey defeated Allada in 1724, occupied the port of Ouidah in 1727, and was in turn forced to pay tribute to Oyo thereafter. These wars accounted for the deportation of many people along the coast of the Bight of Benin.

The Kongo civil wars that lasted intermittently from about 1680 through 1740 also caused instability that led to the enslavement of many people who were deported to the Americas. One group of victims included the followers of the Antonian martyr Beatrice of Kongo, who tried to end the civil wars through pacifist protest, but with tragic consequences. Yet another series of wars related to the spread of militant Islam across West Africa began in the Senegambia region in the late seventeenth century. These wars marked the emergence of Futa Jallon as a jihad state in the highlands of modern Guinea, and the foundation of Futa Toro on the Senegal River in the late eighteenth century. The jihad movement continued into the nineteenth century, especially with the outbreak of war in 1804 in the Hausa states under the leadership of Sheikh Usman dan Fodio. These wars in turn exacerbated political tensions in Oyo, which resulted in a Muslim uprising and the collapse of the Oyo state between 1817 and 1833. One of the consequences of this collapse was the migration southward of refugees, the founding of new strongholds, and intensified warfare among those attempting to resurrect or otherwise replace the collapsed Oyo state. The most notable of these new centers (Ibadan, Abeokuta, and Ijebu) periodically engaged in hostilities, even after the end of the transatlantic trade in slaves in the 1860s.

In addition to these major upheavals, there are many examples of more localized fighting and warfare all along the Atlantic coast, and sometimes European powers intervened on one side or another, often with the aim of obtaining slaves directly in the encounters, or indirectly through the political rewards expected for military assistance. In Angola, moreover, Portugal established a permanent colony at Luanda in the 1590s, and later at other points along the Angolan coast, especially at Benguela in the south. The permanent military presence of Portugal was reflected in alliances and joint military ventures with allies in the interior, with the result that Portugal— more than any other European country—was actually directly involved in the enslavement of Africans. Unlike in Angola, the other wars that produced captives for the slave trade almost always involved African rivals, with little if any direct European participation. Nonetheless, the importation of firearms was an important contributing factor to the intensity of many of the wars and therefore must be recognized as a factor in the increased numbers of people who were enslaved, especially after 1700.[11]

There were also people enslaved as a result of judicial and religious sanctions and punishment that removed criminals and social misfits, or those deemed to be so, from society through enslavement and banishment. In many places, people were used as pawns in credit arrangements, and while those people being held were almost always protected from enslavement by relatives and customary practices that guaranteed the safety of such dependents, there were nonetheless situations in which the arrangements were not honored, and pawned individuals, especially children, were "sold" or otherwise removed from the watchful eyes of relatives and communities. Similarly, there are cases of relatives and other members of communities who for one reason or another were deemed rebellious or uncooperative and were therefore expelled from their homes through enslavement.

Inevitably, there were serious issues of trying to justify enslavement in Africa. People tried to protect their own communities, and various governments and institutions developed means and policies to limit the impact of slavery. Kin were particularly worried about enslavement through kidnapping, which in most places was considered illegal. Also, Muslims were concerned about protecting the freedom of their co-religionists; those who had been born free were supposed to remain so, although that was not always the case. Sometimes captives were ransomed and thereby avoided enslavement, but such actions only encouraged the taking of prisoners in order to obtain the ransom. People, whether Muslims or not, tried to safeguard their own, but tragically were not always able to do so.

As a result of these pressures, the slave trade, and especially the transatlantic trade, had a dramatic impact on Africa, which can be seen on the personal, family, communal, and continental levels. Various biographical accounts have survived that demonstrate the trauma of enslavement and the corresponding impact on the families of the enslaved. Mahommah Gardo Baquaqua, who was enslaved in the interior of the Bight of Benin in the early 1840s, was ransomed once by his family, only to be enslaved another time, spirited to the coast, and sold to Brazil. His older brother had earlier been enslaved, but he was more fortunate and was also ransomed by his kin. The impact is clear: it cost this family a lot of money to protect its own, and then not fully successfully. Similarly, in many places in western Africa, the level of insecurity that could lead to enslavement increased in response to the pressures of the transatlantic trade in enslaved Africans.

The demographic impact of the slave trade on Africa was severe, especially in those areas most fully drawn into the orbit of transatlantic slavery. The death and destruction from war and kidnapping was extensive, as far as can be deduced from the examples that have survived. The old and the very young were often killed or left to starve in the famines that often followed the destruction of military action. Moreover, among those who were enslaved or held for ransom, mortality rates appear to have been high, because people were force-marched long distances. Since many of those who were enslaved were destined to remain in Africa or to be sent across the Sahara to North Africa rather than to the Americas, the full impact of the slave trade and slavery in Africa was even more severe.

It must be emphasized that slavery intrinsically calls forth resistance. Distinctions can be made between moments of open rebellion and the apparent willingness to acquiesce in servitude to avoid punishment or to obtain minor rewards as inducements for appropriate behavior. Resistance also includes expressions of community and coordinated activity, whether expressed through music, dance, religion, belief, food, or language. Resistance implies agency and identity and therefore highlights the individual and group responses to slavery. In North America, the experiences of enslaved Africans and their descendants manifested resistance through flight, uprising, and murder. The African population coalesced around several religious traditions that had been transferred from Africa and that succumbed to the Christian evangelical movements of the late eighteenth century that swept England and North America. The presence of *obeah*, *vodun*, and even Islam reflect the persistence of African traditions in the face of slavery. Musically, there can be no question of the enduring African heritage related to the expressions of the oppressed, their religion, and culture.

Migration

The causes of the migration can be traced to internal African political and social conditions in those parts of western Africa where the enslaved trace their origins. Of course, the European demand for labor for the development of the modern Atlantic world in which European countries, especially Portugal, Spain, Britain, France, and the Netherlands, transported enslaved Africans to their American colonies, was essential. Without that demand, there could not have been a transatlantic slave trade, but there also had to be a willingness to sell, which was related to politics, greed, and power. But that does not explain the willingness of European countries to allow the exploitation of people who were perceived to be different and to allow a racist ideology, nor does it absolve those who participated in the exploitation of people as slaves for any reason and whatever the conditions. However, to understand how this happened, one must examine the conditions in Africa.

First, let us look at the internal political and social conditions in Atlantic Africa, which requires a brief historical overview of the sections of the African coast from where the enslaved traced their origins, from Senegambia in the northwest, south along the Guinea coast to the Bights of Benin and Biafra, and south further along the Loango coast to Kongo and Angola. The political map reveals a dominant pattern for this broad stretch of coast from the sixteenth to the mid-nineteenth centuries—the whole period of the transatlantic slave trade—and that pattern is one of small, centralized states and local federations that governed through secret societies. Even the largest states, such as Asante and Oyo, were reasonably small by modern standards. The consequence of this political fragmentation was the failure to generate methods of government to resist the slave trade. Personal gain and the interests of a small elite supported the slave trade. It is not surprising that the slave trade was closely associated with the political wars of these states and benefited the commercial elites that dominated the trade routes, ports, and secret societies of the federated regions where centralized state institutions were lacking.

The migrating populations can be identified as having their homes in western Africa, from a broad belt along the Atlantic from Senegambia to Angola. The overwhelming majority of enslaved Africans came from two stretches of coast; about nine out of every ten people came either from the region of modern Ghana through Nigeria (known then as the Gold Coast, the Slave Coast, or the Bight of Benin) and the Bight of Biafra, or they came from the coast to the north and south of the Congo River in what is today Congo and Angola. There were some enslaved Africans who came from what are now Sierra Leone, Guinea, Senegal, and the interior regions behind the coast, but they were a small minority of the total migration. The presence of Muslims, often known as Mandingo, is widely known, as is also the presence of Bambara in Louisiana, and rice cultivators from upper Guinea in lowland Carolina, who were brought from the upper Guinea coast and Sierra Leone.

Africans in North America

Hence, the origins of the North American population of Africans can be traced to all the regions of Atlantic Africa. Aside from Mandingos and Bambaras, there were Igbo from the Bight of Biafra who were found in the upper South, while Kongo from the Angola/Congo region were found in all parts of North America. Because of the demographic study of the slave trade, we now have a relatively clear idea of when people came to North America from Africa, from where on the African coast they left, their numbers, the ports of disembarkation, and the relative proportions of men, women, and children and how these figures changed over time. From such information and its correlation with known historical events and contexts in Atlantic Africa, it is possible to impute, and sometimes to substantiate through recorded experiences of individuals, the processes and, indeed, the events that account for the actual people who were enslaved and sold to the Americas. Biographical material exists in many forms and is scattered throughout the diaspora. North America stands out because of the richness of available texts—narratives by and about individuals, some of whom were actually born in Africa, but more often were of the second generation, but who nonetheless continued traditions from their African background.

The principal conditions shaping the forced migration of those who ended up as the black slaves of America related to violence and the threat of violence, from the time of enslavement until death, whether along a trade route, onboard a slave ship, or on a plantation in the Americas. Violence could also, and often did, assume sexual dimensions, rape being common. Sexual violence was extended in Islamic lands to castration, but there was essentially no difference in the ways in which women, and boys onboard ship, were treated—the sexual and personal identity of the individual was denied and only existed for the pleasure of the slave owner or his proxy. Avoidance of violence and resistance to violence were therefore determining characteristics of the responses of the enslaved Africans to the experiences of migration. Individuals attempted to avoid violence through varying degrees of accommodation and co-option that complicates the story of how people resisted bondage.

The types of violence that Africans who were enslaved actually experienced can be classified by context. It appears that a great number of individuals were enslaved in war, either because they were engaged in the actual conflict as soldiers or were civilians captured as the spoils of victory. States and secret societies also organized raids and seizures that resulted in enslavement; these actions suggest degrees and forms of government and hence can be classified as "political," since they may disguise enforcement of law, collection of taxes, or abuse of public office. Manipulation of law, legal procedure, and religious sanction in the form of enslavement also represents a form of public and hence customary, if not constitutional, will. In some cases, those people held as collateral for a loan were sold into slavery to recover the debt, whether or not this was legally acceptable in the local context. Sometimes people seized in wars or raids were already slaves; often, military campaigns allowed the ransoming of captives, which was most likely for those who were free and owned property, or who had families who could pay the redemption price.

The forced movement of enslaved Africans was a fundamental component of the economic development of the frontier of European settlement in the Americas. In North America and elsewhere in the Americas, the use of terror was basic to this mechanism of labor supply. Africans went to areas that were developing economically, often leaving in their wake areas of economic dislocation and desolation in Africa that were a result of slave wars. North America was typical in this regard, since African slave labor was central to several of the most important colonies, particularly South Carolina, Virginia, and Maryland, and indirectly through commerce in other colonies, such as Massachusetts, New York, and Pennsylvania.

The enforced destination of the migrants was to areas where their labor would produce economic development, most importantly to plantations and farms for work in cash-crop agriculture, but also in mining. Africans found themselves in towns and ports as domestic servants; many Africans were urban residents with skilled or semiskilled occupations. They were essential to commerce, serving as porters and teamsters. In eighteenth-century North America, enslaved Africans were concentrated in the agricultural lowlands of South Carolina and Georgia, especially on the Sea Islands, growing rice, lowland cotton, indigo, and other products. In the tidewater region of Virginia and Maryland, they were employed on tobacco farms, while in Louisiana they grew sugar cane. Enslaved Africans and their descendants constituted a sizable portion of the population of New York, Philadelphia, Charleston, and New Orleans, and they were found in numerous towns. Indeed, enslaved Africans were almost everywhere that European settlement was found, so that slaves worked farms and plantations in upstate New York, Rhode Island, and New Jersey, not only in the South. Moreover, any reasonably prosperous family had slaves as domestic servants, whether in Quebec, Boston, Virginia, or New Orleans.

The two most important concentrations of enslaved Africans in North America, the tidewater area of Virginia and Maryland and the lowlands of South Carolina and Georgia, accounted for at least two-thirds of the slaves brought into North America before the end of legal imports of enslaved Africans in 1808.[12] On the basis of data on the voyages of slave ships, it is possible to assess the scale and direction of this migration.

The largest number of Africans in the lowlands of the Carolinas and Georgia came from the Bantu-speaking areas of west-central Africa, representing perhaps one-third of the total number of African immigrants arriving there (34 percent). A substantial number, perhaps 20 percent, came from the area of Senegambia, while the Gold Coast and Sierra Leone each accounted for about 14–15 percent of the total number of enslaved immigrants. There were also substantial numbers of people from the Bight of Biafra and the Windward Coast. By contrast, the greatest number of slaves in the tidewater areas of Virginia and Maryland came from the Bight of Biafra, which accounted for approximately 39 percent of immigrants whose African origins are known. Senegambia accounted for perhaps 21 percent of immigrants to the tidewater, while another 17 percent came from the Bantu regions of west-central Africa. The Gold Coast was also important, with perhaps 10 percent of immigrants coming from there.

Homelands of Immigrants

An examination of the two major importing regions together reveals that 90 percent of the African immigrants in the two major settlement areas came

A view (sepia photo by American School, 19th century) of slave quarters in Savannah, Georgia, ca. 1860. On the eve of the Civil War, the South had a population of approximately nine million people, one-third of whom were slaves. The majority of the white population was made up of yeomen farmers who owned land but no slaves.

from only four regions in Africa. The largest number came from west-central Africa, where languages and cultures were closely related. Many more of these Africans ended up in the lowlands of the Carolinas and Georgia than in the tidewater, but they were prominent in both regions, representing perhaps 29 percent of all immigrants to both regions. The second largest group of immigrants, approximately 18 percent of African arrivals, came from the Bight

Table 7. Origins of Enslaved Africans Shipped to North America

REGION OF ORIGIN	CAROLINAS/ GEORGIA	VIRGINIA/ MARYLAND	N. AMERICA OTHER	N. AMERICA
Senegambia	29,139	14,491	7,166	50,786
Sierra Leone	19,899	2,134	720	22,753
Windward Coast	11,029	2,867	401	14,297
Gold Coast	20,263	6,898	1,802	28,963
Bight of Benin	2,971	1,966	1,984	6,921
Bight of Biafra	13,370	28,542	—	41,912
West Central	47,585	11,072	1,629	60,286
South East Africa	1,118	1,347	295	2,760
Origin unknown	43,921	47,249	8,897	100,067
Total sample	189,295	116,566	22,894	328,755

Data derived from: David Eltis, Stephen Behrendt, David Richardson, and Herbert Klein, *The Atlantic Slave Trade: A Database on CD-Rom* (Cambridge, England: Cambridge University Press, 1999).

of Biafra; these people were mostly Igbo and Ibibio in origins, or in the course of the Atlantic crossing became associated with these predominant groups. While people from the Bight of Biafra were found in both the low country and the tidewater, they were proportionately more numerous in Virginia and Maryland, where they constituted the largest single group. The third largest group, approximately 13 percent, came from the Gold Coast, where Twi was the common language, and most people were identified as Akan. Finally, there was a considerable concentration of people from Sierra Leone, approximately 10 percent of all African immigrants, but they were almost entirely concentrated in the lowlands of the Carolinas and Georgia.

Several distinctive patterns emerge from this demographic profile, although only the broad contours are understood, because the African origins of a substantial number of immigrants, approximately one-third of all immigrants, are not known. Nonetheless, the region of west central Africa stands out; this large region had a population that was closely related in language and culture, often referred to as "Bantu" and incorporating people who spoke Kikongo, Kimbundu, or a similar language. People from west central Africa were heavily represented in the African population of large parts of the Americas, especially Brazil. Hence, North America conformed to this pattern, and it is likely that a significant proportion of arrivals in North America whose origins are not known also came from west central Africa. The predominance of these closely related Bantu-speaking peoples had an important impact on the religion and culture of the enslaved population in North America and elsewhere.

Second, the Senegambia region was prominent in North America, much more so than virtually anywhere else in the Americas, with the possible exception of the small French islands in the Caribbean. Since Senegambia was a region strongly influenced by Islam, more so than any other coastal area of origin for enslaved Africans, there appear to have been more Muslims or people who had been exposed to Islam in North America than anywhere else in the Americas, except for Bahia and other parts of Brazil. The importance of Senegambia was especially pronounced in Louisiana, since many people identified as Bambara and Mandingo went to Louisiana, but they were also clearly present in both the low country of the Carolinas and Georgia and in the tidewater region of Virginia and Maryland. Among those African immigrants who can be identified as coming from Senegambia, adult Muslim males stand out most prominently. Indeed, there are very few references to Muslim women, which reflects what is known about the slave trade in the interior of West Africa, where exports to the coast from the interior were almost entirely males.

Third, the upper South had a considerable concentration of people from the Bight of Biafra, although there were substantial numbers of Biafran immigrants in the lowlands of the Carolinas and Georgia too. It is likely, moreover, that a large portion of the immigrants whose African origins are not known actually came from the Bight of Biafra, since British trade grew substantially in the Bight of Biafra in the eighteenth century, and Britain was the biggest supplier of slaves to North America, sometimes indirectly through transshipments from Jamaica and Barbados. Nonetheless, the size of the population of Igbo and Ibibio origin was substantial, apparently enough to evolve a distinct subculture among the enslaved population. The Bight of Biafra stands out in the demography of the eighteenth-century slave trade because of the relatively high numbers of women in comparison with all other parts of the African coast. Women from the Bight of Biafra were particularly important in giving birth to a new generation in the Americas, in sharp contrast with the virtual lack of women from Muslim areas.

The fourth concentration of peoples included those from Sierra Leone and adjacent parts of the so-called Windward Coast. They were heavily concentrated in the low country, and especially in areas of rice cultivation. While there were some people from this stretch of the African coast in the tidewater region, they were relatively few in number and probably not enough to have as strong an impact on culture and change as in the Carolinas and Georgia.

Noticeably absent or of minor importance is the region of the "Slave Coast"—the Bight of Benin—even though this was one of the most important sources of enslaved Africans for the Atlantic crossing. The region included Yoruba, Ewe/Fon/Allada (so-called Gbe languages) and other people brought from the interior, including Muslims, and the fact that almost none of these people were to be found in North America marks an important difference between the origins of Africans in North America and elsewhere. While the Bight of Benin accounts for some immigrants, they are very few by comparison with their substantial importance in Cuba, Trinidad, and Brazil.

Although the demographic figures are revealing in many respects, the statistics alone disguise the odyssey undertaken by each individual who was forced to cross the Atlantic on a slave ship. Ethnic and regional categories can provide a setting in which to examine the slave trade, but the personal histories of individuals are essential in examining the impact of the slave trade and slavery on society, both in Africa and in the Americas. Biography reveals the experience of African Americans as they became part of the diaspora in North America. It is fortunate that autobiographical and biographical accounts have been recorded for several thousand individuals, and while most accounts relate the experiences of individuals in the nineteenth century, there are some accounts of individuals born in Africa in the eighteenth century that inform our understanding of the defining period of the African Diaspora. Biography presents the voices of the enslaved, whether born in Africa or not, and such information as can be derived from these accounts can be supplemented with information contained in fugitive-slave advertisements, plantation inventories, and probate records. Biographies provide information on the direct impact of the transatlantic slave trade on people.

The discussion of Muslims is enhanced by several biographies that have survived. For example, Muhammad Kaba Saghanughu of Jamaica lived on one plantation, Spice Grove, from 1777 until his death in 1845. He was the leader of the Muslim community in Jamaica, at least since the 1820s, and was the author of an important treatise on prayer that reaffirms the allegiance of the Jamaican Muslims to the Qadiriyya brotherhood. Similar biographical accounts of Muslims have survived from North America, Trinidad, and Brazil.

Resistance to Slavery

Similarly, there are ethnic components to various rebellions and acts of resistance that have to be put in the context of the African background. See, for example, the acts of slave resistance that had clear "ethnic" dimensions, such as the Stono Rebellion, Gabriel's Rebellion, the Bahia Muslim uprising of 1835, and the St. Domingue revolution, with its Kongo background. Similar "ethnic" connections to resistance existed elsewhere. Therefore, the major characteristics of the international slave trade, and especially the place of North America in that trade, are complex. Because of the scale of the migration, and the complexities of the individual experiences that made up that exodus, it is difficult to summarize. However, with respect to North America, the following points are important:

1. The international slave trade to North America, as between Africa and other parts of the Americas, and indeed including the slave trade in the Indian Ocean and the Islamic world at the same time, treated human beings as commodities, buying and selling individuals like any other property. Unlike in other slave systems, however, racial distinctions were used to keep the enslaved population in bondage in the Americas, with the corresponding development of racialized attitudes and racism.

2. The enslaved Africans brought to North America, as elsewhere in the Americas, were considered to be first and foremost workers, and the

degree of power concentrated in the hands of slave owners meant that the enslaved could be worked harder and longer than other laborers. Such exploitation was decidedly to the disadvantage of the health and welfare of the enslaved Africans, who received no wages, minimal clothing and housing, and often had to work overtime to grow food or earn enough to buy food.

3. The degree of power concentrated in the hands of slave owners in North America, as was the case in all slave-based societies, allowed excessive degrees of corporal punishment, the perpetuation of sexual abuse and exploitation, and disregard for kinship, especially in not recognizing relationships arising from paternity. The status of children followed the slave status of the mother, no matter who the father was.

4. Methods of social control were intrinsically associated with racial perceptions, although how racialism developed and how it differed over time and place are important considerations. In North America, any person of identifiable African descent, no matter the degree of "white" ancestry, was deemed "colored," "Negro," or "black," thereby constituting a racial caste, but in other parts of the Americas, racial distinctions were often more complex.

5. The interests of slave owners were in the maximization of profits, which resulted in treating enslaved people as chattels. This treatment was sometimes further exacerbated by psychopathic behavior, social perversity, and political expediency that increased the arbitrariness of master-slave relations.

The most enduring consequence of the migration for the migrants themselves and for the receiving communities was the development of racism, which affected the evolution of a sense of an African American community, with its particular cultural manifestations, attitudes, and expressions. The legacy is apparent in music and art, with considerable impact on religion, cuisine, and language. A literary tradition, which began in song and rhythm, is also noteworthy.

There were enduring consequences of the migration on the communities that suffered the loss of population in Africa. Transformations of society

MPI / Hulton Archive / Getty Images

Male slave in leg chains and iron collar, Louisiana, ca. 1850. Runaways were a constant problem for any slave-based society. Other forms of resistance included working slowly or inefficiently, purposefully misunderstanding instructions, breaking tools, injuring farm animals, feigning illness, and open violence. It has been estimated that more than 250 uprisings or attempted uprisings involving ten or more slaves occurred in the United States in the two centuries before the Civil War.

and economy were caused by involvement in enslavement, slave-trading, and the use of slaves locally within Africa. Places of refuge for those attempting to escape enslavement were developed on such islands of safety as Ganvie, a community built on stilts in the middle of Lake Noue on the lagoons of the Bight of Benin. An enduring legacy of resistance can be seen in the music and art of African immigrants, and in their identification with ethnicity, religion, and race, reflecting common bonds with the cultures of the people who remained in Africa.

The cultural and religious impact of African immigration during the slavery era affected music and expression. It is known that music patterns and rhythms are old, and while the evolution of new styles and changes in instrumentation have affected music, the interconnection of the transatlantic world shows that migrations involve people but also culture. A perspective that does justice to the African background of the modern world demonstrates that "American" culture is not "European" or "African," but its own form, created in a political and economic context of inequality and oppression in which diverse ethnic and cultural influences can be discerned. Moreover, it is clear that influences were both European and African, and in some contexts, Amerindian. Undoubtedly, the transatlantic slave trade was the defining migration that shaped the African Diaspora. It did so through the people it brought, and especially the women who were to give birth to children of the new African American population. In North America, those women include many who can be identified as "Igbo" or "Ibibio," but almost none who were Yoruba, Fon or Hausa, who constituted the slave population leaving the Bight of Benin. There were a considerable number of women in the cargoes leaving west central Africa, so that "Bantu" women, from matrilineal societies, constituted a considerable portion of the fertile population of slave women. Similarly, the immigrant population from Sierra Leone also appears to have had a relatively high proportion of females, which was reflected in fertility rates. These were the women who gave birth to African American culture and society.

The interpretative issues that need to be discussed in presenting the theme of the transatlantic slave trade to the general public and to educators include responsibility, resistance, and reparations. On issues of responsibility, there have to be considerations of who was responsible for the enslavement of individuals in Africa, and whether this enslavement was done through means that were thought to be legal or illegal, whether during acts of war and the taking of political prisoners, or in kidnapping and arbitrary seizure arising from debt or acts perceived to be witchcraft. Responsibility must also be assessed in terms of the merchants and government officials who knowingly or unwittingly sold individuals as slaves for transport across the Atlantic or the Sahara to distant places and unknown hardships and suffering. Responsibility also rests on the shoulders of the merchants and ship crews who carried enslaved Africans to the Americas under barbaric and cruel conditions onboard ship, and on the plantation owners and others whose economic prosperity depended upon the exploitation of slave labor. Ultimately, in the period of slavery and the slave trade, the Atlantic world that included North America arose on the shoulders of African labor, and its development, achieved in the context of slavery and its aftermath, had a clear effect on the modern world economy.

· ·

NOTES

1. David Eltis et al., *The Atlantic Slave Trade: A Database on CD-Rom* (Cambridge, England: Cambridge University Press, 1999); David Eltis, "The Volume and Structure of the Trans-Atlantic Slave Trade: A Reassessment," *William and Mary Quarterly* 58 (2001): 17–46.
2. W. E. B. Du Bois, "The Suppression of the African Slave Trade in the United States of America, 1638–1871" (Ph.D. dissertation, Harvard University, 1895).
3. Philip D. Curtin, "The Slave Trade and the Numbers Game: A Review of the Literature," in *The Atlantic Slave Trade: A Census* (Madison: University of Wisconsin Press, 1969); David P. Henige, "Measuring the Immeasurable: The Atlantic Slave Trade, West African Population and the Pyrrhonian Critic," *Journal of African History* 27 (1986): 295–313; Joseph E. Inikori, ed., *Forced Migration: The Impact of the Export Slave Trade on African Societies* (London: Hutchinson, 1981), 10–22.
4. David Eltis and Stanley L. Engerman, "Was the Slave Trade Dominated by Men?" *Journal of Interdisciplinary History* 23 (1992): 237–57; David Eltis and Stanley L. Engerman, "Fluctuations in Sex and Age Ratios in the Trans-Atlantic Slave Trade, 1663–1864," *Economic History Review* 46 (1993): 308–23; David Geggus, "Sex Ratio, Age and Ethnicity in the Atlantic Slave Trade: Data from French Shipping and Plantation Records," *Journal of African History* 30 (1989): 23–44.
5. Stephan Bühnen, "Ethnic Origins of Peruvian Slaves (1548–1650): Figures for Upper Guinea," *Paiduema* 39 (1993): 57–110; Michael Angelo Gomez, *Exchanging Our Country*

Marks: *The Transformation of African Identities in the Colonial and Antebellum South* (Chapel Hill: University of North Carolina Press, 1998); Gwendolyn Hall, *Slavery and African Ethnicities in the Americas: Restoring the Links* (Chapel Hill: University of North Carolina Press, 2005); P. E. H. Hair, "Ethnolinguistic Continuity on the Guinea Coast," *Journal of African History* 8 (1967): 247–68; Robin Law, "Ethnicity and the Slave Trade: 'Lucumi' and 'Nago' as Ethnonyms in West Africa," *History in Africa* 24 (1997): 205–19; Paul E. Lovejoy and David V. Trotman, "Enslaved Africans and Their Expectations of Slave Life in the Americas: Towards a Reconsideration of Models of 'Creolisation,'" in *Questioning Creole: Creolisation Discourses in Caribbean Culture*, edited by Verene A. Shepherd, Kamau Brathwaite, and Glen L. Richards (Kingston, Jamaica: Ian Randle, 2002), 9–42.

6. Sheila Lambert, ed., *House of Commons Sessional Papers of the Eighteenth Century* (Wilmington, Del.: Scholarly Resources, 1975).

7. Olaudah Equiano, *The Interesting Narrative and Other Writings* (New York: Penguin, 1995); Robin Law and Paul E. Lovejoy, eds., *The Biography of Mahommah Gardo Baquaqua: His Passage from Slavery to Freedom in Africa and America* (Princeton, N.J.: Markus Wiener Publisher, 2001); Barry Unsworth, *Sacred Hunger* (New York: Doubleday, 1992).

8. Herbert S. Klein and Stanley L. Engerman, "Long-Term Trends in African Mortality in the Trans-Atlantic Slave Trade," *Slavery and Abolition* 18 (1997): 36–48; Raymond L. Cohn, "Deaths of Slaves in the Middle Passage," *Journal of Economic History* 45 (1985): 685–92; Philip D. Curtin, "Epidemiology and the Slave Trade," *Political Science Quarterly* 83 (1968): 190–216; Joseph C. Miller, "Mortality in the Atlantic Slave Trade: Statistical Evidence on Causality," *Journal of Interdisciplinary History* 11 (1980): 385–423; Joseph C. Miller, "Overcrowded and Undernourished: The Techniques and Consequences of Tight-Packing in the Portuguese Southern Atlantic Slave Trade," in *De la traite à l'esclavage*, edited by Serge Daget (Paris: L'Harmattan, 1988); Joseph C. Miller, *Way of Death: Merchant Capitalism and the Angolan Slave Trade, 1730–1830* (Madison: University of Wisconsin Press, 1988); Richard B. Sheridan, "The Guinea Surgeons on the Middle Passage: The Provision of Medical Services in the British Slave Trade," *International Journal of African Historical Studies* 14 (1981): 601–25; Stephen D. Behrendt, "The British Slave Trade, 1785–1807: Volume, Profitability, and Mortality" (Ph.D. dissertation, University of Wisconsin, 1993); Philip Morgan, "The Cultural Implications of the Atlantic Slave Trade: African Regional Origins, American Destinations and New World Developments," *Slavery and Abolition* 18 (1997): 98–121.

9. Paul E. Lovejoy and David Richardson, "The Business of Slaving: Pawnship in Western Africa, c. 1600–1810," *Journal of African History* 42 (2001): 67–89.

10. Albert van Dantzig, "Effect of the Atlantic Slave Trade on Some West African Societies," *Revue française d'histoire d'outre-mer* 62 (1975): 252–69; Robin Law, "Slaves, Trade, and Taxes: The Material Basis of Political Power in Precolonial West Africa," *Research in Economic Anthropology* 1 (1978): 37–52.

11. Joseph C. Miller, "Central Africa during the Era of the Slave Trade, c. 1490s–1850s," in *Central Africans and Cultural Transformations in the American Diaspora*, edited by Linda Heywood (Cambridge, England: Cambridge University Press, 2001); John K. Thornton,

"The Slave Trade in Eighteenth Century Angola: Effects on Demographic Structures," *Canadian Journal of African Studies/Revue canadienne d'études africaines* 14 (1980): 417–27.

12. Roger T. Anstey, "The Volume of the North American Slave-Carrying Trade from Africa, 1761–1810," *Revue française d'histoire d'outre-mer* 62 (1975): 47–66.

BIBLIOGRAPHY

Adamu, Mahdi. "The Delivery of Slaves from the Bight of Benin in the Eighteenth and Nineteenth Centuries." In *The Uncommon Market: Essays in the Economic History of the Atlantic Slave Trade*, edited by H. A. Gemery and J. S. Hogendorn. New York: Academic Press, 1979.

Adediran, Biodun. "Yoruba Ethnic Groups or a Yoruba Ethnic Group? A Review of the Problem of Ethnic Identification." *Africa: Revista do Centro de Estudos Africanos da USP* 7 (1984): 57–70.

Anstey, Roger T. "The Volume of the North American Slave-Carrying Trade from Africa, 1761–1810." *Revue française d'histoire d'outre-mer* 62 (1975): 47–66.

Behrendt, Stephen D. "The British Slave Trade, 1785–1807: Volume, Profitability, and Mortality." Ph.D. dissertation, University of Wisconsin, 1993.

Binder, Wolfgang, ed. *Slavery in the Americas*. Würzburg, Germany: Königshausen & Neumann, 1993.

Bühnen, Stephan. "Ethnic Origins of Peruvian Slaves (1548–1650): Figures for Upper Guinea." *Paideuma* 39 (1993): 57–110.

Clarkson, Thomas. "Essay on the Inhumanity of the Slave Trade." Honours Degree, Cambridge University, 1785.

Cohn, Raymond L. "Deaths of Slaves in the Middle Passage." *Journal of Economic History* 45 (1985): 685–92.

Colclanis, Peter A., ed. *The Atlantic Economy during the Seventeenth and Eighteenth Centuries: Organization, Operation, Practice, and Personnel*. Columbia: University of South Carolina Press, 2005.

Crane, Elaine F. "'The First Wheel of Commerce': Newport, Rhode Island, and the Slave Trade, 1760–1776." *Slavery and Abolition* 1 (1980): 178–98.

Curtin, Philip D. "Epidemiology and the Slave Trade." *Political Science Quarterly* 83 (1968): 190–216.

——. "The Slave Trade and the Numbers Game: A Review of the Literature." *The Atlantic Slave Trade: A Census*. Madison: University of Wisconsin Press, 1969.

——, ed. *Africa Remembered: Narratives by West Africans from the Era of the Slave Trade*. Madison: University of Wisconsin Press, 1967.

Curto, José C., and Raymond R. Gervais. "The Population History of Luanda during the Late Atlantic Slave Trade, 1781–1844." *African Economic History* 29 (2001): 1–59; 30 (2002): 15–162.

Curto, José C., and Paul E. Lovejoy, eds. *Enslaving Connections: Changing Cultures of Africa and Brazil during the Era of Slavery*. Amherst, N.Y.: Humanity Books, 2004.

————, eds. *Enslaving Spirits: The Portuguese-Brazilian Alcohol Trade at Luanda and its Hinterland.* Leiden, Netherlands: Brill, 2004.

Curto, José C., and Renée Soulodre-La France, eds. *Africa and the Americas: Interconnections during the Slave Trade.* Trenton, N.J.: Africa World Press, 2005.

van Dantzig, Albert. "Effect of the Atlantic Slave Trade on Some West African Societies." *Revue française d'histoire d'outre-mer* 62 (1975): 252–69.

Drescher, Seymour. *Econocide: British Slavery in the Era of Abolition.* Pittsburgh, Pa.: University of Pittsburgh Press, 1977.

Du Bois, W. E. B. "The Suppression of the African Slave Trade in the United States of America, 1638–1871." Ph.D. dissertation, Harvard University, 1895.

Eltis, David. *The Rise of African Slavery in the Americas.* Cambridge, England: Cambridge University Press, 2000.

————. "The Volume and Structure of the Trans-Atlantic Slave Trade: A Reassessment." *William and Mary Quarterly* 58 (2001): 17–46.

Eltis, David, Stephen Behrendt, David Richardson, and Herbert S. Klein. *The Atlantic Slave Trade: A Database on CD-Rom.* Cambridge, England: Cambridge University Press, 1999.

Eltis, David, and Stanley L. Engerman. "Fluctuations in Sex and Age Ratios in the Trans-Atlantic Slave Trade, 1663–1864." *Economic History Review* 46 (1993): 308–23.

————. "Was the Slave Trade Dominated by Men?" *Journal of Interdisciplinary History* 23 (1992): 237–57.

Equiano, Olaudah. *The Interesting Narrative and Other Writings.* 1789; New York: Penguin, 1995.

Fage, J. D. "Slaves and Society in Western Africa, c. 1445–c. 1700." *Journal of African History* 21 (1980): 289–310.

Florentino, Manolo G. "About the Slaving Business in Rio de Janeiro, 1790–1830: A Contribution." In *Pour l'histoire du Brésil: Hommage à Katia de Queirós Mattoso,* edited by François Crouzet, Philippe Bonnichon, and Denis Rolland. Paris: L'Harmattan, 2000.

Geggus, David. "Sex Ratio, Age and Ethnicity in the Atlantic Slave Trade: Data from French Shipping and Plantation Records." *Journal of African History* 30 (1989): 23–44.

Gilroy, Paul. *The Black Atlantic: Modernity and Double Consciousness.* Cambridge, Mass.: Harvard University Press, 1993.

Gomez, A. Michael. *Black Crescent.* Cambridge, England: Cambridge University Press, 2005.

————. *Exchanging Our Country Marks: The Transformation of African Identities in the Colonial and Antebellum South.* Chapel Hill: University of North Carolina Press, 1998.

————, ed. *Diasporic Africa: A Reader.* New York: New York University Press, 2005.

Hair, P. E. H. "Ethnolinguistic Continuity on the Guinea Coast." *Journal of African History* 8 (1967): 247–68.

Hall, Gwendolyn. "Senegambia during the French Slave Trade to Louisiana." *Africans in Colonial Louisiana: The Development of Afro-Creole Culture in the Eighteenth Century.* Baton Rouge: Louisiana State University Press, 1992.

———. *Slavery and African Ethnicities in the Americas: Restoring the Links*. Chapel Hill: University of North Carolina Press, 2005.

Henige, David P. "Measuring the Immeasurable: The Atlantic Slave Trade, West African Population, and the Pyrrhonian Critic." *Journal of African History* 27 (1986): 295–313.

Herskovits, Melville J. "On the Provenience of New World Negroes." *Social Forces* 12 (1933): 247–62.

———. "The Significance of West Africa for Negro Research." *Journal of Negro History* 21 (1936): 15–30.

Heywood, Linda, ed. *Central Africans and Cultural Transformations in the American Diaspora.* Cambridge, England: Cambridge University Press, 2002.

Hofstee, Erik J. W. "The Great Divide: Aspects of the Social History of the Middle Passage in the Trans-Atlantic Slave Trade." Ph.D. dissertation, Michigan State University, 2001.

Hogendorn, Jan, and Marion Johnson. *The Shell Money of the Slave Trade.* Cambridge, England: Cambridge University Press, 1986.

Hurston, Zora Neale. "Cudjoe's Own Story of the Last African Slaver." *Journal of Negro History* 12 (1927): 648–63.

Inikori, Joseph E. *Africans and the Industrial Revolution in England: A Study in International Trade and Economic Development.* Cambridge, England: Cambridge University Press, 2002.

———, ed. *Forced Migration: The Impact of the Export Slave Trade on African Societies.* London: Hutchinson, 1981.

Klein, Herbert S. "The European Organization of the Slave Trade." *The Atlantic Slave Trade.* Cambridge, England: Cambridge University Press, 1999.

———. *The Middle Passage: Comparative Studies in the Atlantic Slave Trade.* Princeton, N.J.: Princeton University Press, 1978.

Klein, Herbert S., and Stanley L. Engerman. "Long-Term Trends in African Mortality in the Trans-Atlantic Slave Trade." *Slavery and Abolition* 18 (1997): 36–48.

Lambert, Sheila, ed. *House of Commons Sessional Papers of the Eighteenth Century.* Wilmington, Del.: Scholarly Resources, 1975.

Law, Robin. "Ethnicity and the Slave Trade: 'Lucumi' and 'Nago' as Ethnonyms in West Africa." *History in Africa* 24 (1997): 205–19.

———. *Ouidah: The Social History of a West African Slaving "Port," 1727–1892.* Athens: Ohio University Press; Oxford: James Currey, 2004.

———. "Royal Monopoly and Private Enterprise in the Atlantic Trade: The Case of Dahomey." *Journal of African History* 18 (1977): 555–77.

———. *The Slave Coast of West Africa, 1550–1750: The Impact of the Atlantic Slave Trade on an African Society.* Oxford: Clarendon Press, 1991.

———. "Slaves, Trade, and Taxes: The Material Basis of Political Power in Precolonial West Africa." *Research in Economic Anthropology* 1 (1978): 37–52.

———, ed. *Source Material for Studying the Slave Trade and the African Diaspora.* Stirling, Scotland: Centre of Commonwealth Studies, University of Stirling, 1997.

Law, Robin, and Paul E. Lovejoy, eds. *The Biography of Mahommah Gardo Baquaqua: His Passage from Slavery to Freedom in Africa and America*. Princeton, N.J.: Markus Wiener Publisher, 2001.

Law, Robin, and Silke Strickrodt, eds. *Ports of the Slave Trade (Bights of Benin and Biafra)*. Stirling, Scotland: Centre of Commonwealth Studies, University of Stirling, 1999.

Lovejoy, Paul E. *Ecology and Ethnography of Muslim Trade in West Africa*. Trenton, N.J.: Africa World Press, 2005.

——. "Ethnic Designations of the Slave Trade and the Reconstruction of the History of Trans-Atlantic Slavery." In *Trans-Atlantic Dimensions of the Ethnicity in the African Diaspora*, edited by Paul E. Lovejoy and David Trotman. London: Continuum, 2002.

——. *Slavery, Commerce, and Production in the Sokoto Caliphate of West Africa*. Trenton, N.J.: Africa World Press, 2005.

——. *Transformations in Slavery: A History of Slavery in Africa*. Cambridge, England: Cambridge University Press, 2000.

——, ed. *Identity in the Shadow of Slavery*. London: Cassell Academic, 2000.

——, ed. *Slavery on the Frontiers of Islam*. Princeton, N.J.: Markus Wiener Publisher, 2004.

Lovejoy, Paul E., and J. S. Hogendorn. "Slave Marketing in West Africa." In *The Uncommon Market: Essays in the Economic History of the Atlantic Slave Trade*, edited by H. A. Gemery and J. S. Hogendorn. New York: Academic Press, 1979.

Lovejoy, Paul E., and David Richardson. "The Business of Slaving: Pawnship in Western Africa, c. 1600–1810." *Journal of African History* 42 (2001): 67–89.

——. "The Initial 'Crisis of Adaptation': The Impact of British Abolition on the Atlantic Slave Trade in West Africa, 1808–1820." In *From Slave Trade to Legitimate Commerce: The Commercial Transition in Nineteenth-Century West Africa*, edited by Robin Law. Cambridge, England: Cambridge University Press, 1995.

Lovejoy, Paul E., and David V. Trotman. "Enslaved Africans and Their Expectations of Slave Life in the Americas: Towards a Reconsideration of Models of 'Creolisation.'" In *Questioning Creole: Creolisation Discourses in Caribbean Culture*, edited by Verene A. Shepherd, Kamau Brathwaite, and Glen L. Richards. Kingston, Jamaica: Ian Randle, 2002.

Manning, Patrick, ed. *Slave Trades, 1500–1800: Globalization of Forced Labour*. Aldershot, England: Variorum, 1996.

Miller, Joseph C. "Central Africa during the Era of the Slave Trade, c. 1490s–1850s." In *Central Africans and Cultural Transformations in the American Diaspora*, edited by Linda Heywood. Cambridge, England: Cambridge University Press, 2001.

——. "Mortality in the Atlantic Slave Trade: Statistical Evidence on Causality." *Journal of Interdisciplinary History* 11 (1980): 385–423.

——. "Overcrowded and Undernourished: The Techniques and Consequences of Tight-Packing in the Portuguese Southern Atlantic Slave Trade." In *De la traite à l'esclavage*, edited by Serge Daget, 2:395–424. Paris: L'Harmattan, 1988.

——. *Way of Death: Merchant Capitalism and the Angolan Slave Trade, 1730–1830*. Madison: University of Wisconsin Press, 1988.

Minchinton, Walter E. "Characteristics of British Slaving Vessels, 1698–1775." *Journal of Interdisciplinary History* 20 (1989): 53–82.

Morgan, Philip. "The Cultural Implications of the Atlantic Slave Trade: African Regional Origins, American Destinations and New World Developments." *Slavery and Abolition* 18 (1997): 98–121.

Mouser, Bruce L. "Trade, Coasters, and Conflict in the Rio Pongo from 1790–1808." *Journal of African History* 14 (1973): 45–64.

Palmer, Colin A. "From Africa to the Americas: Ethnicity in the Early Black Communities of the Americas." *Journal of World History* 6 (1995): 223–37.

Patterson, Orlando. *Slavery and Social Death: A Comparative Study.* Cambridge, Mass.: Harvard University Press, 1982.

Richardson, David. "The Costs of Survival: The Transport of Slaves in the Middle Passage and the Profitability of the 18th-Century British Slave Trade." *Explorations in Economic History* 24 (1987): 178–96.

——. "Shipboard Revolts, African Authority, and the Atlantic Slave Trade." *William and Mary Quarterly* 58 (2001): 69–92.

Rodney, Walter. "Slavery and Other Forms of Social Oppression on the Upper Guinea Coast in the Context of the Atlantic Slave Trade." *Journal of African History* 7 (1969): 431–43.

——. "Upper Guinea and the Significance of the Origins of Africans Enslaved in the New World." *The Journal of Negro History* 54 (1969): 327–45.

Searing, James F. *West African Slavery and Atlantic Commerce: The Senegal River Valley, 1700–1860.* Cambridge, England: Cambridge University Press, 1993.

Sheridan, Richard B. "The Guinea Surgeons on the Middle Passage: The Provision of Medical Services in the British Slave Trade." *International Journal of African Historical Studies* 14 (1981): 601–25.

Taylor, Eric Robert. "If We Must Die: A History of Shipboard Insurrections during the Slave Trade." Ph.D. dissertation, University of California, Los Angeles, 2000.

Thornton, John. *Africa and Africans in the Making of the Atlantic World, 1400–1800.* Cambridge, England: Cambridge University Press, 1998.

——. "The Slave Trade in Eighteenth Century Angola: Effects on Demographic Structures." *Canadian Journal of African Studies/Revue canadienne d'études africaines* 14 (1980): 417–27.

Unsworth, Barry. *Sacred Hunger.* New York: Doubleday, 1992.

Warner-Lewis, Maureen. "Posited Kikoongo Origins of Some Portuguese and Spanish Words from the Slave Era." *América Negra* 7 (1997): 83–97.

CHRONOLOGY

1441   The explorer Antam Goncalves seizes Moors near Cape Blanc in West Africa and carries them back to Portugal as slaves.

1442   The Portuguese build forts along the western coast of Africa and begin to engage in a slave trade.

ca. 1445   The Portuguese introduce slavery to the Madeiras, and by 1501 there are 2,000 slaves working on sugar plantations on the islands.

1490   The Portuguese and Kongolese nobles begin to cultivate sugar on the island of São Thomé, using African slaves from Kongo.

1491   The Castilians begin to grow sugar on the Canary Islands, at first using enslaved natives, and later enslaved Africans acquired from the Portuguese.

1501   Nicolas de Ovando, the colonial governor of Hispaniola, receives authorization from the Spanish Crown to import enslaved Africans; the first group arrives the following year.

1506   Using slave labor, the Spanish begin to produce sugar in the Greater Antilles.

1510   A Portuguese ship carries enslaved Africans to Brazil to labor on sugar plantations.

1521   December: The first recorded incident of a slave insurrection in the western hemisphere occurs when enslaved Africans rise up on Hispaniola.

1542   Spain outlaws the enslavement of Amerindians, and as a result, the African slave trade intensifies.

1619   August: The first blacks arrive at the British colony of Jamestown. Although they are not termed "slaves," they are considered to be war captives and thus subject to indefinite servitude.

1621   Willem Usselinx and other Dutch merchants charter the Dutch West India Company to establish colonies and transport slaves to the New World.

1629   The French begin to import enslaved Africans into St. Kitts.

1630   English settlers use enslaved Africans to cultivate sugar on Barbados.

ca. 1660 There are approximately 100,000 enslaved Africans in the West Indies but only about 5,000 in the North American mainland colonies.

1672   The Royal African Company is granted a monopoly over the English slave trade.

1700   An estimated 28,000 enslaved Africans are in the British North American colonies.

1750   The British North American colonies have approximately 236,000 slaves.

1778   A special commission established by the British Parliament begins to investigate the conduct of the transatlantic slave trade.

1787   Under Article I, Section 9 of the U.S. Constitution, the transatlantic slave trade is prohibited as of 1808.

1807   British Parliament prohibits the transatlantic slave trade; the ban takes effect on March 1, 1808.

1807–08 The U.S. Congress bans the transatlantic slave trade to the United States and its territories; the ban takes effect on January 1, 1808.

1814   The Netherlands officially ends its involvement in the transatlantic slave trade.

1817   At the prompting of the British government, Spain and Portugal each agree to end the transatlantic slave trade north of the equator.

1817   The French government officially ends its participation in the transatlantic slave trade.

1820   The Spanish government abolishes the transatlantic slave trade south of the equator.

1829   Mexico abolishes slavery.

1830   Brazil signs a treaty with Great Britain and Portugal ending its participation in the slave trade south of the equator; the treaty is not consistently enforced.

1833   August 1: The British Parliament passes the Emancipation Act, abolishing slavery throughout the British Empire. Within five years all slaves in British colonies—but not British Territories—are freed.

1839   Under the Palmerston Act, the British Royal Navy is given the right of search and seizure of ships suspected of carrying enslaved Africans; subsequent negotiations with individual countries, including Portugal, the United States, and others, extend this right of search to Portuguese vessels and ships of other countries suspected of carrying slaves to the Americas.

1848   The French government abolishes slavery in all its colonies, but slavery continues unabated in French Africa.

1851   The Queiróz Law outlaws the African slave trade to Brazil.

1860   The Netherlands enacts a statute abolishing slavery in all Dutch colonies; the law takes effect in 1863.

1867   The transatlantic slave trade, in operation since 1502, ends when the last shipload of African slaves arrives in Cuba. It is estimated that a total of 12 million Africans were sent to the New World as slaves.

1873   The Spanish government abolishes slavery in Puerto Rico.

1886   The Spanish government abolishes slavery in Cuba.

1888   May 13: Brazil is the last country in the western hemisphere to end slavery; the *Lei Aurea* (Golden Law) frees approximately 750,000 Brazilian slaves.

GLOSSARY

Abolition. The movement to abolish slavery that began in various countries in the eighteenth century. Though slave trading was outlawed by Great Britain and the United States in 1807 and abolished in British colonies in 1838, slavery was declared illegal by various states in the U.S., beginning with Vermont in 1777, before it was finally abolished throughout the country in 1865, and before slavery was abolished in Brazil in 1888.

Akan. Ethnic term for people in modern Ghana, including Asante (Ashanti), Fante, and others who speak the Twi language.

Bight of Benin. Region of the coast of southwestern Nigeria, République du Benin, and Togo; also called the "Mina" Coast and the "Slave Coast."

Bight of Biafra. Region of the Niger River delta and the Cross River basin of southeastern Nigeria and Cameroon.

Cowries. Small sea shells from the Indian Ocean used as money in West Africa, and also used in making jewelry.

Creole. A term often referring to people born in the Americas of African, European, or mixed background; also, by extension, people born in port towns around the Atlantic, including Africa; also, a linguistic term referring to the mixed languages of such populations.

Gbe. A linguistic term referring to several related languages in the Bight of Benin, including Fon (Dahomey), Allada, Ewe, and Mahi.

Gold Coast. The region of modern Ghana, named because of gold available in the interior.

Jihad. Muslim holy war, specifically the wars of the eighteenth and nineteenth centuries in West Africa, including those founding the states of Futa Jallon, Futa Toro, and Sokoto.

"Middle Passage." A reference to the transatlantic crossing of enslaved Africans.

"Mina" Coast. A term referring to the "Slave Coast" or Bight of Benin and the Gold Coast, named after Elmina Castle, built by the Portuguese in 1482 for use in gold trade and later used to warehouse slaves for transport across the Atlantic.

Manilas. Bracelets imported into the Bight of Biafra and used as money.

Senegambia. The region incorporating the Senegal and Gambia Rivers in the western Sudan.

"Slave Coast." The area of West Africa from what is now Ghana to southwestern Nigeria, which served as the principal trading center for African slaves from about 1550 to about 1750.

African Americans and Native Americans

Barbara Krauthamer

Abstract

The following essay discusses the history of African/African American and Native American interactions and relations in North America from the eighteenth century through the present day. It provides an introduction to this broad subject that traces the contact between newly arrived Africans and the indigenous peoples of North America in the British and Spanish colonies, and then highlights important moments for relations between the two groups in the eighteenth and nineteenth centuries as well as the present day. The essay is designed to offer readers a summary of the extensive scholarly literature in this field, from the earliest works by Carter G. Woodson to recent studies in literary analysis, critical legal theory, and contemporary art. Over the years, certain key themes have emerged in studies of African American/ Native American relations, and the works discussed in this essay examine the central events and issues related to them.

The articles and book chapters discussed below are drawn mainly from three disciplines—history, anthropology, and literature—to ensure ample coverage of a broad subject. The material includes older, classic pieces, such as work by Woodson, as well as newer contributions. All of the works expose the reader to primary sources, original research, and scholarly analysis. The history and anthropology articles address subjects such as intermarriage between Indians and Africans in colonial New England; trade relations between enslaved Africans and free Indians in French Louisiana; Creek Indians' early practices of slaveholding; cross-cultural identification between African Americans and Native Americans in the nineteenth century; the creation of maroon communities among the Seminoles in antebellum Florida; and conflicts between African Americans and Native Americans over the meaning of "Indian" identity in the late nineteenth century. Work in the field of legal studies highlights the ways in which law and social institutions have created racial categories, laws, and policies that influenced relations between Africans, African Americans, and Native Americans. Finally, articles in the fields of art history and literature discuss artistic and literary representations of African/African American/Native American identity and relationships. Together, works from these various disciplines allow readers to gain a broad knowledge of the field and identify particular areas of interest.

A Long, Unwritten Chapter

"One of the longest unwritten chapters of the history of the United States is that treating of the relations of the Negroes and Indians." In 1920, with these words, the eminent scholar of African American history Carter G. Woodson inaugurated the study of Africans' and African Americans' contact and interactions with Native Americans in North America in the essay "The Relations of Negroes and Indians in Massachusetts." This essay provides readers with a broad range of scholarship on this history and offers an interdisciplinary perspective by bringing together works by historians, anthropologists, literary scholars, and a creative artist. The works discussed point to the wide range of conditions that have influenced nearly five centuries of contact between African Americans and Native Americans at different times and places. The breadth and diversity of this history make it almost impossible to make any broad generalizations about the relations between African Americans and

Hulton Archive / Getty Images

Born in 1875 into a family of ex-slaves in New Canton, Virginia, Carter Woodson rose to become known as "The Father of Black History," and specifically the history of African Americans in the United States. Woodson's determination to further his education was evident from an early age, but the needs of his family meant that he was required to work on the land for most of the year. At age seventeen, Woodson moved to Huntington intending to study at the Douglass High School, but again the need to earn a living intervened, and instead he worked as a miner. At twenty he finally entered high school, and in less than two years he graduated. Finally armed with academic credentials that matched his early promise, Woodson became a teacher, returning to Douglass High School in 1900 as the school's principal, at age twenty-five. He held this position for three years, and then traveled the world, working and studying in Asia and Europe, before returning to America to study at the University of Chicago in 1908 and Harvard in 1912. Graduating with a Ph.D. in history, he set out to record and document the history of African Americans. Woodson helped found a number of mediums that intended to highlight and promote African American history, starting the Association for the Study of Negro Life and History in 1915, establishing the *Journal of Negro History* (still published today as the *Journal of African American History*) in 1916, and a decade later developing the idea for Negro History Week. Today that celebration has been extended to the entire month of February. Woodson died in 1950, at the age of seventy-five. Many of the institutes he helped to create still champion and celebrate the dissemination of African American history in American society.

Indians, and, indeed, one should be wary of sweeping conclusions, which neglect the variegated nature of the interactions.

Africans in Colonial America

The earliest Africans to arrive in North America were among the large sixteenth-century expeditions under the leadership of Spanish explorers and *conquistadores*, who journeyed to the Americas hoping to find sea routes to Asia as well as gold and riches. By the early 1500s, Spanish and Portuguese traders had already begun purchasing goods and slaves along the West African coast, and some of these enslaved Africans were compelled to serve as sailors, servants, and soldiers. Consequently, the parties of Spanish soldiers who attacked the indigenous empires in the Americas, such as the Aztecs in Mexico and the Incas in Peru, included some enslaved African men.

Spanish explorers' accounts of North America reveal the presence of Africans in the early expeditions into North America. Enslaved Africans seized opportunities to rebel, and Spanish accounts suggest that they sometimes escaped to live among the indigenous populations. Perhaps the best known episode of early African contact with indigenous peoples in North America is the account of the Spanish-speaking slave named Esteban. In the summer of 1527, five ships under the command of Pánfilo de Narváez set out from Spain and arrived in the spring of the following year on the coast of present-day Florida. Esteban was one of the men in this expedition. The Indians in the region fought to repel the invaders and succeeded in breaking up the group and separating them from their supply ships. Most of the Spanish party perished on the Gulf Coast, but local Indian communities incorporated the few survivors, most likely retaining them as servants or subordinates. As late as 1534, four survivors were held by Indians on the coast of present-day Texas. Esteban was one of the survivors, along with Alvar Núñez Cabeza de Vaca, the leader of the exploration, who penned the amazing account of their escape and subsequent two-year trek across the southwest before reaching Mexico City in 1536.

The Spanish viceroy of Mexico, Antonio de Mendoza, recognizing Esteban's skills as a translator and guide, purchased him and gave him to the Spanish friar named Fray Marcos de Niza who had been selected to lead an expedition into the southwest. Several Indians and Africans, including Esteban, were pressed into service, and the entire party traveled north from Mexico City into the area that is now Arizona, where the Spanish hoped to find gold and riches. Esteban and a small group of the Indian servants or slaves arrived among peoples who were most likely a Zuni community in western New Mexico. Zuni leaders, already aware of the devastation wrought on indigenous peoples by European diseases and Spanish enslavement of Indians, refused to extend hospitality to Esteban, withholding food and water and seizing his trade goods. Esteban was killed shortly after his arrival, along with the Indians who had accompanied him. Those who survived carried the news of the deaths back to Fray Marcos de Niza.

Through the rest of the sixteenth century, Spanish expeditions in North America, especially in the southeast, included enslaved Africans and brought Africans into contact with Native Americans. Spanish outposts in present-day New Mexico were established in the midst of Indian settlements and included free and enslaved Africans. While there are several studies examining the lives of free and enslaved Africans in the Spanish colonies, few focus specifically on Africans' interactions and relationships with indigenous peoples. Dedra McDonald's article "Intimacy and Empire," however, provides a comprehensive overview of African-Indian relations in Spanish colonial New Mexico, the northernmost region of New Spain, from the sixteenth through the eighteenth centuries. She discusses instances in which Africans and Indians joined forces against Spanish governmental authorities, and also considers intermarriage and the ensuing cultural exchange within mixed African and Indian families. Africans and Native Americans encountered each other across the Spanish empire. In 1565, the Spanish established a garrison at St. Augustine, Florida, and African slaves were shipped there as laborers within the fort and as household servants of the Spanish residents. Enslaved Africans, however, often fled their Spanish masters and resettled within nearby Indian communities. During the seventeenth century, Spanish imperial ambitions in the southeast continued to bring Africans and Indians into contact with each other in Florida and the surrounding region.

Imperial conflicts in the southeast became increasingly violent after British proprietors established the Carolina colony in 1663 and thus threatened the Spanish hold in Florida. Since the 1619 arrival of enslaved Africans in the British North American colonies, British planters and colonists used enslaved men as laborers and, when necessary, to defend colonial settlements against attackers. Both the British and Spanish relied upon the men among their Indian allies and enslaved Africans to fight on behalf of the European powers. Participating in the bloody waves of raids and retaliation allowed African men to gain a keen appreciation of the geopolitical conflicts between the Spanish and English, and also to acquire detailed knowledge about the region's geography. This information proved useful to those slaves who escaped bondage in Carolina and made their way to either Indian settlements or Spanish Florida; in 1693 a royal proclamation granted sanctuary to runaway slaves from British colonies who arrived in Florida.

Historian Jane Landers has written extensively about the intertwined Spanish and African history of colonial Florida and has also charted the movement of African peoples between Florida and Spain's Caribbean colonies.[1] Her work reveals the ways in which Spanish colonial interests brought Africans and Indians into contact, and sometimes conflict, in Florida. She also offers valuable descriptions and analyses of the communities and institutions that free and enslaved Africans created for themselves within the Spanish colonies. In her article "Gracia Real de Santa Teresa de Mose" on the history of the free black town in Spanish Florida (also called Fort Mose), Landers examines the ways in which runaway African and African American slaves skillfully navigated their way through the Spanish-English imperial contest and secured their freedom and refuge in the Spanish colony. In developing their own community, former slaves forged kinship and friendship relations with the local slave, free-black, Indian, and white communities in nearby St. Augustine.[2] Spanish law and custom, Landers explains, acknowledged slaves' legal and moral personhood. The law afforded certain privileges and protections to slaves, and runaway slaves used Spanish colonial legal and religious institutions to their own advantage.

For many slaves, the hardships of daily life meant that escape was a constant temptation. European colonists referred to runaway slaves as maroons, and many escapees settled in the jungles and inaccessible regions of the Caribbean islands and elsewhere, forming communities and developing their own culture, traditions, and languages. As slavery matured, the chances of escape decreased, particularly on the plantations of the South, where slaveowners would use bloodhounds to hunt escapees down. Once recaptured, the individual in question would usually be severely punished.

Conditions in the English colonies, however, differed in important ways from those of Spanish Florida. In *Suspect Relations*, her study of colonial North Carolina, historian Kirsten Fischer traces the ways in which colonial-era categories of race, gender, and class worked to create social hierarchies that were defined and perpetuated in the law and in daily life. Eighteenth-century European and Anglo-American beliefs that differences in appearance signaled cultural, intellectual, and moral distinctions and hierarchies would develop by the nineteenth century into biological conceptions of race and racial difference. Fischer describes how, through the colonial period, Euro-Americans became less interested in cultural or environmental differences and increasingly embraced the belief that human difference was inherent and inheritable, and could be observed and assessed in physical appearance. Physical characteristics, furthermore, were associated with intellectual capacity and morality. These conceptions of human difference coalesced in racial theories that identified specific racial categories and arranged them in what was assumed to be a "natural" hierarchy. Euro-Americans' racial theories thus justified the enslavement of Africans and also allowed for the oppression of Native Americans.

Kirsten Fischer's study of race and gender ideologies in colonial North Carolina explores the ways Anglo-Indian relations were informed by European and Indian ideas about gender, race, and power. Her work is an important reminder that Euro-American ideas about Africans and African Americans were informed in part by ideas about Native Americans. As she explains, colonial legislators responded to the marriages and intimate relations between Africans and Indians by establishing laws regulating marriage and property ownership. A 1723 law, for example, levied taxes on the children born to Indian-African couples, and later laws imposed a tax on any white man or woman who married someone of Indian-African parentage. Laws also created stark racial categories that equated color and ancestry with legal status, and the exclusive association of blackness with permanent, inheritable enslavement obscured people's mixed African and Indian heritage.[3]

During the initial phases of European colonialism, many Native Americans had little interest in, or use for, Euro-American ideas about racial categories and hierarchies and instead continued to identify themselves and others by factors such as kinship, language, and culture. Some Native American peoples, consequently, initially regarded Africans as not unlike Europeans, because both were outsiders whose presence in North America sparked profound demographic, environmental, social, and political changes in the lives of Native Americans.[4] The arrival of Europeans in North America, of course, brought previously unknown diseases to Native Americans. Nearly two centuries of Europeans' imperial conquest in North America entailed continually shifting diplomatic and military alliances, and bloody conflicts with Indians. Colonial investment in plantation agriculture both altered the physical environment and informed the Euro-American quest for control over Indians' land.

In his article "The Racial Education of the Catawba Indians," for instance, historian James H. Merrell indicates that Catawbas most likely first encountered Africans and Europeans during de Soto's expedition across the southeast. As slaves and soldiers in this military contingent, African men would have been well versed in Spanish customs and language, making them virtually indistinguishable from their European comrades in the eyes of Native Americans. Visible physical differences between Africans and Spaniards, Merrell indicates, would have been far less important to the Catawbas than their apparent cultural similarities, especially their joint participation in the invasion of Native America. Catawbas, like many other southeastern Native peoples, identified foreigners and enemies not in terms of "race," or the presumption of inherent biological differences, but in terms of language, kinship, and culture. Thus, Catawbas viewed other Indian peoples in the same way they perceived newly arrived Europeans and Africans—as strangers or outsiders.

These attitudes persisted among the Catawbas, who in the early eighteenth century retained control over the interior of South Carolina and thus encountered Euro-Americans when British traders entered their territory to broker exchanges of goods for the deerskins hunted by Indian men. British traders usually traveled and worked with the enslaved black men, but the conditions of their lives and labor on the frontier precluded a rigid racial hierarchy and stark distinctions between master and slave. Consequently, from the Catawbas' vantage, the British traders and black slaves who entered Catawba territory appeared united in purpose. And, as Merrell explains, when

British colonists confronted hostile Indians, including Catawbas, during the Yammassee War of 1715, they enlisted male slaves in the fight against their Indian attackers, and this, too, linked blacks and whites in Catawbas' eyes and experiences. Behavior proved more important than appearance to the Catawbas in understanding the newcomers who settled around them.

Merrell examines the complexity of Catawba interactions with, and ideas about, African Americans. He begins by arguing for the importance of shifting the focus away from white people's attitudes about Indians to Indian people's ideas about, and actions toward, the foreigners who entered their societies. He presents Indians not as they were seen by Euro-Americans, but as they defined themselves and, in turn, others whom they encountered in the southeast. Furthermore, Merrell's work moves beyond the broad generalizations found in earlier scholarship and popular knowledge and considers the particular historical circumstances that informed Catawba–African American interactions and the Catawbas' increasing anti-black sentiment in the nineteenth century. Challenging earlier assumptions that the Catawbas' antipathy towards blacks was innate or that it was entirely orchestrated by white colonists, Merrell demonstrates the ways in which Catawbas assessed changing demographic and political conditions during the colonial era and after the Revolution. Their initial wariness of both British traders and their black slaves gradually gave way to routine, informal contact with blacks as Anglo-American settlers pushed into the Catawbas' territory. By the early nineteenth century, when Anglo-American slaveholders strove to build a society based on strict racial hierarchy, Catawbas increasingly embraced Anglo-American notions of black inferiority to ensure that they would not be racially marked with the stigma of blackness. In his discussion of this later period, Merrell cautions his readers to pay close attention to the different historical conditions that informed Catawbas' ideas and actions toward African Americans in eighteenth- and nineteenth-century South Carolina. His case study about the Catawbas, furthermore, is instructive when considering other Indian peoples, as it demonstrates the importance of historical context and specificity and explicates the limits of broad, ahistorical generalizations.

Extensive and often intimate relations between African Americans and Indians were not confined to the Southern colonies but occurred across colonial America, although the circumstances varied by region and time. In eighteenth-century New England, for example, demographic conditions played an important role in shaping the relationships between Native Americans and African Americans. The number of Indian men in Massachusetts, for example, declined in the first decades of the century primarily because of their participation in colonial wars in the northeast. At the same time, greater numbers of enslaved African men were arriving in the region. Anglo-American laws that ensured the subordination and servitude of Indians and Africans created conditions that promoted contact between Indians and Africans who worked together as household servants, or encountered each other as fellow laborers in New England cities. Carter G. Woodson's article referred to earlier, "The Relations of Negroes and Indians in Massachusetts," discussed intermarriage between African Americans and Indians by examining census data and legal documents. Although Woodson's work reflects an early twentieth-century, and now outdated, attention to the physical traits associated with racial categorization, his work endures as a pioneering study of African American–Indian relations.

More recently, historian Daniel Mandell has investigated the history of intermarriage between Indians and African Americans in eighteenth- and nineteenth-century Massachusetts in his article "Shifting Boundaries of Race and Ethnicity." Mandell's work considers the demographic, economic, and social conditions that fostered personal relationships between African Americans and Indians in the eighteenth century, and also pays attention to white New Englanders' responses to the ensuing generations of biracial populations. Indian peoples, too, had a range of responses to black people and intermarriage between blacks and Native Americans. Some peoples, such as the Mohegans and Narragansetts, grew increasingly hostile to black and biracial people in the nineteenth century. The expansion of African American communities in New England's cities, however, offered people with Indian and African American ancestry social and economic opportunities that they could not find elsewhere.

All of the scholars discussed above pay close attention to the ways in which European colonialism created conditions that brought Africans and Native Americans into contact, but also formulated racial categories that aimed to differentiate black people and Indians and promote and maintain distance between the two groups. The article by anthropologist Jack D. Forbes "The Manipulation of Race, Caste and Identity" stands out for its insistence that scholars of the history of race and racism in the Americas include both Native Americans and peoples of mixed ancestry in their analyses. Forbes carefully traces the development of racial and racist categories and explicates the connections between colonialism, slavery, and Euro-Americans' reliance on racial categories as a means of excluding and exploiting specific groups of people. In his article, Forbes follows the trajectory of racial and racist thought and practice beyond the colonial era into the nineteenth century and discusses the ways in which people of mixed parentage were identified in historical documents, but have been neglected in historical scholarship. Forbes concludes his article with a call to combat racism and to uncover the historical connections between supposedly separate peoples.

The work of anthropologist Karen I. Blu also addresses the complexity of a population of people with diverse ancestry. Like Forbes, Blu pays close attention to the ways in which Indian peoples understood the dominant system of racial categorization and used those categories to suit their own purposes. Her book *The Lumbee Problem*, a study of the Lumbee people in Robeson County, North Carolina, challenges prevailing assumptions about the unchanging nature of racial categories and about the parameters of Indianness. She seeks to show the shifting ways in which the Lumbees, who in the nineteenth century were sometimes labeled as "free Negroes," defined themselves over time, often in response to the dominant society's racial attitudes. She argues for an understanding of the Lumbees "as American Indians and as Southerners" because both factors influenced the ways they understood themselves and the world in which they lived.[5]

Southern Indians and Slavery

Many historians of Native Americans in the southeast have also underscored Indians' participation in the antebellum Southern institution of chattel slavery. In the first half of the nineteenth century, many Cherokee, Choctaw,

Chickasaw, and Creek Indians owned, bought, and sold black slaves as property and exploited black slaves' labor to produce profitable staple crops such as cotton. Theda Perdue's book *Slavery and the Evolution of Cherokee Society, 1540–1866* stands out as one of the earliest comprehensive histories of black enslavement in a southern Indian nation.

Too often, nineteenth-century white Americans' misperceptions of Indians' economic and labor patterns have informed popular assumptions about slavery in the southern Native nations. Impressions that Indians lacked a well-structured economy and sophisticated understanding of profit and property gained strength during the early nineteenth century and quickly informed U.S. Indian policy. Lingering versions of these ideas continue to appear in some accounts of Native slaveholding. Euro-American chroniclers of Native peoples in the southeast brought their own ideas about gender and work to bear on their assessments of Indians' sexual division of labor, particularly men's control of resources and women's economic productivity. Among the southern Native peoples, women bore the primary responsibility for agricultural labor and a wide range of other tasks that were central to their communities' subsistence and trade. Women's agricultural work included growing food crops; gathering nuts, berries, and tubers; making sugar and salt; and catching fish. Additionally, they accompanied Native men during the hunting season, building winter camps, preserving meat, and preparing deerskins for trade in the Euro-American market. The scope of women's labor and its fundamental importance to Native societies led many white American observers to conclude that Indian women were drudges or beasts of burden.

In the eyes of both elite policymakers and local white populations in the south, Native men who spent their time hunting rather than farming demonstrated their racial inferiority through their seemingly backward and stunted gender roles. Shortly after the Presbyterian missionary Joseph Bullen arrived in 1799 in Big Town, a Chickasaw village on the upper Tombigbee River near Tupelo, he wrote about the town's inhabitants, "Labour is done by the women, hunting by the men." Anglo-American men, believing in the economic and social values of agrarianism, regarded hunting as a leisure activity and did not comprehend either its place in Native peoples' subsistence and trade economies or its metaphysical meanings. In the early nineteenth century, the differences between Native and Anglo-American-gendered definitions of labor proved to be of tremendous consequence. Prominent white intellectuals and politicians, steeped in the gendered ideologies of republicanism, dismissed Native women's agricultural production and emphasized Native men's unwillingness or inability to perform the labor of "civilized men." It was not simply that Indian men were content to remain idle and dependent on their wives' labor, but also that they failed to "[transform] nature into property"—this marking Indians as racially inferior to white people.[6] Early nineteenth-century white observers determined that the extent of Native women's agricultural and productive labor signaled Native men's failure to assume command of economic activity and resources, and these limitations would appear in greater relief when white observers assessed Indians' slave ownership.

Indian men's purchase of black slaves was rarely heralded by white observers as an unequivocal sign of their "civilization." Rather, white observers regularly identified Indians' slaveholding patterns as indicative of their tenuous grasp on the social and economic meanings of property, especially that increasingly vital category of property in the antebellum South—black slaves. One critic, for example, charged that Cherokee men had only acquired slaves as a measure to avoid working.[7] Whites found Native men's acquisition of slaves suspect not only because it allowed them to forgo agricultural work, but also because many Native slaveholders did not harness black people's labor for the production of commodity crops, namely, cotton. In 1842, after touring the Choctaws' new home in the Indian Territory, Major Ethan Allen Hitchcock wrote from Doaksville, a Choctaw town, "The full-blood Indian rarely works himself and but few of them make their slaves work. A slave among wild Indians is almost as free as his owner."[8] Both Native men and women slaveholders were scrutinized by white observers, and similar criticisms were leveled by U.S. Indian agent Benjamin Hawkins against Creek women who did not manage their households as efficient sites of domestic labor. One woman, Hawkins noted, allowed her slaves so much autonomy that "They do nothing the whole winter but get a little wood, and in the summer they cultivate a scanty crop of corn barely sufficient for bread."[9] In the United States, the racial ideology buttressing slavery produced, and was produced by, the dehumanization of black people and the exploitation of their productive and reproductive labor. The law denied black humanity, but it was the endless and inventive daily acts of terror wrought on black people's bodies and souls that constituted the crushing weight of chattel slavery. When men such as Hawkins and Hitchcock looked at Indian societies, however, they did not see the systematic degradation and exploitation of black people; instead they witnessed black women and men possessing their own bodies, labor, and families—alarming spectacles that contradicted the principles of race, gender, and property informing the social and economic order of the antebellum South.

Interested and attentive observers did, however, pay close attention to those Native slaveholders whose behavior more closely resembled that of white slaveholders. As Hitchcock explained, slaves owned by "half-breeds" were worked and disciplined in ways that indicated they were "slaves indeed."[10] In 1838, the commissioner of Indian Affairs, reporting on conditions in the Indian Territory, wrote that wealthy Choctaw "half-breeds" were operating thriving cotton plantations.[11] Pseudoscientific disciplines such as phrenology and craniometry emerged in the antebellum era and cloaked white supremacy in academic respectability by explaining both chattel slavery and the drive to dispossess southern Indians of their lands to make way for the expanding cotton kingdom as natural and inevitable. Yet, while nearly two centuries of racial thought and legislation reconstructed blackness as an immutable and inheritable mark of inferiority and servitude that endured even across the generations of children resulting from interracial sex, considerable room existed for Indians to dilute and transcend their presumed racial inferiority through intermarriage with whites. During the first decade of the century, Thomas Jefferson eagerly endorsed intermarriage between Indians and whites as a means of hastening both Indians' "civilization" and the peaceful transfer of land from Native peoples to the United States. "You will mix with us by marriage," he told one delegation of Indians in 1808.[12] Even after Jeffersonian "civilization" programs gave way to Jacksonian Removal, ideas about the salubrious effects of white people's genetic makeup—"blood" or "breed" in the parlance of pseudoscientists—on Indians' cultural and racial position did not fade away entirely. Reformers and confirmed racists of the early nineteenth century concurred: "half-breed" Indians who owned slaves attested to the established racial index by confirming both the inferiority of blackness and the power of whiteness.

Until recently, historians studied slavery in the Indian nations primarily by comparing it to slavery in the Southern states to assess Indians' similarity to or deviance from the slaveholding practices of white Americans.[13] Positing Southern plantation slavery as the norm, scholars drew on sources such as Benjamin Hawkins and Ethan Allen Hitchcock to identify the ways in which the material conditions of slavery in the Indian nations differed from those in the Southern states. Accepting the premise that Indians lacked an awareness of, and interest in, the accumulation of property, historians concluded that because most Indian slaveholders did not force their slaves to raise commodity crops on large plantations, they practiced a mild or benign form of slavery. Southern Native peoples, scholars contended, had merely imitated whites when they adopted slavery, but hindered by an innate racial aversion to producing wealth, developed an aberrant version of chattel slavery. In the same vein, the early historiography attributed the growing number of plantations and the increasingly restrictive slave codes in the Indian nations during the 1840s and 1850s to the presence of "half-breed" or "mixed-blood" men, the sons of Euro-American men and Indian women, and, like nineteenth-century racial theorists, equated their commitment to deriving wealth from property ownership with their racial makeup, specifically whiteness.[14]

Such reductive formulations, however, have no explanatory weight and are deceptive, replicating the racial hierarchies of the nineteenth century and obscuring the array of conditions and contingencies that informed Native peoples' attitudes toward, and practices of, slaveholding, property ownership, and commodity production. Personal experience coupled with social and political exigencies, rather than the fact of biological parentage, shaped Native slaveholders' views about race, slavery, and property. First, although a number of southeastern Indians had one white parent, usually a father, southeastern Indian peoples did not identify themselves with the racial categories and ideology used by white Americans. Because many southeastern indigenous peoples traced lineage and identity through the mother's male relatives, people with white fathers were regarded and understood themselves as Indian. Before the nineteenth century, furthermore, Indian peoples in the southeast had institutions of slavery that subordinated and degraded the enslaved without dehumanizing them and reducing them to the status of property. Patterns of slaveholding changed during the early nineteenth century, but the shifts cannot be simply attributed to the presence of slaveholders who had a white parent. Within recent years, several younger scholars have produced historical and anthropological studies that investigate the history of slavery in southern Indian nations and pay careful attention to both the specific circumstances that shaped slavery and the ways in which enslaved African Americans attempted to control their own lives. Tiya Miles's book *Ties That Bind: The Story of an Afro-Cherokee Family in Slavery and Freedom* focuses on the intricate and intimate family relationships that emerged from the union of Doll, a black woman, and Shoe Boots, a Cherokee man, and linked generations of free and enslaved black people and their Cherokee relatives.

Historian Claudio Saunt studies slavery and relations between blacks and Indians in the Creek nation.[15] His article "The English Has Now a Mind to Make Slaves of Them All" examines the Creek Indians' reactions to Anglo-American slaveholders through the eighteenth century. Creeks, he explains, were initially alarmed by the emergence of plantation slavery in South Carolina "because it violated their notion of just power."[16] Many Creeks, consequently, refused to return runaway slaves to English authorities. By the middle of the century, however, Creeks' ideas and practices of property ownership had changed, increasingly allowing for individual acquisition of personal wealth. Thus, greater numbers of Creeks looked to the ownership of slaves to bolster their property holdings and financial interests. In his article, Saunt explores the Creeks' changing attitudes towards slavery and black people and situates this particular history within the broader context of Southern history.

Equally attuned to the connections between African American, Native American, and Southern history, Daniel Usner considers the spread of cotton plantations across Mississippi in the late eighteenth and early nineteenth centuries. In his article "American Indians on the Cotton Frontier," Usner describes how, for centuries, Choctaws and Chickasaws had occupied the region that would become the states of Mississippi and Alabama in 1817 and 1819, respectively. As white planters and slaveholders moved into these new states, local Indian populations faced dramatic changes and responded carefully and deliberately to the new conditions.

Early in the nineteenth century, Choctaw women worked as seasonal laborers on cotton plantations, suggesting that they worked alongside enslaved African American women and men.[17] In some instances, slaves who learned about nearby Indian settlements successfully ran away to these communities, where they sometimes found permanent refuge from bondage. Usner tracks the decline in the deerskin trade between Indians and white Americans as the cotton economy expanded, but also notes that some Indians in Mississippi purchased slaves and became cotton planters.[18] The history of enslavement and the lives of the enslaved in the Choctaw and Chickasaw nations remains understudied, although Clara Sue Kidwell's book *Choctaws and Missionaries in Mississippi, 1818–1918* addresses the presence of black people in the Choctaw nation. Although Usner's work does not focus specifically or extensively upon the relations between blacks and Choctaws or Chickasaws in Mississippi, his work makes an important contribution to Southern history, because it foregrounds the intersections of African American and Native American history.

The expansion of plantation agriculture into the Deep South and the concomitant emergence of a domestic slave trade that channeled enslaved people from the upper South to the lower South is not only a central chapter in African American history but one fundamental to Native American history. This is among the central themes in Claudio Saunt's article referred to earlier.[19] The growth of plantation slavery in large measure fueled white Southerners' calls for the dispossession of Indians' land in the South. Patrick Minges's article "Beneath the Underdog" provides a general overview of slavery in the southern Indian nations and includes a brief but important description of slaves' experiences during Indian removal. Under the federal government's program for the relocation of the Cherokee, Creek, Choctaw, Chickasaw, and Seminole nations from Georgia and the Gulf states to the Indian Territory, Indians with means were able to transport their property, including their slaves, to the west. Consequently, scores of enslaved black people, as well as free blacks in the Indian nations, made the forced trek commonly known as the Trail of Tears. Often, slaves were put to work by their masters and by the federal officials overseeing the removal process, and slave men and women drove wagons, tended livestock, and cooked meals for the other emigrants. This issue is also addressed in Tiya Miles's book.[20]

The late William G. McLoughlin was a prolific historian of southern Indians and wrote a great deal about black–Indian relations, specifically slavery and the relations between Indian masters and black slaves. His article "The Choctaw Slave Burning" provides an important counter to the assumption that Native Americans were always humane masters and did not abuse or exploit their slaves. In this piece, McLoughlin follows the story of Richard Harkins, a prominent Choctaw slaveholder who was murdered in December 1858 in the Indian Territory. After Harkins's death was discovered, his wife and relatives questioned their slaves and determined that he had been murdered by an enslaved man named Prince, who committed suicide after confessing. Lucy, an enslaved woman who reportedly instigated the events, was executed by burning as punishment for her participation. The incident commanded great attention not only because it was a dramatic act of slaves' resistance but also because both Harkins and Lucy belonged to a church organized by the American Board of Commissioners for Foreign Missions. In the 1850s the issue of slavery became increasingly inflammatory as a highly vocal and visible abolitionist movement lambasted the Christian religious denominations that continued to minister to slaveholders and openly sanction slavery. The moral and political schisms were so great, in fact, that the Methodist and Baptist churches split into Northern and Southern branches, abolitionist and proslavery respectively, in the 1840s. McLoughlin examines the debates and conflicts that took place within the Presbyterian church over the local church's responses to Harkins's murder and Lucy's execution. His article does not directly address the issue of slaves' resistance, however, but it certainly provides detailed accounts of Lucy's and Prince's efforts to subvert their master's authority, and offers a window onto the violence that punctuated enslaved people's lives in the Indian Territory.

Enslaved people's lives in the southern Indian nations have been covered in great detail by Daniel F. Littlefield, and his books should be consulted by anyone interested in gaining a solid understanding of African Americans' lives in the Cherokee, Chickasaw, Creek, and Seminole nations.[21] His article "Slave 'Revolt' in the Cherokee Nation, 1842," cowritten with Lonnie E. Underhill, discusses an important episode of slave resistance against Cherokee slaveholders in the Indian Territory. In the autumn of that year, over one hundred slaves fled their Cherokee masters and headed southwest, most likely towards Mexico. In this article, Littlefield and Underhill provide a brief review of the Cherokee slave code, pointing to restrictive and punitive laws against free and enslaved blacks that likely motivated this episode of collective resistance. This was not the only occasion on which large numbers of slaves attempted to rebel against slavery and their Indian masters. Seven years later, in 1849–1850, the Black Seminole Gopher John along with the Seminole leader Wild Cat led a contingent of Seminoles, Black Seminoles, and runaway slaves out of the Indian Territory to Mexico, where they established a permanent settlement with the assistance of the Mexican government. According to Littlefield and Underhill, by 1851 approximately three hundred enslaved people had attempted to run away from the Indian Territory.

Africans and Seminoles in Florida

One of the most fascinating chapters in nineteenth-century Southern history concerns the extensive interactions and relations between African Americans and Seminole Indians in Florida from the 1800s through the 1840s. Historian Kevin Mulroy's work examines the history of black–Seminole relations and focuses on the people known as Black Seminoles or Seminole maroons, runaway slaves who formed communities in Florida by forming strategic alliances and personal relationships, including marriage, with Seminole Indians.[22] During the first decade of the nineteenth century, white Americans hoped to wrest Florida from Spanish control to gain the territory for the United States and also to rid the region both of the maroons and the Indians, who encouraged and assisted runaway slaves from American plantations.

During the War of 1812, however, British forces were eager to harbor runaway slaves and employ their services, as well as those of Indians, against the

Americans. A British naval officer directed the construction of an armed fort on top of a cliff at the mouth of the Apalachicola River in 1814–1815. The fort, known as the Negro Fort, attracted runaway slaves from South Carolina and Georgia. After the war ended, blacks and Indians remained in the garrison and ambushed U.S. naval vessels that attempted to make their way up the river. In the summer of 1816, U.S. forces destroyed the fort and, as Mulroy writes, "smashed the African power base on the Apalachicola."[23] Still, as Mulroy explains, the destruction of the fort did not eradicate the extensive and determined maroon communities in the surrounding region. Subsequent conflicts between white Southerners and maroons and Indians became known as the First Seminole War, which lasted from 1817 to 1819. The United States acquired Florida from Spain in 1819 and then sought to relocate the Seminoles within Florida and prevent them from harboring any more fugitive slaves.

By the 1830s, after Congress passed the Indian Removal Act, Seminoles and maroons feared they would be removed from Florida. When the Seminoles met with representatives of the federal government, they relied on bilingual maroons, such as a man named Abraham (a black leader of a maroon community), who served as interpreters. During the 1830s and 1840s, Seminoles and maroons resisted removal and fought the United States military in what was known as the Second Seminole War (1835–1842).

Mulroy's work details the Second Seminole War and the subsequent removal of the Seminoles and maroons from Florida to the Indian Territory, the region that would become part of Oklahoma. Mulroy contends that the maroons were an ethnically distinct group apart from Seminole Indians. Other scholars, however, have argued that the long history of intermarriage and fictive kinship between black people and Seminoles means that people of African American descent in the Seminole nation are not a separate racial group from those of Native American descent. This is an ongoing debate at both the academic and grassroots levels, and Mulroy's work stands as an important contribution to the growing body of scholarship on black–Seminole relations.

The dramatic political implications of African Americans' extensive contact with Seminoles are revealed in James Sefton's article "Black Slaves, Red Masters, White Middlemen" on the political and legal consequences of the Second Seminole War. Sefton traces the convoluted and often contradictory policies formulated by U.S. military officers regarding the fate of runaway slaves in Florida and of slaves seized from white masters by Indian warriors. As Sefton carefully illustrates, conflicts between Indians, runaway slaves, and U.S. military officers over the status of runaway and captured slaves sparked debates over slavery at the highest levels of the federal government. In their efforts to end the Second Seminole War and secure the removal of the Seminoles and maroons from Florida, congressmen had to consider the actions and demands of black and Indian warriors who insisted upon recognizing maroons as free people. Sefton's article points, consequently, to the ways in which maroons' and Seminoles' determination to exert control over their lives informed and influenced political debate in the halls of Congress. Few other scholars have paid close attention to this issue or have considered the extent to which antebellum political debates over the expansion and future of Southern slavery necessarily entailed debate over the fate of Native Americans in the South.

The rich history of the Black Seminoles has been the focus of anthropological as well as historical investigation. Anthropologist Rebecca Belle Bateman's article "Naming Patterns in Black Seminole Ethnogenesis" examines the naming patterns in Black Seminole families living in the Indian Territory during the decades after removal and argues that the evidence points to African-derived practices that resemble a Kongo-Angolan system of naming. Her study thus links the history of African Americans' relations with Native Americans in North America to a broader history of the African Diaspora through the late nineteenth century.

Other scholars interested in Black Seminoles have turned their attention to those who did not remove from Florida to the Indian Territory, but instead fled Florida for the Bahamas. In his article "The Seminole Negroes of Andros Island Revisited," Harry Kersey, Jr., traces the lives of the Black Seminoles who either secured passage on commercial vessels or managed to transport themselves by canoe from Florida to the Bahamas. Using Bahamian newspapers from the 1850s as one of his sources, Kersey follows the story of a Black Seminole young man named Ben who emigrated from Florida to the Bahamas. Anthropologist Rosalyn Howard has studied the present-day experiences of the descendants of Black Seminoles in the Bahamas in her book *Black Seminoles in the Bahamas*. Although Howard is less interested in charting the history of African Americans' relationships with the Seminoles, her book adds another important diasporic dimension to the field of African American–Native American relations.

African Americans and Native Americans in the United States, 1865–1907

In 1861, after the Confederacy's secession from the United States, Southern politicians, especially those in states on the western borders of the Confederacy, such as Arkansas and Texas, turned their attention to the slaveholding Indian nations in the Indian Territory. Eager to secure their allegiance during the war, the Confederate government dispatched Albert Pike of Arkansas to the Indian Territory to negotiate treaties with the Choctaw, Chickasaw, Cherokee, Creek, and Seminole nations. Many, but not all, leaders of the nations were receptive to Pike's overtures because a number of leaders felt as though they had been abandoned by the Union when military exigencies prompted the withdrawal of Union troops from the Indian Territory, and the closing of government stores and posts in the region. Factions of the Cherokee, Chickasaw, Choctaw, and Creek nations' leaders sided with the Confederacy, while other factions within each of these four nations, along with the entire Seminole nation, remained loyal to the Union. Detailed histories of Native Americans' participation in the Civil War can be found in a now classic series of documentary histories by Annie Heloise Abel that have recently been reprinted.[24] Although outdated in their characterizations of Native American cultures, the works offer extensive passages from government records and letters that detail the debates and decisions of Indian leaders during the Civil War. During the course of the war, some black men from the Indian nations joined with loyal Indians to fight on the Union side, and the all-black regiments that were formed in Kansas included some former slaves from the Indian Territory.

After the Civil War, African Americans' future status and rights in the sovereign Indian nations were not explicated by the Thirteenth Amendment

(1865) and the emancipation of slaves in the United States. Instead, these matters were determined in the course of one and a half years of treaty negotiations between the Indian nations and the United States. Although only a few African American men played a limited role in the treaty-making process, the debates and issues raised about freed people's future rights and status affected all black people in the Indian nations immediately after the war and for generations to come. In September 1865, leaders of both the Confederate and loyal Creek factions journeyed from the Indian Territory to Fort Smith, Arkansas, where they met with the commission appointed by the federal government for the purpose of negotiating peace treaties with each of the nations in the Territory. Of all the representatives from the slaveholding Indian nations, only the loyal Creeks were accompanied by delegates from their nation's African American population. By mid-morning on September 8, 1865, Oktarharsars Harjo, the head chief of the loyal Creeks; various lower chiefs; Harry Island, the Creeks' African American interpreter; and the black delegates Ketch Barnett, John McIntosh, Scipio Barnett, Jack Brown, and Cow Tom presented themselves before the federal commission appointed to settle matters in the Indian Territory. Angie Debo's books on the post-emancipation period in the Indian Territory are particularly outdated in their depiction of black people, but provide a considerable amount of information about particular African Americans and their efforts to secure freedom and citizenship rights for former slaves in the Indian nations.[25] Daniel F. Littlefield's books are especially useful for readers interested in the history of emancipation and post-emancipation black life in the Indian Territory.[26] The article by Donald A. Grinde, Jr., and Quintard Taylor, entitled "Red vs. Black: Conflict and Accommodation in the Post Civil War Indian Territory, 1865–1907," provides a clear and concise summary of this history, detailing the conditions of African Americans' lives in the Indian nations in the years after emancipation, when they struggled to gain the full rights of citizenship in the Indian nations.

In 1866, each of the five nations entered a new treaty with the United States. The postwar treaties contained specific provisions designed to punish the Indians for their disloyalty. The penalties, moreover, benefited the United States. Each nation was compelled to cede large sections of land to the United States, and agreed to allow the construction of railroads across their territory as well. Additionally, the nations were to abolish slavery and provide for the freedpeople's "incorporation into the tribes on an equal footing with the original members."[27] Incorporation meant that the freedpeople were to be granted the status and rights of full and equal citizens. Grinde and Taylor outline some of the conflicts that emerged as former slaves pursued their rights in the Indian nations.[28] Although the 1866 treaties have not been studied in depth by legal scholars, other works have examined freedpeople's efforts to establish themselves as free citizens in the Indian nations.[29]

During the second half of the nineteenth century, the federal government pursued policies designed to circumscribe Indian nations' sovereignty and land claims, leading to the acquisition of the Indian Territory from the Native American nations and the creation of the state of Oklahoma in 1907. With the passage of the Dawes Act in 1887 and then the Curtis Act in 1898, Congress created laws that allowed for the federal government to divide the Indian nations' land into allotments of private property. Reflecting a late nineteenth-century preoccupation with racial and ethnic identity, the laws also created new categories of racial identity for the purposes of allotting land to Native Americans and regulating the subsequent sale and taxation of that land. The newly created racial categories also extended to the former slaves in the Indian nations, who were all labeled as "freedmen"—which erased many black people's family connections to Native Americans.

Michael Elliott's article "Telling The Difference" offers an overview of the legal definitions of racial identities in the second half of the nineteenth century, and provides an important discussion of the ways in which white jurists attempted to create racial categories and equate racial identity with legal rights for African Americans and Native Americans. His work covers the period immediately preceding the Civil War and extends into the late nineteenth century. It points to the ways in which dominant definitions of blackness and Indianness were often linked in the ideas and policies of white lawmakers and politicians. Other scholars who have addressed these issues include Murray R. Wickett and David Chang. Wickett's book-length study *Contested Territory* examines interracial and intraracial politics in the Indian Territory after the Civil War through the end of the nineteenth century. While Indians and their former slaves acquired ownership of some land through the allotment process, the bulk of the land in the Indian Territory was made available to white settlers from the United States. David Chang's doctoral dissertation "From Indian Territory to White Man's Country" examines in great detail former slaves' efforts to become landowners in the Indian Territory and then in Oklahoma, and discusses the meanings of land ownership to black people in the late nineteenth and early twentieth centuries. The second chapter of Chang's dissertation focuses on former slaves in the Creek nation, and on their acquisition of land in the Indian Territory in the late nineteenth century.

Other scholars who have turned their attention to black people's cultural, family, and political ties to Indian nations include historians Laura Lovett and Celia Naylor-Ojurongbe. Celia Naylor-Ojurongbe's article "Born and Raised among These People" uses the ex-slave narratives collected during the 1930s under the aegis of the Works Progress Administration (WPA) to discern black people's multifaceted connections to Native Americans. She focuses specifically on the narratives of those black men and women who were owned by Indian slaveholders, some of whom also had family connections to their Indian masters. She reveals the deeply rooted cultural ties black people had to particular Indian communities and shows how this cultural identification informed former slaves' sense of political connectedness to specific Indian nations. Laura Lovett takes a different approach by considering the meanings of Native American ancestry to those black people who did *not* have a personal or familial history of enslavement in an Indian nation. In her article "African and Cherokee by Choice," she argues that some black people used their claims of Indian ancestry to challenge the theories of inherent racial difference that were used to justify legal and customary patterns of segregation and anti-black discrimination. Black people who embraced their Indian ancestry, she suggests, refused to be pigeonholed into a stark racial category assigned to them by segregationists and instead attempted to show the complexity and diversity of people's cultural and ancestral heritage. Lovett also considers the ways in which African Americans in New Orleans appropriated symbols of Native American resistance in their Mardi Gras parades to enhance the presentation of black opposition to segregation and anti-black violence.

One little-known arena where African Americans and Native Americans continued to encounter and interact with each other is Hampton University. Established in Virginia in 1868 by General Samuel Chapman Armstrong, the son of American missionaries in Hawaii, Hampton Normal and Agricultural Institute was founded for the education of former slaves. In 1878, a decade after its creation, however, Hampton Institute accepted both black and Indian students. One of the most famous Hampton students, Booker T. Washington, served for a while as the "dorm father" for a group of Native American students.[30] Native Americans from across the country attended the school through the 1920s, but they were largely segregated from the black students in the dining halls, dormitories, classrooms, and the chapel. Abraham Makovsky's article "Experience of Native Americans at a Black College" examines the Indian students' experiences at Hampton, considering both the difficulties they faced and the possibilities for cross-cultural exchange between black and Indian students.

Current Issues in African American–Native American Relations

One of the central issues confronted by persons of African American and Native American descent is the question of how Indian identity is defined in official contexts, such as by a tribal government, and in people's daily lives and social relations. Debates over how to best define Indianness also inform Native peoples' interactions with each other and with the federal government, and this complicated question has generated much debate. For many Native Americans, including those who identify with their African American heritage, the issue dates back to the late nineteenth century, when federal policies established categories of Indian identity based on blood quanta. The 1887 General Allotment Act, known as the Dawes Act, dissolved Native American nations' land claims and established the federal government's right to assign parcels of land to Indians as individually owned private property. The size of the land allotments depended on the individual's age and marital status; children and unmarried adults received less land than heads of families. In the five slaveholding Indian nations (Cherokee, Choctaw, Chickasaw, Creek, and Seminole), land was allotted to Indians and black people, specifically former slaves and their descendants. David Chang's work referred to earlier discusses the acquisition of land allotment by freedpeople in the Creek and Seminole nations.

The Dawes Act not only compelled changes in patterns of property ownership but also divided Indians within specific tribes or nations into racial categories based on blood quantum or degree of Indian ancestry. In the late nineteenth and early twentieth centuries, many white intellectuals and reformers turned their attention to the cultural and biological identities of Native Americans, as well as immigrants from southern and eastern Europe, and devised plans for facilitating their assimilation into the American mainstream. Native Americans' capacity for abandoning indigenous culture and assimilating into the dominant Euro-American culture was linked to their Indian ancestry and thus blood quantum. Reflecting the presumed superiority of whiteness and inferiority of Indianness, the Dawes Act divided Indians by their blood quanta and imposed specific restrictions on individuals' property rights based on their categorization. For example, those who were classified as "full bloods" were assumed to lack the intellectual and moral fiber to run their own lives, and their land allotments were to be held in trust by the Secretary of the Interior for twenty-five years. Those classified as "mixed blood," which referred to white, not black ancestry, were believed to be competent to manage their own affairs, and thus had ownership and control over their land allotments. Readers interested in learning more about the Dawes Act and the systems of classification by blood quanta should consult works by Frederick Hoxie and Thomas Biolsi.[31]

The articles by Terry Wilson, Circe Sturm, Ward Churchill, and Ann McMullen address the historical and present-day issues of using blood quanta as a means for determining Indian identity.[32] In his article "The Crucible of American Indian Identity," Ward Churchill (Keetowah Band Cherokee), a prominent scholar and activist, is expressly critical of the notion of blood quanta because it is premised on racial hierarchy and links cultural identity to ancestry rather than to individual and group experience and self-identification. In the first sections of the article, Churchill provides an overview of indigenous peoples' historical patterns of determining individual

identity and belonging in an Indian community. He, like many other scholars, maintains that prior to their contact with Europeans, Native American
peoples distinguished themselves by culture rather than by notions of biology, and outsiders were incorporated into a particular society through rituals
of marriage or fictive kinship, and thus, Churchill writes, "genealogy rather
than genetics was the core component of society composition."[33] These patterns of determining individual and group identity persisted through much
of the eighteenth century, although many Indian peoples' practices changed
gradually over time. Churchill provides a number of examples of the ways in
which Native peoples continued to rely on their own notions of culture rather
than on Euro-American conceptions of biology and race to inform individual
and group identity. One such example is the case of Jim Beckwourth, a black
man who was incorporated into a Crow Indian community and married a
Crow woman named Still Water. Because of his cultural and kin ties to the
Crows, Churchill explains, Beckwourth rose to a prominent leadership position in the Crow society. Churchill takes a critical stance toward the federal
government's imposition of the dominant American racial ideology with its
early twentieth-century policies of determining identity by blood quanta, and
also expresses concern that some Native peoples have adopted this system of
identifying themselves and each other in terms of blood quanta.

Anthropologist Circe Sturm examines the implications of the Dawes
Act's racial classification scheme in the lives of former slaves in the Cherokee Nation. In both her article "Blood Politics, Racial Classification and
Cherokee National Identity" and her book *Blood Politics*, Sturm explores the
workings of federal policy and also the ways in which Cherokees and African
Americans understood the imposed changes and responded to them. In her
article, Sturm suggests that many Cherokees have resented their own racial
subordination in the dominant racial framework, but simultaneously rely on
racial categories to exclude people of African American descent from their
communities. After providing a detailed summary of the history of emancipation and freed slaves' struggles for citizenship in the Cherokee Nation, she
goes on to discuss the federal government's racial classification of Indians
and African Americans in the Cherokee Nation during the late nineteenth-
century era of the Dawes Act.

The land-allotment process entailed compiling a census, or roll, of each Indian nation, and individuals were classified as Indians by blood, Intermarried Whites, and Freedmen; the final category included former slaves and their descendants as well as those African Americans who had been free during the period of slavery. Classifying all black people as "Freedmen" created a gulf between African Americans and Indians and also ignored those people who had both African American and Native American ancestry. In the decades after emancipation and the abolition of slavery, many Cherokees had opposed freedpeople's citizenship rights in the Cherokee Nation, and continued to challenge black people's status and rights as citizens during the enrollment and allotment processes. Sturm's article provides a well-detailed discussion of the ways in which leaders of the Cherokee Nation continued their efforts to exclude black people—former slaves and their descendants—from the rights and status of citizenship that had been established by the Cherokees' 1866 treaty with the United States. Her analysis reaches well beyond the nineteenth century, however, and covers events through the twentieth century. Sturm illustrates the ways in which Cherokees formulated definitions of their cultural and political identities by employing biological notions of race to exclude African Americans. She suggests that "many Cherokees express contradictory consciousness" because they oppose anti-Cherokee discrimination on the basis of biological definitions of race, or "blood," while using these same conceptions of race and blood to block the recognition of black people as Cherokee.

Debates over biology or "blood" and the connections between ancestry and cultural and political identities are not limited to the issue of African American–Native American relations and intermarriage. Both Terry Wilson and Ann McMullen consider the legacy of late nineteenth-century racial classification schemes in the context of both African American–Native American relations and Indians' intragroup relations in the past and present. In her article "Blood and Culture," McMullen addresses the intertwined issues of blood and culture as they are understood by Native Americans in southeastern New England. She discusses the ways in which the Mohegans, Pequots, Narragansetts, Wampanoags, and Nipmucs evaluate the meanings and relevance of "blood" and culture to individual and group identity. McMullen provides a clear historical background of each group, illustrating the conditions that fostered interaction and intermarriage with African Americans, and to a far lesser degree Euro-Americans, through the nineteenth century. The article then presents McMullen's observations and conclusions, drawn from her anthropological fieldwork from 1990 to 1994, about the ways in which Native peoples in southeastern New England have considered the meanings of physical appearance, ancestry, cultural practices, and external racism in their efforts to define themselves as Indians.

Terry Wilson's article "Blood Quantum" addresses the many complexities of understanding the historical and present-day issues of race, blood, and cultural identity for Native Americans. He denounces the notion of blood quanta as an appropriate index of cultural identity and explicates its connections to Euro-Americans' nineteenth- and twentieth-century racial ideologies and belief in white superiority. He discusses the ways in which dominant ideas about Indian identity and blood quanta have been primarily concerned with Native Americans' white ancestors. Wilson argues that the federal government's late nineteenth-century system of classifying Indians by blood quanta rested on the belief in white superiority, and thus the relative superiority of those who had white ancestors. This focus on whiteness, he explains, has obscured the history of African American–Native American relations, specifically the unions between black and Indian people, and continues to deny the presence of people who claim both African American and Native American ancestry.

Wilson, like Churchill and Sturm, also addresses the ways in which Native Americans have adopted the ideas and categories of blood quanta to define Indian identity. Although he is critical of the notion of blood quanta as a measure of cultural identity, he accepts the fact that many Native peoples employ it as a means of identifying themselves and each other. Wilson reflects on how he has "deal[t] with mixed-blood Indian status, personally and professionally" and also provides both anecdotal accounts and quantitative data reflecting his students' efforts to grapple with the implications of linking biology and cultural identity. He discusses the ways in which notions of "blood" serve to marginalize people of mixed ancestry, including those whose ancestors were from different Native groups as well as those who have African American or

Euro-American ancestors. Although Wilson clearly expresses his opposition to the notion and use of blood quanta as a measure of cultural and political identity, he writes that he expects that these ideas will remain salient in both the dominant society and in Native communities. At the same time, however, he concludes by stating that he believes that self-identification and cultural involvement, rather than "blood," are the most important markers of individual and group identity for Indians today.

Readers interested in learning more about the present-day issues faced by people of African American and Native American descent are encouraged to read the essay by Ron Welburn (Assateague Gingaskin, Cherokee, and African American). Dr. Welburn is a professor of English literature, specializing in Native American literature and American Studies, and is also a published poet. In his essay "A Most Secret Identity," Welburn discusses his life experiences as a person of African American and Native American descent, and challenges racial thinking that diminishes the legitimacy of African American–Native American people's self-identification with their Indian ancestors.

African Americans and Native Americans in Art and Literature

A number of authors and artists have explored the meanings and expressions of the historical, cultural, and familial ties between African Americans and Native Americans. Works of fiction and visual art have drawn on documented histories to create characters that embody the hopes, frustrations, and contradictions that scholars have explored in other fields. In her essay "If You Know I Have a History, You Will Respect Me," literary scholar Sharon Holland writes about the ways in which the intersecting and overlapping experiences of African Americans and Native Americans and those of mixed ancestry emerge in contemporary fiction. She discusses works by Leslie Marmon Silko, Alice Walker, and the late Michael Dorris, and she focuses on the writings of Silko and Nettie Jones, whose novel *Mischief Makers* "chronicles four generations of an Afro-Native family living in Michigan from 1920 to 1950."[34] Works of literature by these authors, Holland suggests, allow readers to imagine and understand the complex and sometimes contradictory identities of persons who explore and embrace the rich intersections of African Americans' and Native Americans' experiences. Readers interested in learning more about African American–Native American literature and literary scholarship are encouraged to read the volume of essays entitled *When Brer Rabbit Meets Coyote*, edited by literary scholar Jonathan Brennan.

The visual artist Betye Saar creates works of art that challenge the stereotypes and brutality of racism by examining the power of images both to do harm and to soothe. In 2002–2003, an exhibition of Saar's work entitled "Colored: Consider the Rainbow" showcased pieces that explore the multiple meanings of skin color in African American history. In her work, Saar examines, for instance, the ways in which color-related words have been used as racial epithets against black people, and she confronts the ways in which African Americans differentiate themselves by complexion. In one series of collages, Saar turns her attention to the relationships between African Americans and Native Americans. She points to common experiences of marginalization and oppression, and suggests the rich spiritual and cultural resources that nurtured both blacks and Indians when they faced extreme oppression and violence. In the collages, Saar presents familiar images from the African American and Native American pasts. The images evoke experiences and memories of hardship, but also of endurance, and signal the theoretical and actual intersections of African American and Native American experiences. The excerpts from the exhibition catalog, which was written by art historian Dr. Leslie King-Hammond, offer a detailed description and analysis of Saar's work and provide readers with a close analysis of Saar's artistic approach to the historical, cultural, and personal connections between African Americans and Native Americans.[35]

Conclusion

Over the course of more than eighty years, scholars from a range of disciplines have created a rich body of work that explores African American and Native American interactions and relations. Much of this scholarship focuses on Native peoples in the southeast, northeast, and the Indian Territory/Oklahoma, but also suggests possibilities for new directions in this field of inquiry. Important work was done by early scholars whose efforts were mainly directed toward locating documents and assembling information to provide a foundation of knowledge. More recent generations of scholars have set out in new directions, examining the subject of black–Indian relations from different vantages and with new interpretive and analytical frameworks. Together, older and newer works combine to offer interested readers a range of views and conclusions and reveal the developments in scholarly understandings of African American and Native American cultural, social, and political history. Important areas that await future research have already been identified in conferences, dissertations, and current works-in-progress. Such areas include, but are not limited to, the "Africanization" of Indian peoples in the colonial southeast; black women's experiences of slavery and freedom in Indian nations; interactions between black soldiers and Indian peoples in the nineteenth-century southwest. As new areas of inquiry are opened, and as scholars and interested readers continue to exchange ideas across disciplines, awareness of both the intersections between Native American and African American history and the diasporic implications of this overlap will continue to grow and to inspire students, teachers, researchers, writers, artists, and activists.

· ·

NOTES

1. Jane Landers, *Black Society in Spanish Florida* (Urbana: University of Illinois Press, 1999).
2. Jane Landers, "Gracia Real de Santa Teresa de Mose: A Free Black Town in Spanish Colonial Florida," *American Historical Review* 95 (1990): 11.
3. Kirsten Fischer, "Cross-Cultural Sex in Native North Carolina," in *Suspect Relations: Sex, Race, and Resistance in Colonial North Carolina* (Ithaca, N.Y.: Cornell University Press, 2002), 86.
4. James Merrell, "The Racial Education of the Catawba Indians," *Journal of Southern History* 50 (1984): 364–83.
5. Karen I. Blu, "Where Did They Come From and What Were They Like Before?" *The Lumbee Problem: The Making of an American Indian People* (Cambridge, England: Cambridge University Press, 1980), 4, 36.

6. Robert F. Berkhofer, Jr., *The White Man's Indian: Images of the American Indian from Columbus to the Present* (New York: Alfred A. Knopf, 1978), 138.

7. Theda Perdue, "Native Women in the Early Republic: Old World Perceptions, New World Realities." In *Native Americans and the Early Republic*, edited by Frederick E. Hoxie, Ronald Hoffman, and Peter J. Albert (Charlottesville: University of Virginia Press, 1999), 118–19.

8. Daniel F. Littlefield Jr., *The Chickasaw Freedmen: A People without a Country* (Westport, Conn.: Greenwood Press, 1980), 16.

9. Benjamin Hawkins, "December 25, 1796," in *Letters, Journals, and Writings of Benjamin Hawkins*, edited by C. L. Grant (Savannah, Ga.: Beehive Press, 1980); and Barbara Krauthamer, "Kinship and Freedom: Fugitive Slave Women's Incorporation into Creek Society," in *New Studies in the History of American Slavery*, edited by Stephanie M. H. Camp and Edward E. Baptist (Athens: University of Georgia Press, 2005).

10. Littlefield, Jr., *Chickasaw Freedmen*.

11. Office of Indian Affairs, *Annual Report of the Commissioner of Indian Affairs* (Washington, D.C.: U.S. Government Printing Office, 1838), 73.

12. Reginald Horsman, "The Indian Policy of an 'Empire for Liberty,'" in *Native Americans and the Early Republic*, edited by Frederick E. Hoxie, Ronald Hoffman, and Peter J. Albert (Charlottesville: University of Virginia Press, 1999), 50.

13. Early studies of slavery in the southern Indian nations, especially those written between the 1930s and 1960s, added to the emerging scholarship in African American history and provided an important complement to works that emphasized the frequency of alliance and intermarriage between blacks and Indians enslaved by European colonists, and between runaway slaves and the Indians who harbored them. Most notable are anthropologist Melville Herskovits's findings that significant percentages of African Americans in the 1920s claimed Native ancestry (Melville J. Herskovits, *The American Negro: A Study in Racial Crossing* [1928; Bloomington: Indiana University Press, 1964] and *The Anthropometry of the American Negro* [1930; New York: Haskell House Publishers, 1970]). Consistent with most scholarly works about Native Americans written during the first half of the twentieth century, these initial studies of slavery offered particularly flat depictions of Indians, suggesting that they simply replicated the Euro-American system of slavery and racist ideology that unfolded around them (Wyatt F. Jeltz, "The Relations of Negroes and Choctaw and Chickasaw Indians," *Journal of Negro History* 33 [1948]: 24–37; J. H. Johnston, "Documentary Evidence of the Relations of Negroes and Indians," *Journal of Negro History* 14 [1929]: 21–43; Kenneth Wiggins Porter, "Relations between Negroes and Indians within the Present Limits of the United States," *Journal of Negro History* 17 [1932]: 287–367; Kenneth Wiggins Porter, "Notes Supplementary to 'Relations between Negroes and Indians,'" *Journal of Negro History* 18 [1933]: 282–321; William S. Willis, "Divide and Rule: Red, White, and Black in the Southeast," *Journal of Negro History* 48 [1963]: 157–76. For a detailed discussion of this historiography, see Tiya Miles and Barbara Krauthamer's "Africans and Native Americans," in *The Blackwell Companion to African American History*, edited by Alton Hornsby (Oxford: Blackwell Publishers, 2004);

for an insightful treatment of the studies conducted by Melville Herskovits, with the assistance of Zora Neale Hurston, that explores the reasons why African Americans valued Native ancestry during the first half of the twentieth century, see Laura Lovett's "'African and Cherokee by Choice': Race and Resistance under Legalized Segregation" (*American Indian Quarterly* 22 [1998]: 203–29).

14. This is a variation on what Ward Churchill describes as the "article of faith among historical interpreters that mixed-bloods served as something of a Trojan Horse within indigenous societies during the era of Euro-American conquest, undermining their cohesion and thereby eroding their ability to resist the onslaught effectively" (Ward Churchill, "The Crucible of American Indian Identity: Native Tradition versus Colonial Imposition in Postconquest North America." *American Indian Culture and Research Journal* 23 [1999]: 39–67). In the literature on the southern nations and slavery, however, adoption of Euro-American economic and social patterns is not categorized as destructive to Native sovereignty or culture, but is implicitly treated as "progress" despite the moral opprobrium of slavery and racism. James Merrell's work offered a critical intervention by revealing Native people's thoughts over time (Merrell, "Racial Education").

15. Claudio Saunt, *A New Order of Things: Property, Power, and the Transformation of the Creek Indians, 1733–1816* (Cambridge, England: Cambridge University Press, 1999).

16. Claudio Saunt, "The English Has Now a Mind to Make Slaves of Them All," *American Indian Quarterly* 22 (1998): 159.

17. Daniel H. Usner Jr., "American Indians on the Cotton Frontier: Changing Economic Relations with Citizens and Slaves in the Mississippi Territory," *Journal of American History* 72 (1985): 305.

18. Ibid., 315.

19. Saunt, "The English Has Now a Mind to Make Slaves of Them All."

20. Tiya Alicia Miles, *Ties That Bind: The Story of an Afro-Cherokee Family in Slavery and Freedom* (Berkeley: University of California Press, 2005).

21. Daniel F. Littlefield Jr., *Africans and Seminoles: From Removal to Emancipation* (Westport, Conn.: Greenwood Press, 1977), *The Cherokee Freedmen: From Emancipation to American Citizenship* (Westport, Conn.: Greenwood Press, 1978), *Africans and Creeks: From the Colonial Period to the Civil War* (Westport, Conn.: Greenwood Press, 1979); and *The Chickasaw Freedmen: A People without a Country* (*Africans and Creeks*).

22. Kevin Mulroy, "Florida Maroons" and "Immigrants from Indian Territory," in *Freedom on the Border: The Seminole Maroons in Florida, the Indian Territory, Coahuila, and Texas.* (Lubbock: Texas Tech University Press, 1993).

23. Ibid., 15.

24. Annie Heloise Abel, *The American Indian as Slaveholder and Secessionist* (1915; Lincoln: University of Nebraska Press, 1992), *The American Indian in the Civil War, 1862–1865* (1919; Lincoln: University of Nebraska Press, 1992), and *The American Indian and the End of the Confederacy, 1863–1866* (1925; Lincoln: University of Nebraska Press, 1993).

25. Angie Debo, *And Still the Waters Run* (Princeton, N.J.: Princeton University Press, 1940); and *The Road to Disappearance* (Norman: University of Oklahoma Press, 1941).

26. Littlefield, *Africans and Seminoles*; *Cherokee Freedmen*; *Africans and Creeks*; and *Chickasaw Freedmen*.

27. D. N. Cooley, *Report of the Secretary of the Interior*, 39th Congress, 1st session, October 20, House Executive Document 1, Washington, D.C., 1865.

28. Donald Grinde and Quintard Taylor, "Red vs. Black: Conflict and Accommodation in the Post Civil War Indian Territory, 1865–1907," *American Indian Quarterly* 8 (1984): 211–27.

29. Minnie Thomas Bailey, *Reconstruction in Indian Territory: A Story of Avarice, Discrimination, and Opportunism* (*Reconstruction in Indian Territory*); Barbara Krauthamer, "Blacks on the Borders: African-Americans' Transition from Slavery to Freedom in Texas and the Indian Territory, 1836–1907" (Ph.D. dissertation, Princeton University, Princeton, N.J., 2000); Claudio Saunt, "The Paradox of Freedom: Tribal Sovereignty and Emancipation during the Reconstruction of Indian Territory," *Journal of Southern History* 70 (2004): 63–95.

30. Lovett, "'African and Cherokee by Choice,'" 205.

31. Frederick E. Hoxie, *A Final Promise: The Campaign to Assimilate the Indians, 1880–1920* (Lincoln: University of Nebraska Press, 1984); Thomas Biolsi, *Deadliest Enemies: Law and the Making of Race Relations on and off Rosebud Reservation* (Berkeley: University of California Press, 2001).

32. Terry P. Wilson, "Blood Quantum: Native American Mixed Bloods," in *Racially Mixed People in America*, edited by Maria P. Root (Newbury Park, Calif.: Sage Publications, 1992); Circe Sturm, "Blood Politics, Racial Classification and Cherokee National Identity: The Trials and Tribulations of the Cherokee Freedmen," *American Indian Quarterly* 22 (1998): 230–58; Churchill, "Crucible of American Indian Identity"; Ann McMullen, "Blood and Culture: Negotiating Race in Twentieth-Century Native New England," in *Confounding the Color Line: The Indian–Black Experience in North America*, edited by James F. Brooks (Lincoln: University of Nebraska Press, 2002).

33. Churchill, "Crucible of American Indian Identity," 38.

34. Nettie Jones, *Mischief Makers* (New York: Weidenfeld & Nicolson, 1989); Sharon Holland, "If You Know I Have a History, You Will Respect Me: A Perspective on Afro-Native American Literature," *Callaloo* 17 (1994): 334–50.

35. Leslie King-Hammond, "Bitter Sweets: Considering the *Colored* Rainbow Universe of Betye Saar," in *Betye Saar: Colored: Consider the Rainbow* (New York: Michael Rosenfeld Gallery, 2002).

BIBLIOGRAPHY

Abel, Annie Heloise. *The American Indian and the End of the Confederacy, 1863–1866*. 1925; Lincoln: University of Nebraska Press, 1993.

——. *The American Indian as Slaveholder and Secessionist*. 1915; Lincoln: University of Nebraska Press, 1992.

——. *The American Indian in the Civil War, 1862–1865*. 1919; Lincoln: University of Nebraska Press, 1992.

Bailey, Minnie Thomas. *Reconstruction in Indian Territory: A Story of Avarice, Discrimination, and Opportunism.* Port Washington, N.Y.: Kennikat Press, 1972.

Bateman, Rebecca Belle. "Naming Patterns in Black Seminole Ethnogenesis." *Ethnohistory* 49 (2002): 227–57.

Bearss, Edwin C. "The Civil War Comes to Indian Territory, 1861: The Flight of Opothleyoholo." *Journal of the West* 11 (1972): 9–42.

Bennett, Herman L. *Africans in Colonial Mexico: Absolutism, Christianity, and Afro-Creole Consciousness, 1570–1640.* Bloomington: Indiana University Press, 2003.

Berkhofer, Robert F., Jr. *The White Man's Indian: Images of the American Indian from Columbus to the Present.* New York: Alfred A. Knopf, 1978.

Biolsi, Thomas. *Deadliest Enemies: Law and the Making of Race Relations on and off Rosebud Reservation.* Berkeley: University of California Press, 2001.

Blu, Karen I. "Where Did They Come From and What Were They Like Before?" *The Lumbee Problem: The Making of an American Indian People.* Cambridge, England: Cambridge University Press, 1980.

Brennan, Jonathan, ed. *When Brer Rabbit Meets Coyote: African–Native American Literature.* Urbana: University of Illinois Press, 2003.

Brooks, James F., ed. *Confounding the Color Line: The Indian-Black Experience in North America.* Lincoln: University of Nebraska Press, 2002.

Chang, David. "From Indian Territory to White Man's Country: Race, Nation, and the Politics of Land Ownership in Eastern Oklahoma, 1889–1940." Ph.D. dissertation, University of Wisconsin-Madison, 2002.

Churchill, Ward. "The Crucible of American Indian Identity: Native Tradition versus Colonial Imposition in Postconquest North America." *American Indian Culture and Research Journal* 23 (1999): 39–67.

Cooley, D. N. *Report of the Secretary of the Interior,* 39th Congress, 1st session, October 20, House Executive Document 1, Washington, D.C., 1865.

Debo, Angie. *And Still the Waters Run.* Princeton, N.J.: Princeton University Press, 1940.

———. *The Road to Disappearance.* Norman: University of Oklahoma Press, 1941.

Doran, Michael F. "Negro Slaves of the Five Civilized Tribes." *Annals of the Association of American Geographers* (Sept. 1978): 335–50.

Elliott, Michael A. "Telling the Difference: Nineteenth-Century Legal Narratives of Racial Taxonomy." *Law and Social Inquiry* 24 (1999): 611–36.

Fischer, Kirsten. "Cross-Cultural Sex in Native North Carolina." In *Suspect Relations: Sex, Race, and Resistance in Colonial North Carolina.* Ithaca, N.Y.: Cornell University Press, 2002.

Forbes, Jack D. *Black Africans and Native Americans: Color, Race, and Caste in the Evolution of Red-Black Peoples.* Oxford: Blackwell Publishers, 1988.

———. "The Manipulation of Race, Caste and Identity: Classifying Afro-Americans, Native Americans and Red-Black People." *Journal of Ethnic Studies* 17 (1990): 1–51.

Grinde, Donald, and Quintard Taylor. "Red vs. Black: Conflict and Accommodation in the Post Civil War Indian Territory, 1865–1907." *American Indian Quarterly* 8 (1984): 211–27.

Halliburton, Rudi, Jr. *Red over Black: Black Slavery among the Cherokee Indians*. Westport, Conn.: Greenwood Press, 1977.

Hawkins, Benjamin. "December 25, 1796." In *Letters, Journals, and Writings of Benjamin Hawkins*, edited by C. L. Grant, 29. Savannah, Ga.: Beehive Press, 1980.

Herskovits, Melville J. *The American Negro: A Study in Racial Crossing*. 1928; Bloomington: Indiana University Press, 1964.

———. *The Anthropometry of the American Negro*. 1930; New York: Haskell House Publishers, 1970.

Holland, Sharon P. "If You Know I Have a History, You Will Respect Me: A Perspective on Afro-Native American Literature." *Callaloo* 17 (1994): 334–50.

———. *Raising the Dead: Readings of Death and (Black) Subjectivity*. Durham, N.C.: Duke University Press, 2000.

Horsman, Reginald. "The Indian Policy of an 'Empire for Liberty.'" In *Native Americans and the Early Republic*, edited by Frederick E. Hoxie, Ronald Hoffman, and Peter J. Albert. Charlottesville: University of Virginia Press, 1999.

Howard, Rosalyn. *Black Seminoles in the Bahamas*. Gainesville: University Press of Florida, 2002.

Hoxie, Frederick E. *A Final Promise: The Campaign to Assimilate the Indians, 1880–1920*. Lincoln: University of Nebraska Press, 1984.

Jeltz, Wyatt F. "The Relations of Negroes and Choctaw and Chickasaw Indians." *Journal of Negro History* 33 (1948): 24–37.

Johnston, J. H. "Documentary Evidence of the Relations of Negroes and Indians." *Journal of Negro History* 14 (1929): 21–43.

Jones, Nettie. *Mischief Makers*. New York: Weidenfeld & Nicolson, 1989.

Kersey, Harry A., Jr. "The Seminole Negroes of Andros Island Revisited: Some New Pieces of an Old Puzzle." *Florida Anthropologist* 34 (1981): 169–76.

Kidwell, Clara Sue. *Choctaws and Missionaries in Mississippi, 1818–1918*. Norman: University of Oklahoma Press, 1995.

King-Hammond, Leslie. "Bitter Sweets: Considering the *Colored* Rainbow Universe of Betye Saar." In *Betye Saar: Colored: Consider the Rainbow*, 7, 10–11. New York: Michael Rosenfeld Gallery, 2002.

Krauthamer, Barbara. "Blacks on the Borders: African-Americans' Transition from Slavery to Freedom in Texas and the Indian Territory, 1836–1907." Ph.D. dissertation, Princeton University, Princeton, N.J., 2000.

———. "Kinship and Freedom: Fugitive Slave Women's Incorporation into Creek Society." In *New Studies in the History of American Slavery*, edited by Stephanie M. H. Camp and Edward E. Baptist. Athens: University of Georgia Press, 2005.

Landers, Jane. *Black Society in Spanish Florida*. Urbana: University of Illinois Press, 1999.

———. "Gracia Real de Santa Teresa de Mose: A Free Black Town in Spanish Colonial Florida." *American Historical Review* 95 (1990): 9–30.

Littlefield, Daniel F., Jr. *Africans and Creeks: From the Colonial Period to the Civil War*. Westport, Conn.: Greenwood Press, 1979.

——. *Africans and Seminoles: From Removal to Emancipation.* Westport, Conn.: Greenwood Press, 1977.

——. *The Cherokee Freedmen: From Emancipation to American Citizenship.* Westport, Conn.: Greenwood Press, 1978.

——. *The Chickasaw Freedmen: A People without a Country.* Westport, Conn.: Greenwood Press, 1980.

Littlefield, Daniel F., Jr., and Mary Ann Littlefield. "The Beams Family: Free Blacks in Indian Territory." *Journal of Negro History* 61 (1976): 16–35.

Littlefield, Daniel F., Jr., and Lonnie Underhill. "Slave 'Revolt' in the Cherokee Nation, 1842." *American Indian Quarterly* 3 (1977): 121–31.

Lovett, Laura. "African and Cherokee by Choice." *American Indian Quarterly* 22 (1998): 203–29.

Makofsky, Abraham. "Experience of Native Americans at a Black College: Indian Students at Hampton Institute, 1878–1923." *Journal of Ethnic Studies* 17 (1989): 31–46.

Mandell, Daniel. "Shifting Boundaries of Race and Ethnicity." *Journal of American History* 85 (1998): 466–501.

May, Katja. *African Americans and Native Americans in the Creek and Cherokee Nations, 1830s to 1920s: Collision and Collusion.* New York: Garland Press, 1996.

McDonald, Dedra S. "Intimacy and Empire: Indian–African Interaction in Spanish Colonial New Mexico, 1500–1800." *American Indian Quarterly* 22 (1998): 134–57.

McLoughlin, William G. "The Choctaw Slave Burning: A Crisis in Mission Work among the Indians." *Journal of the West* 13 (1974): 113–27.

McMullen, Ann. "Blood and Culture: Negotiating Race in Twentieth-Century Native New England." In *Confounding the Color Line: The Indian–Black Experience in North America,* edited by James F. Brooks. Lincoln: University of Nebraska Press, 2002.

Merrell, James. "The Racial Education of the Catawba Indians." *Journal of Southern History* 50 (1984): 364–83.

Miles, Tiya Alicia. *Ties That Bind: The Story of an Afro-Cherokee Family in Slavery and Freedom.* Berkeley: University of California Press, 2005.

Miles, Tiya, and Barbara Krauthamer. "Africans and Native Americans." In *The Blackwell Companion to African American History,* edited by Alton Hornsby. Oxford: Blackwell Publishers, 2004.

Minges, Patrick. "Beneath the Underdog: Race, Religion and the Trail of Tears." *American Indian Quarterly* 25 (2001): 453–82.

Mulroy, Kevin. "Florida Maroons" and "Immigrants from Indian Territory." In *Freedom on the Border: The Seminole Maroons in Florida, the Indian Territory, Coahuila, and Texas.* Lubbock: Texas Tech University Press, 1993.

Naylor-Ojurongbe, Celia. "Born and Raised among These People." In *Confounding the Color Line: The Indian-Black Experience in North America,* edited by James F. Brooks. Lincoln: University of Nebraska Press, 2001.

——. "'More at Home with the Indians': African-American Slaves and Freedpeople in the Cherokee Nation, Indian Territory, 1838–1907." Ph.D. dissertation. Duke University, 2001.

Office of Indian Affairs. *Annual Report of the Commissioner of Indian Affairs*. Washington, D.C.: U.S. Government Printing Office, 1838.

Palmer, Colin A. *Slaves of the White God: Blacks in Mexico, 1570–1650*. Cambridge, Mass.: Harvard University Press, 1976.

Perdue, Theda. "Native Women in the Early Republic: Old World Perceptions, New World Realities." In *Native Americans and the Early Republic*, edited by Frederick E. Hoxie, Ronald Hoffman, and Peter J. Albert. Charlottesville: University of Virginia Press, 1999.

———. *Slavery and the Evolution of Cherokee Society, 1540–1866*. Knoxville: University of Tennessee Press, 1979.

Phelps, Eawson A., ed. "Excerpts from the Journal of the Reverend Joseph Bullen, 1799 and 1800." *Journal of Mississippi History* 17 (1955): 262.

Porter, Kenneth W. "Negro Guides and Interpreters in the Early Stages of the Seminole War, December 28, 1835–March 6, 1837." *Journal of Negro History* 35 (1950): 174–82.

———. "Notes Supplementary to 'Relations between Negroes and Indians.'" *Journal of Negro History* 18 (1933): 282–321.

———. "Relations between Negroes and Indians within the Present Limits of the United States." *Journal of Negro History* 17 (1932): 287–367.

Riordan, Patrick. "Seminole Genesis: Native Americans, African-Americans, and Colonists on the Southern Frontier from Prehistory through the Colonial Era." Ph.D. dissertation, Florida State University, 1996.

Saunt, Claudio. "The English Has Now a Mind to Make Slaves of Them All." *American Indian Quarterly* 22 (1998): 157–81.

———. *A New Order of Things: Property, Power, and the Transformation of the Creek Indians, 1733–1816*. Cambridge, England: Cambridge University Press, 1999.

———. "The Paradox of Freedom: Tribal Sovereignty and Emancipation during the Reconstruction of Indian Territory." *Journal of Southern History* 70 (2004): 63–95.

Sefton, James E. "Black Slaves, Red Masters, White Middlemen: A Congressional Debate of 1852." *Florida Historical Quarterly* 51 (1972): 113–28.

Spear, Jennifer. "Colonial Intimacies: Legislating Sex in French Louisiana." *William and Mary Quarterly* 60 (2003): 75–98.

Sturm, Circe. *Blood Politics: Race, Culture, and Identity in the Cherokee Nation of Oklahoma*. Berkeley: University of California Press, 2002.

———. "Blood Politics, Racial Classification and Cherokee National Identity: The Trials and Tribulations of the Cherokee Freedmen." *American Indian Quarterly* 22 (1998): 230–58.

Usner, Daniel H., Jr. "American Indians on the Cotton Frontier: Changing Economic Relations with Citizens and Slaves in the Mississippi Territory." *Journal of American History* 72 (1985): 297–317.

———. *Indians, Settlers, and Slaves in a Frontier Exchange Economy: The Lower Mississippi Valley before 1783*. Chapel Hill: University of North Carolina Press, 1992.

Welburn, Ron. "A Most Secret Identity: Native American Assimilations and Identity Resistance in African America." In *Confounding the Color Line: The Indian-Black Experience in North America*, edited by James F. Brooks. Lincoln: University of Nebraska Press, 2002.

Wickett, Murray R. *Contested Territory: Whites, Native Americans, and African Americans in Oklahoma, 1865–1907*. Baton Rouge: Louisiana State University Press, 2000.

Willis, William S. "Divide and Rule: Red, White, and Black in the Southeast." *Journal of Negro History* 48 (1963): 157–76.

Wilson, Terry P. "Blood Quantum: Native American Mixed Bloods." In *Racially Mixed People in America*, edited by Maria P. Root. Newbury Park, Calif.: Sage Publications, 1992.

Woodson, Carter. "The Relations of Negroes and Indians in Massachusetts." *Journal of Negro History* 5 (1920): 45–57.

CHRONOLOGY

1527–28	The expedition led by Spanish conquistador Pánfilo Narváez, and including Estevan, an African slave, travels to America. It arrives in April 1528 in what is now Florida.
1619	August: Africans first arrive in the English colonies in North America.
1693	November 7: Charles II, king of Spain, issues a royal proclamation extending freedom to black slaves who run away from the British colonies to Spanish Florida.
1738	March–November: Spanish authorities in Florida establish a new town, Gracia Real de Santa Teresa de Mose, known as Fort Mose.
1814–15	April: Blacks and Indians construct the Negro Fort on Prospect Bluff.
1816	July 27: U.S. forces attack and destroy the Negro Fort and surrounding Indian settlements.
1817–19	First Seminole War.
1819	July: United States acquires Florida from Spain with the Adams-Onis Treaty.
1835–42	December 28, 1835: Second Seminole War begins.
1850	June: Wild Cat and John Horse lead a party of about 200 Seminoles, including Black Seminoles, from the Indian Territory to Mexico.
1865	April: Civil War ends.
1865	December: The Thirteenth Amendment outlaws slavery; 4 million enslaved African Americans are emancipated.
1865–66	Autumn/Winter: Treaties between the United States and the Cherokee, Chickasaw, Choctaw, Creek, and Seminole nations emancipate black slaves owned by these Indians.
1868	Hampton Normal and Agricultural Institute established for educating former slaves.
1878	Hampton Institute establishes program for Native Americans to attend the school.
1887	February 8: Dawes Act passed by U.S. Congress.
1898	June 28: Curtis Act passed by U.S. Congress.

GLOSSARY

Curtis Act. On June 28, 1898, Congress passed "An Act for the Protection of the People of Indian Territory," generally known as the Curtis Act after its sponsor, Senator Charles Curtis. This law applied to the Indian nations that had been exempted from the Dawes Act, and directed the Dawes Commission to move ahead with the allotment of their land even without tribal consent. The law authorized the Dawes Commission to "adopt any other means by them deemed necessary" in order to implement the division of the Indians' land into allotments. Many Indians in the Indian Territory resisted the Curtis Act by refusing to enroll on the Dawes Rolls. Many black people in the Cherokee, Choctaw, Chickasaw, Creek, and Seminole nations also protested the law because it limited the amount of land allotted to former slaves and their descendants.

Dawes Act. Congress passed the Dawes Act, named for its author, Senator Henry Dawes of Massachusetts, on February 8, 1887. Also known as the General Allotment Act, the law allowed for the president to take the land held as common property by Indian nations and break it into small allotments to be owned by individuals. In order to receive an allotment, people in each Indian nation were required to enroll with the Bureau of Indian Affairs, which compiled the names in lists known as the "Dawes Rolls." The law specified how much land people would receive. A head of a family, for example, was to receive 160 acres, while a single person over the age of eighteen would receive 80 acres. The stated intent of the Dawes Act and similar, subsequent legislation was purportedly to protect Native Americans' land rights, especially during the late nineteenth-century land rushes in the West. In practice, however, there were many instances when the outcome was quite different. Indians were often given land allotments in desert regions that were unsuitable for farming or raising livestock, and unscrupulous speculators conspired to cheat Indians out of their titles to valuable land. Many Indians, furthermore, were denied access to resources such as credit and the tools, animals, seed, and other supplies necessary to subsist as farmers. Some Indian peoples were initially exempt from the Dawes Act's provisions. The law did not extend to the land in the Indian Territory claimed by the Cherokees, Creeks, Choctaws, Chickasaws, Seminoles, Osages, Miamies, Peorias, Sacs, and Foxes, nor did it apply to the Seneca Nation's reservations in New York, nor to the Sioux Nation's land in Nebraska. The exemptions were overruled by subsequent legislation passed by Congress in the 1890s.

Fort Mose. Between March and November of 1738, Spanish authorities in Florida established a fortified town approximately two miles north of St. Augustine, and called it Gracia Real de Santa Teresa de Mose. This town, known as Fort Mose, became home to the black men and women who ran away from slavery in the English colonies and sought refuge in Spanish Florida. The men of Fort Mose served in the Spanish militia, defending Spain's colony against attacks by the British and their Indian allies. During the War of Jenkin's Ear in 1739, British forces attacked Fort Mose, but Spanish forces consisting of blacks, Indians, and Spaniards recaptured the fort in a bloody battle on June 14, 1740.

Hampton University. Located in Virginia, Hampton Normal and Agricultural Institute was founded in 1868 by Brigadier General Samuel Chapman Armstrong, the twenty-nine-year-old son of missionary parents, to provide education for recently emancipated African American young men and women. Early support for the school came from the American Missionary Association; the United States Bureau of Refugees, Freedmen and Abandoned Lands (the Freedmen's Bureau); and northern philanthropists. In 1878, Hampton established a course of education for Native American students that was implemented for over forty years. The school's name was changed to Hampton Institute in 1924, and was changed again in 1984 to Hampton University.

Indian Territory. The region known as "Indian Territory" in the northern part of what is now Oklahoma was set aside in 1834 as the home to the five southern Indian nations—Cherokee, Choctaw, Chickasaw, Creek, and Seminole—after their forced removal from Georgia and the Gulf states in the 1830s and 1840s. Throughout the nineteenth century, other Indian nations were also relocated to the Indian Territory. Until the late nineteenth century, the Indian Territory was home to Native Americans and the African Americans who had been enslaved and emancipated in Indian nations. At the end of the century, federal legislation terminated the Indian nations' land claims, making much of the land available to white people, and the region once known as Indian Territory was merged with Oklahoma Territory to become the state of Oklahoma in 1907.

Maroons. Fugitive slaves in the Americas were called maroons, a term that may derive from the Spanish word *cimarrón*, meaning "wild" or "untamed." Extensive, permanent maroon communities developed in places such as Jamaica and Brazil, but maroon settlements also emerged in North America. Maroons established remote, defensible settlements, and survived by planting small crops and, sometimes, raiding slaveholders' plantations. Men assumed leadership roles within the communities, directing women's agricultural and domestic labor and leading other men in battles against slaveholders or Native American enemies. In many instances, however, maroons forged military alliances and social relationships, including marriage, with nearby Indian peoples, as was the case with the Seminole Indians and runaway slaves in Florida.

Negro Fort. Located on Prospect Bluff above the Apalachicola River in Spanish Florida, the Negro Fort was constructed by the British during the winter of 1814–1815 to entice runaway slaves and Seminole and Redstick Indians to fight in the War of 1812. Approximately 2,800 people, predominantly men, lived at Prospect Bluff. By the spring of 1815, the heavily armed fort was surrounded by a ten-foot-wide and four-foot-deep moat, had a parapet that stood fifteen feet high and was eighteen feet thick, and had cannons and mortars mounted on the ramparts. Over the following year, slaves continued to run away to the fort. The continued escape of slaves, and the visibly strong military alliance between runaway slave men and Indian men aggravated and alarmed American slaveholders and government officials. In July 1816, American gunboats advanced towards the fort, and on July 27 gunfire was exchanged between the fort and U.S. vessels. The fort was destroyed when a red-hot cannonball fired from one of the American gunboats landed in the fort's powder magazine. Most of the fort's residents successfully escaped to nearby Seminole towns, but approximately forty people lost their lives in the fort.

Seminole Wars. The First Seminole War broke out in the summer of 1817 when maroons and Seminole Indians opposed white slaveholders' efforts to retrieve the fugitive slaves living among the Indians in Spanish Florida. Together, blacks and Indians raided white-owned plantations in the United States, stealing property and helping slaves escape. Andrew Jackson led the United States forces as they invaded Spanish Florida to defeat the black-Indian alliance in 1818. Jackson's victory resulted in the U.S. acquisition of

Florida from Spain by 1819. The Second Seminole War began on December 28, 1835, when maroon warriors inspired Seminole warriors to oppose the federal government's plans for removing the Seminoles from Florida and relocating them in the West. This war lasted until August 1842, when the Seminoles and maroons were finally removed to the Indian Territory.

Afro-Latinos

Agustín Laó-Montes

Abstract

This collection traces the development of Afro-Latino culture resulting from the African Diaspora. The vast population denominated "Afro-Latino" constitutes the largest component of the African Diaspora in the Americas. Demographic calculations range between 70 and 150 million, depending on who is considered African-descended.[1] A significant percentage of African descendants in Latino America identify themselves as belonging to some sort of "brown" or "mulatto" category. In this essay, Afro-Latinos are defined as all peoples of substantive African descent who belong either by birth, descent, or residence to the world region that we call Latino America.[2] In this sense, Afro-Latinos form a diaspora within a diaspora, and as a product of the global dispersal of African peoples, particularly within the Atlantic system, they have multiple ties and diverse identities—locally, nationally, regionally, and globally. Indeed, Afro-Latino history comprises a complex constellation of diasporas—a set of local histories that are linked by common trajectories of uprooting, enslavement, and resistance; by experiencing racism and engaging in antiracist struggles; and by national and transnational efforts to obtain justice and emancipation.

Afro-Iberia and the Simultaneous Invention
of Europe, Africa, and the Americas

A general overview of Afro-Latino history, culture, and politics extends at least to the European Middle Ages on the Iberian Peninsula. The presence of sub-Saharan Africans in the Iberian Peninsula can be traced to antiquity, but we have clearer evidence of it in the context of the invasion of the Islamic region called al-Andalus by African Muslims in the early eighth century and the establishment of the great Abbasid Caliphate centered in Cordoba from 750 to 1258. This particular subregion was an Islamic stronghold and thus destined for the historic clash with Christendom. In this highly contested terrain of military, cultural, and religious wars, sub-Saharan Africans were mostly used as soldiers or slave laborers. The so-called *Reconquista*, a name used to signify the nearly eight centuries of conflict between Islamic and Christian armies to control Iberia, led the Moors (the Northern Africans who dominated the peninsula) to integrate sub-Saharan soldiers into their armies. Indeed, by the late Middle Ages the Iberian Peninsula was a diverse cultural land, a contact zone of a plurality of civilizations, religions, and cultural traditions. The great divides there between Islam, Judaism, and Christianity provided the conditions for Christian protoracial discourses of "purity of blood."

By 1250 most of the Iberian Peninsula was occupied by Christian forces that later established the earliest modern European absolutist states and empires, namely, Spain and Portugal. Influenced by Arabic mercantilism, the Portuguese and the Spanish took advantage of their proximity to West Africa, developing trade relationships with the African continent that extended the circuits of the African slave trade to Europe, and initiating plantation agriculture partly based on African slave labor. Consequently, after 1492, when the Spaniards initiated the conquest of the Americas, a diversity of peoples of African descent who already were part of the Iberian world came in its wake. But even more important, the European exploration of the Americas created the conditions for a profound expansion and development of the slave trade and the plantation agriculture that had been initiated by the Portuguese and the Spaniards.

The conquest of the Americas and the introduction of the slave trade established the conditions for the forced transportation of millions of people from the African continent to the Americas. The great majority of the Africans who came to the Americas were brought as slaves to work in mines and on the plantations that were crucial for the growth of the rising capitalist world economy.

The Making of Afroamerica

The first Africans who came to the Americas as slave labor in 1502 were brought to Hispaniola (now the island that is composed of Haiti and the Dominican Republic) by the Spaniards. After the relatively rapid decline of indigenous populations, due primarily to disease, the slave trade with Africa became massive, and plantations based on African slave labor became the first forms of industrial production in the rising capitalist system. Thus from the early sixteenth century to the late nineteenth century, the slave trade brought millions of sub-Saharan Africans to the Americas. The majority of them came to the region that is now called Latin America and the Caribbean. Since the times of slavery, and especially since the early twentieth century, there have also been abundant migrations of Afro-descendants inside Latin America, within the Caribbean and Central America, and to the United States.

Afro-descendants (including both blacks and mulattos) constituted the majority of the population in many Latin-American countries during the eighteenth and nineteenth centuries.[3] However, state-sponsored demographic policies geared toward whitening national populations and culture in the late nineteenth century significantly diminished the proportion of black and brown populations in places such as Argentina and Southern Brazil. Nonetheless, the historic strongholds of the African Diaspora in the Americas, the countries and regions in which the indigenous population was relatively small and wherein the plantation complex was significantly established, remained as the key sites for Afro-Latino diasporas. Characteristics changed over time, but places such as Brazil, Cuba, Colombia, and Haiti/Hispaniola have been important centers since the very beginnings of the Africanization of the Americas.

In the eighteenth century, given that Haiti was the richest colony founded on plantation slave labor, and in light of the tremendous significance of the Haitian Revolution both in the cultures and politics of slave resistance and in the restructuring of colonial societies and racial capitalism, the events in Saint Domingue should be regarded as central to the history of the African Diaspora in the Americas.[4] The fear felt by the Haitian masters spread across the diaspora, establishing a memory of revolutionary success and a feasible hope of liberty in the African-slave cultures of resistance throughout the Americas. Arguably, the Haitian Revolution (1791–1804 and beyond) not only inaugurated the very idea of *Négritude* (as observed by Aimé Césaire) but also initiated an African-descendant transnational racial politics.

Since the nineteenth century, the Afro-Latino population was concentrated in Cuba and Brazil, which were the largest and, to a large extent, the most influential black cultures of Latin America. Brazil and Cuba share the peculiarity of experiencing a boom both in slave immigration and in plantation agriculture throughout the nineteenth century, even after the legal abolition of the slave trade.[5] The results were that many more Africans came to Brazil and Cuba than to any other place in the Americas. The sheer numbers and the late arrivals from the African continent had important implications for the strength and significance of African-diasporic expressive cultures (for example, music, dance, and religion), and eventually for the emergence of particularly black public spaces and racial politics in Cuba and Brazil.

By the beginnings of the nineteenth century a nascent constellation of African American settlements can be identified within the emerging region of Ibero-America. People of African descent were spread throughout the region, ranging from Mexico to Argentina. But the main concentration of Afro-Latinos was in countries such as Brazil, Cuba, Colombia, Panama, Dominican Republic, Puerto Rico, and Venezuela, and in subregions (some rural but others urban) of Central America (for example, Garifunas in Honduras and Guatemala), Ecuador, Peru, and Uruguay. The combined effect of everyday resistances to slavery, slave revolts and insurrections, and the abolitionist movement along with wars of independence, were the main

Illustration of a Brazilian slave auction, ca. 1850. Brazil was the last country in the western hemisphere to abolish slavery. Following passage of the Emancipation Act in 1833, the British government made concerted efforts to make Brazil follow suit. The Aberdeen Law of 1845 authorized the Royal Navy to search Brazilian vessels suspected of participating in the slave trade. Five years later Brazil officially ended its participation in the transatlantic slave trade. It was not until 1888, however, that the former Portuguese colony emancipated its slaves.

factors behind the myriad processes of emancipation and the abolition of slavery in the Americas. In their search for empowerment, the Afro-diasporic subjects who inhabited those worlds created a distinct cultural identity within the Ibero-American component of the Black Atlantic that might be called

Afroamerica and Afro-Latino/America by means of their quotidian struggles and practical affirmations of memory, self, and culture.[6]

The Historical Production of Afro-Latino America: From the Wars of Independence to Struggles for Equal Citizenship

The everyday fight to claim their humanity and to affirm their right to a memory, a culture, and fair conditions of life led to a unity among African descendants in Latin America, who constituted an underclass. The middle strata, composed of mulattos and free blacks, were also crucial in the organization of black publics with their own intellectuals, publications, pedagogical spaces, meeting places, and small businesses. These "Afro" or "black" social spaces and cultural-political settings were a historical foundation for the participation of African-descendants in the wars of independence, and subsequently in the processes of state formation and regionalization that created Latin America itself. Indeed, the history of Latin America can be written in terms of the African Diaspora, while the history of Afroamerica can be told from the specific perspective of the Afro-Latino diasporas within it.[7] For instance, the wars against the Spanish empire that achieved independence for the territories that later were organized as Latin American nations were largely seen by African descendants as an opportunity for the abolition of slavery and for the creation of more democratic forms of citizenship. However, this was not the case for Euro-American Creole elites, who defined themselves as superior to blacks and Indians. In the African-diasporic historical narrative, the protagonists were not simply leaders from the Creole elites, like Simón Bolívar and José de San Martín; they were also from the black masses who composed the pro-independence armies, and who fought within various arenas for a more democratic political, economic, and cultural contract.

From the standpoint of African-descendants, the wars between Spain and the Creoles in the early nineteenth century can be interpreted as a contest between two white (European and Euro-American) dominant classes fighting for hegemony, in which both offered them concessions of relative freedom and societal inclusion in exchange for military and political support. Consequently, even though most African-descendants fought in the independence armies, some were recruited by the imperial forces. With the important exception of the War for Cuban Independence, for the most part blacks remained as simple rank-and-file soldiers and did not become high officers or political and intellectual leaders in the movements for independence. The Cuban situation, the exception that confirms the rule, is revealing about the racial politics that configured the emerging nation-states as well as the region. After the Haitian Revolution, Cuba became the richest plantation colony, with the largest base of slave labor. The formidable profits from sugar-cane cultivation, along with the fear of another major slave insurrection, kept the Cuban plantocracy loyal to the Spanish colonial state until the end of the nineteenth century. When the Cry of Yara began the first war for independence in 1868, both the free colored peoples (blacks and mulattos) and the slaves were numerous enough and organized enough to play a key role in the movement. After much struggle and negotiation, the army for Cuban independence achieved the peculiarity of not only constituting a majority of people of color but also of having black and mulatto officers up to the rank of general. This circumstance accounts for the particularly antiracist discourse that gained prominence in nineteenth-century Cuban nationalism, which was eloquently articulated by revolutionary writer José Martí and by Afro-Cuban revolutionary general Antonio Maceo. (Aline Helg argues, on the other hand, that even after the revolution, a "myth of racial equality" prevailed, and that discrimination against mulattos and blacks was widespread.)[8]

In general, African-descendants played a significant role in the historical movement for independence of the territories in Latin America. As rank-and-file soldiers, they fought in the frontline while they negotiated emancipation from slavery and citizenship in the nascent nations. In a few countries, such as Ecuador, Venezuela, and Mexico, Afro-Latinos also became military, political, and intellectual leaders. In Mexico, revolts in the early nineteenth century led by Afro-Indio (or Afro-Mestizo) leaders such as Miguel Hidalgo y Costilla and José María Morelos Pavón demonstrated how struggles for racial and economic justice continued after independence. The continuation of these struggles in the emerging Latin American nation-states against the racial, class, and patriarchal domination created by European imperialism is analyzed by Anibal Quijano with regard to the concept of the "coloniality of power."[9] After independence, the nascent Latin American nations remained economically subordinate in a capitalist world economy dominated by the British. Also, within each nation-state of the region, *negros*, *indios*, and *mulatos* (*castas*) remained economically, politically, and culturally subordinate in relation to the white Creole elites, who declared themselves heirs of Europe and the West in the Americas. The movements for independence prepared the way for the gradual abolition of slavery. However, the persistent condition of ethnoracial subordination, cultural devalorization, and class inequality that defined blacks and indigenous peoples as second-class citizens in the newly formed Latin American nations framed a new historical constellation of racial, social, and cultural struggles for substantive citizenship in which Afro-Latinos played a key role.

As in the move toward independence, the process of building modern liberal polities in Latin America did not have exactly the same meaning for African-descendants that it had for the white (and light mestizo) Creole elites. By the late nineteenth century, most Latin American countries (with the important exceptions of Brazil, Cuba, and Puerto Rico) had abolished slavery. The new claims for racial democracy and social justice for African-descendants were defined in terms of the inclusion and equality of black citizens in all domains of national life, from the cultural to the political. In the formal and institutional domain of politics in the nineteenth century, Afro-Latinos were, for the most part, kept as clients of the liberal and conservative parties that shared political power. In general, Afro-Latino struggles for citizenship constituted significant forces in the historical contests for democratization.

An important arena of struggle was the cultural, given the devalorization of African-diasporic cultural forms and religious practices by European-influenced state policies and ecclesiastical doctrines. In places like Brazil and Cuba, where African-diasporic religions were fundamental in the everyday life of many African-descendants, Afro-religious organizations, such as the *terreiros* in Brazil and the *cabildos* in Cuba, had to struggle to survive against the vilification and even legal censure to which they were subjected. Afro-Latinos also developed their own public spaces for intellectual expression and development, including newspapers, academies, and social clubs that were led by the middle stratum, many of whom were mulattos. In Cuba, by the late nineteenth century, the social and political organization of Afro-Cubans had obtained national coordination with the creation of the Central Directory of the Colored Race. Cuba provides a clear example of the formation of two distinct yet entangled domains of Afro-Latino life, one led by a westernized middle-class intelligentsia who acted within the formal channels of state and civil society, the other adopting the values of the working-class Afro-Cuban neighborhoods. These two distinct yet intertwined Afro-Latino domains of middle-class intellectual culture and popular culture composed in their dialectical relationship the historical substratum of the cultural production of African-descendants in Latin America.

Another principal historical terrain of conflict and self-affirmation for Afro-Latinos was the economic arena, given that after the abolition of slavery the majority of blacks remained in the lower echelons of labor, both in the rural areas and in cities. Thus, in places such as Puerto Rico and Cuba, African-descendants, who constituted a large proportion of the working classes, played a crucial role in the organization of the labor movement. By the end of the nineteenth and the beginning of the twentieth century, booming urbanization caused mass migrations of African-descendants from country to city. This in turn created urban working classes and working-class neighborhoods largely composed of African-descendants; it also caused the mass unemployment and substantive marginalization of rights for a significant percentage of the black population. These urban settlements also spawned the Afro-Latino urban cultures that eventually had national and transnational impact—developments that were to a large extent facilitated by the growth of culture industries in the last half of the twentieth century.

The Emergence of Afro-Latino Politics and the Rise of Black Expressive Cultures

Thus the stage was set early in the twentieth century for the creation of the first political organizations that explicitly advocated a racial politics for the empowerment of people of color: the Partido Independiente de Color (1908) in Cuba and the Frente Negra Brasileira (1931) in Brazil. Several historical conditions framed the rise of African-descendants in Latin America. The first was the 1898 Spanish-Cuban-American-Filipino (SCAF) War (called the Spanish American War) that marked both the rise of the United States as a world power and the concept of Latino/Americanism, developed by intellectuals and statesmen from the Ibero-America region.

The SCAF War marked U.S. political-economic domination in the hemisphere, and the establishment of forms of colonial and neocolonial power in the Caribbean and Central America. Puerto Rico was annexed as a colony with the legal title of "unincorporated territory," while Cuba was kept as a neocolony under the Platt Amendment. In the new U.S. imperial discourse, the Caribbean and Central America became a "backyard" for which specific categories of negative racial classification were developed. The racialized divide between "Anglos" and "Latinos," which was originally a product of the imperial competition between the British and the French, became more central and relevant in the context of 1898 in the Americas. Creole-white elites from both the United States and Latin American countries claimed in various ways to be the heirs of the West in the Americas. In their claims for intellectual, aesthetic, and moral hegemony (in the case of Latin Americans), they defined their identities as distinct from other elite peoples and took particular care to separate themselves from the underclasses—notably blacks, Indians, and Asians. This hemispheric divide of identity and difference articulated by the Creole elites established the parameters of U.S. imperial discourse on the one hand, and of hegemonic Latino/Americanism on the other. In this historical conjuncture, Cuba and Puerto Rico, as the only remaining colonies of Spain in the Americas, had a particular path. Cuban and Puerto Rican anticolonial activists had organized the Cuban Revolutionary Party in New York City in 1892. José Martí, the most lucid anticolonial and antiracist Latin American voice of the period, lived one-third of his short life in New York, where he wrote some of his most important essays, including *Nuestra America*, a foundational text of Latino/Americanism. As observed before, Martí was a product of the democratic strength of Afro-Cubans in the anticolonial movement that launched three liberation wars from 1868 to

1898. In the same vein, Martí should be analyzed as a trans-American voice speaking from U.S.-Latino settlements to the whole hemisphere, and thus representing a critical Latino/Americanism that defended the predicament of *castas* such as *el indio* and *el negro* against all dominant powers. In this sense, it is crucial to notice the role of Afro-Puerto Ricans, such as Arturo Alfonso Schomburg and Sotero Figueroa in the Club dos Antillas, which was one of the main clubs of the movement for Cuban and Puerto Rican independence in New York in the late nineteenth century and was mostly composed of Afro-Antilleans.

In Cuba, the twentieth century began with the establishment of a re-public in which Afro-Cubans were subjected to racism and class domination from both U.S. and Cuban regimes. The claims for equal citizenship, and the democratic definition of nationhood that was negotiated during the independence, suffered a serious setback. In this context, the National Directory of Societies of People of Color coordinated a strand of racial politics advocating equal rights, resources, and recognition for Afro-Cubans and their integration into a democratic nation-building process. However, the blatant racism infecting all aspects of social life, from income distribution and employment to political power and de facto segregation, motivated a sector of Afro-Cuban political activists and labor leaders to organize the first political party in the Americas with an explicit agenda of empowerment for people of color. The Partido Independiente de Color was founded in 1908 and lasted until 1912, when after having been declared illegal because it was organized on the basis of race, a large percentage of its constituency was massacred by the military forces of the Cuban state.

Generally speaking, the collective action that can be characterized as Afro-Latino racial politics during the first part of the twentieth century did not take the form of independent political organizations or of a politics for black empowerment; it was manifested more as claims for rights and resources through the main political parties and labor unions. Afro-Latino organizations developed informally, primarily in the cultural sphere and at the local level. Thus, the success in developing, maintaining, and affirming their cultural forms and practices constitutes a mode of Afro-Latino racial politics that opposed the official policies of modernization endorsed by those who sought to eliminate

African-diasporic cultures that were seen as backward. The Creole ruling classes and intellectuals who presided over the young Latin American nations promoted policies of modernization predicated on the racist reasoning of the times, including the rising "science" of eugenics and social Darwinism. The civilizing mission guiding the racial, cultural, and economic policies of Latin American states, which were also an expression of the global configurations of the coloniality of power, implied a tacit equation between modernization and whitening. Hence, in the first part of the twentieth century, Latin-American governments, most successfully Argentina and Brazil, gave Europeans incentives, such as good jobs and cheaper transportation, to immigrate in order to change the racial balance of the population. The net effect was an increased marginalization of Afro populations in places where the effort was successful, such as Argentina, Uruguay, and the south of Brazil.

The increase in global and regional migrations in the period between the world economic crisis of the 1870s, the first Great War accompanied by two revolutions (the Mexican in 1910 and the Russian in 1917), and the Great Depression of the 1930s also brought migratory movements of the African Diaspora in the Americas. The mass migrations of West Indians to Central America and the Hispanic Caribbean (especially Cuba and the Dominican Republic), primarily as a labor force to build the Panama Canal and as a rural proletariat for the United Fruit Company, altered the pattern of Afro-Latino diasporas. Another important element within this migratory wave was the thousands of Haitians who emigrated primarily to the eastern part of Cuba, mostly to work in the sugar-cane industry. Eastern Cuba became a trans-Caribbean African-diasporic subregion that was centered on the city of Santiago. This migration partly explains why the Universal Negro Improvement Association led by Marcus Garvey (who visited Cuba twice during the period) had more than 300,000 registered members in Cuba. There still are several communities in eastern Cuba that assert Haitian ancestry and speak Haitian Creole along with Spanish; many of their members practice a Cuban variant of Haitian Vodun, as well as music and dance similar to those performed in today's Haiti. Many people who belong to this particular historical lineage still claim a double national identity as both Haitian and Cuban, thus pursuing a path of identification defined as African-diasporic and trans-Caribbean.

In certain regions of Costa Rica, which was not an Afro-Latino bastion, West Indian labor migrations to staff the United Fruit Company facilitated the creation of what became a vibrant Afro-Latino community with its own cultural production (for example, literature) and political movement centered on the coastal city of Limón. In a similar fashion, Afro-Central American communities emerged in Guatemala, Honduras, Nicaragua, and Panama. In Honduras, Guatemala, Belize, and Nicaragua, there was also an older history of Garifuna (in old anthropology, Black Carib) settlements since the late eighteenth century, when the British colonists expelled them from the island of San Vicente (ca. 1789) after they realized that this group of African-diasporic maroons and Carib Indians were virtually impossible to colonize. The Garifunas are quintessentially diasporic people, given that they maintain a transnational ethnic identity while keeping distinct national identities, such as Guatemalan, Belizean, and Honduran. In sum, a new wave of migrations within the Americas redrew the geography and the historical terrains of Afroamerica in general, and of Afro-Latino diasporas in particular.

An important event was the 1937 massacre of close to twenty thousand Haitians in the Dominican Republic by order of the dictator Rafael Leonidas Trujillo, who had aggressively campaigned for a negrophobic definition of Dominican identity, founded on anti-Haitian sentiments. Trujillo's dictatorship was instrumental in developing a peculiar strand of anti-black racism in the Dominican Republic based on proclaiming and disparaging blackness as a trait of Haiti and the Haitians, while developing a Hispanophile discourse of Dominican nationality and nomenclature in which all Dominicans of color were classified as some sort of "Indian." In the Dominican Republic during the early twentieth century, there were relatively large immigrations from the Anglophone Caribbean, especially to work in the sugar-cane industry in San Pedro de Macorís. Several thousands of these new immigrants, who eventually were called *Cocolos* in Dominican popular parlance, also joined the ranks of Garvey's Universal Negro Improvement Association. Anti-black fear directed against West Indian immigrants was a phenomenon not restricted to the Dominican Republic. In fact, in Panama, a place that eventually became a keystone of Afro-Latino organization, on national as well as hemispheric scales, a historical tension between West Indians (or Antilleans) and Afro-Hispanics had entailed much negotiation to consolidate a unified national movement of Afro-descendants.

The period between the Great Depression of the 1930s and World War II shook the structures of the world and reconfigured Latin American societies. For instance, changes in the countryside that entailed reconfiguration of land into large *latifundia,* loss of land by black peasantries, and the emergence of a rural proletariat of African-descendants resulted in large migrations from country to city and the organization of urban settlements that became a locus of Afro-Latino culture and politics. The urbanization of African-descendants and the concomitant rise of urban black popular cultures were key factors in the emerging process of Afroamericanization of Latin American public cultures in various nations and in the whole region.

Three elements are crucial to the explanation of how Afroamerican cultural practices, especially in the domains of music and dance but also in other aspects of culture, such as literature, the visual arts, performance arts, and religion, came to occupy a central position in Latin American culture. The first element, which is the foundation, was the struggles of African-descendants to affirm and defend their cultural practices as valid expressions of national culture, against the force of hegemonic discourses and cultural policies that characterized them as atavistic. These struggles, at once racial, social, and cultural, were launched by the black and mulatto urban middle classes, but also by African-descendants from the working classes and those marginalized from formal employment who lived in the *barrios,* the nascent *favelas* in Rio de Janeiro, or the *solares* in La Habana. The second factor was the rise of culture industries such as radio, music-recording, entertainment, commercial magazines, and film that facilitated the spread of black music and dance in various national and transnational contexts (noticeably from Brazil, Cuba, and Puerto Rico to U.S. Afro-North American and Afro-Latino metropolitan centers, and especially New York City). The third factor was the organization of transnational networks of Afroamerican intellectuals, artists, writers, and political activists, who cultivated a cosmopolitan culture of the African Diaspora.

The specific roles and participation of Afro-Latinos in the cosmopolitan webs of the African Diaspora in the 1930s and 1940s still needs to be

Hulton Archive / Getty Images

Dominican dictator General Rafael Leonidas Trujillo (*center*) and his brother, President Hector Trujillo (*right*), take the salute during a military parade, ca. 1958. An army officer trained by the U.S. Marines, Trujillo seized power in the Dominican Republic following a military revolt in 1930. Although he brought a level of peace and economic prosperity to his country, Trujillo terrorized his people by crushing their civil and political liberties and murdering his opponents. He remained in absolute control of the country until his assassination in 1961. The Trujillo years in the Dominican Republic were marked by fervent racism directed toward persons of African descent.

researched. A productive angle is to explore the lifelong project and the multiple engagements of Afro-Puerto Rican Arturo Alfonso Schomburg, a Puerto Rican–born mulatto who founded what still is the most important archive of black history in the world, was a pillar of the Harlem Renaissance, and became president of the American Negro Academy. The differential construction of Schomburg's biography by Puerto Rican, black American, and Afro-Caribbean intellectuals reveals how distinct diaspora discourses define their subject. In Puerto Rico Schomburg is barely known, while in

U.S.-Puerto Rican memory he is highly regarded, and U.S. black historians remember him as a black archivist. Some historians argue that Schomburg abandoned Hispanic Caribbean militancy after 1898 and eventually let go of his Puerto Rican identity in favor of an African-diasporic one. But an analysis of Schomburg's work and projects yields a more nuanced view of his multiple locations and loyalties. His long-lasting commitment to what we now call Afro-Latinidades can be clearly seen in his struggle for inclusion of Afro-Cubans and Puerto Ricans in organizations such as the Negro Society for Historical Research, and of Afro-Hispanic writers in anthologies of black literature. His research on Africans in early modern Spain pioneered the current revision of European history as multiracial. His advocacy for translation of Afro-Latino writers like Nicolás Guillén revealed his contributions to scholarship on the African Diaspora. Indeed, Schomburg could not give up his Afro-Latino identity, because his blackness was often contested in light of his Puerto Rican origin and light skin color. Schomburg was able to maintain good relations with such people as W. E. B. Du Bois, Marcus Garvey, Claude McKay, and Alain Locke, with whom he had basic disagreements. In fact, his project of black cosmopolitanism based on a recognition of diversity and complexity in the multiple racial regimes and cultural practices that composed the global African Diaspora challenged narrow notions of both Africanness and *Latinidad*. In sum, he was a "transamerican intellectual" who promoted a diasporic project in which identity and community were conceived through and across difference.

A telling example of powerful diasporic reciprocity involving three cultural movements in three key nodes of a cosmopolitan network of black intellectuals, cultural creators, and political activists in the early twentieth century is provided by the Harlem Renaissance, the Négritude movement, and Afro-Cubanismo. An important relationship in this black cosmopolitan diasporic world was between Cuban writer Nicolás Guillén and Langston Hughes; their friendship, intellectual exchange, mutual translation of poetry, and reciprocal introduction to their respective national and linguistic contexts eloquently exemplify African-diasporic solidarity. In Mexico, the Instituto de Estudios Afroamericanos was organized in the early 1940s and published a short-lived magazine called *Afroamerica*.[10] The association and magazine were launched and supported by a trans-American group of intellectuals of (or for) the African Diaspora that included Euro-Cuban Fernando Ortiz, Afro-Cubans Nicolás Guillén and Romulo Lachatanere, Brazilian Gilberto Freyre, Haitian Jacques Roumain, Mexican Gonzalo Aguirre Beltrán, Martiniquean Aimé Césaire, Trinidadian Eric Williams, U.S. blacks Alain Locke and W. E. B. Du Bois, and anthropologist Melvin Herskovits.[11]

Latin-American Populism, Developmentalism, and Discourses of Mestizaje: Contested Terrains of Racial/Social/Cultural Politics and Policy

After World War II, the capitalist nations entered into a period of restructuring. New forms of global governance were designed under the umbrella of the United Nations, together with newly created institutions of global capitalism, such as the International Monetary Fund and the World Bank. In Latin America, political and economic crises of the interwar period and especially the Great Depression resulted in the demise of the oligarchic state and the emergence of populist states and developmentalist policies. Latin American populism implied political pacts and developmentalist policies more inclusive than before, involving a degree of income redistribution. The populist movement in Latin American politics, which can be traced to the late 1930s with the government of Getúlio Vargas in Brazil and which reached its peak in the 1940s and 1950s with the leadership of charismatic figures such as Juan Perón in Argentina, Rómulo Betancourt in Venezuela, and Muñoz Marín in Puerto Rico, was the product of vibrant movements for democracy and social justice. Afro-Latino claims of full citizenship embedded in demands for rights, recognition, and resources were an important element within the set of demands addressed by populist regimes. Hence, it should not be a surprise that populist parties and governments were often accused of favoring blacks and Indians. Nonetheless, the same ambiguities and contradictions that we can observe in the class politics and policies of Latin American populism can be ascribed to the associated policies of their racial discourses. The new nationalisms advocated by populist movements did not admit real differences within the popular bloc. Consequently, the specificity of Afro-Latino difference (say Afro-Brazilian or Afro-Venezuelan) was diluted within the national-popular bloc. In this vein, the ethnoracial ideology that articulated such vision was the discourse of mestizaje that emerged as hegemonic since the late 1930s and 1940s, and whose main intellectual progenitors were José Vasconcelos in Mexico, Gilberto Freyre in Brazil, and Fernando Ortiz in Cuba. According to this narrative of the history for each nation and for the whole Latin American region, Latin American peoples and nations are the hybrid product of cultural Americanist discourses. They remain basically European, despite the progressivist significance attributed to "races" and cultures, according to which white Euro-American characteristics are assumed to be dominant, while the cultural history of indigenous peoples and the influence of the African experience are the least important elements.

The historic turn from the oligarchic state to the populist state can also be represented as a shift from a racial state of whitening to a racial politics of browning. The strong social movements that brought the populist state into being fought against racial discrimination, for redistribution of income, and for democratization of polity and culture. As a result, policies against discrimination and for racial inclusion were introduced in countries such as Venezuela, Brazil, and Costa Rica, at the same time that Afro-Latino political organizations were formed in Brazil, Cuba, and Uruguay. In tune with these changes, there was a fair growth in the percentage of Afro-Latinos gaining literacy, finishing school, and going to universities. There was also a significant increase of Afro-Latinos in public employment. The pressing need for public employment for Afro-Latinos was also an indication of persistent inequalities and of discrimination in the labor market, despite its growing dependency on the black lower class. The growth of Afro-Latino working classes also entailed increased participation and leadership in the labor movements that gained special political significance in places like Cuba and Brazil. Brazil, Cuba, and Puerto Rico were also the only three countries from which we have statistics that specify race and ethnicity for the first half of the twentieth century. In these three cases, but especially in Brazil and Cuba, there was a substantial shift from "black" to "brown" in census identification from the 1940s to the 1960s, which indicates more of a change in self-identification (fewer people want to identify as black and more want to call themselves some sort of mulatto or mestizo) than a profound process of *mestizaje* or *mulataje*.

To take a different perspective, the exponential growth and rising centrality of culture industries and the beginning of mass media facilitated the shift of Afro-Latino cultural expressions (especially music and dance) from the margins into the center of public culture. This phenomenon that musicologist Robin Moore called the "nationalization of blackness" in the context of Cuba could also be observed in the development of diasporic and global webs of cultural production and circulation.[12] In the late 1940s and 1950s, the clearest case of this sort of globalization of African-diasporic/Afro-Latino cultural genres was the mambo, which became a staple of music and dance from Cuba and Mexico City to New York and Los Angeles to Europe and Japan. The bebop revolution in jazz belongs to the same musical lineage of African-diasporic cosmopolitanism that created what Robert Farris Thompson calls the "cultural revolution" of the mambo. In New York City in the 1950s, next to the Palladium (known as "The Home of Mambo") stood Birdland (a main venue for bebop at the time), where a strand of Afro-Cuban jazz called Cu-Bop was played by Afro-Cuban musicians like Mario Bauza. The common claim that the collaboration in New York of Afro-Cuban musician Chano Pozo with Afro-North American musician Dizzy Gillespie in recording the classic song "Manteca" was a founding moment of the bebop, demonstrates how overlapping Afroamerican diasporas can join to create new cultural genres in the context of the world city.

The Sixties: Global Movements and New Afro-Latino Politics, Identities, and Cultures

Generally speaking, by the late 1950s and early 1960s the populist movements had failed to fulfill their goals of fair income distribution, democratization of political life, and conciliation of class and ethnoracial inequalities and conflicts. But by the early 1970s, the conjuncture of social movements that challenged all the forms of power in the modern capitalist world (class, ethnoracial, cultural, gender, sexual, geopolitical) had important implications for Afro-Latinos. The Black Freedom movement in the United States, and the movements of decolonization in Africa and Asia inspired a racial politics of liberation that prompted many Afro-Latinos to develop claims against racism and for black empowerment while engaging in anti-imperialist and anticapitalist movements. This impulse toward change took a variety of forms and developed a plurality of distinct projects. The resulting activity ranged from local gestures to recognize and legitimize African-diasporic cultural practices and historical memory against hegemonic Eurocentric racist narratives of nation and region, to the organization of transnational conferences to set an agenda for Afro-Latinos and coordinate political efforts. Organizations were formed in Brazil, Panama, and Venezuela, while research centers were developed and educational initiatives took place in Costa Rica and Colombia. International conferences began to articulate these initiatives; the first major one was held in 1977 in Colombia, followed by Brazil in 1982, Ecuador in 1984, and Uruguay in 1994. Several other conferences were also organized, some of which constituted regional associations, as with Afro-Central Americans. In sum, a historical motion was created for the emergence of Afro-Latino movements at the local, national, regional, and hemispheric levels and connected to larger formations of the global African Diaspora that are still in place today.

Reconfigurations of Afro-Latino/America in the Age of Neoliberal Globalization

With the beginning of the 1980s, the demise of the development project as a strategy to promote growth and welfare in the world economy converged with the decline of U.S. hegemony (political, economic, cultural) in the global system. The establishment and worldwide dissemination of neoliberal economic policies promoting a free market, open economies in favor of investment and trade for transnational corporations, along with political platforms minimizing state social spending and economic regulation had devastating effects on the lives of thousands of Afro-Latinos. In addition to the exacerbation of the already existing tendencies to undermine the landed property

Meyer Liebowitz / Hulton Archive / Getty Images

Members of the Young Lords Party, a Puerto Rican activist group, stand in front of a medical truck they hijacked in East Harlem, New York City, June 1970. The origins of this group date to 1967 (and perhaps earlier) when it was founded in Chicago as a Puerto Rican equivalent of the Black Panthers. Initially called the Young Lords, members later changed the name to Young Lords Organization and then Young Lords Party. Another group that emerged from the Young Lords was the Marxist-Leninist Puerto Rican Revolutionary Workers Organization. The Young Lords had chapters in several major U.S. cities.

of small and medium peasantries, neoliberal globalization also entailed the privatization and commodification of resources and goods (such as water and rain forests) that were either nationally owned and/or relatively untouched by capitalism. In this manner, subregions inhabited by Afro-Latinos, such as the Pacific Coast of Colombia and Esmeralda in Ecuador, which had been relatively free from being colonized in the search for profits, became a target of capitalist exploitation of land, labor, and natural resources. Consequently, since the 1990s there has been an emergence of social movements in these places at the same time that there was a plea for a recognition of their African-descendant identity, memory, and culture in the national context. There are claims by these Afro-Latinos against capitalist attempts to expropriate their land and exploit their labor, while they mobilize in favor of biodiversity, ecological integrity, and the right to remain in their place. A similar movement of African-diasporic self-affirmation, accompanied by ecological claims against land appropriation and against the expropriation of residents' rights by transnational corporations, is also taking place in the Mangrel sector of Piñones in the town of Loíza, Puerto Rico, where every year in October on the anniversary of Columbus's landing in the West Indies, they organize a festival named "Cultural Bridge from Africa to Piñones" as part of an annual campaign against racism.

New modes of social politics at the close of the twentieth century opened political space for the emerging Afro-Latino movements. The United Nations' 2001 Conference against Racism in Durban, South Africa, was a crucial occasion for Afro-Latino movements. It offered the opportunity not only to build networks and to achieve greater coordination but also to discuss and negotiate historical projects and political agendas. The goal was to achieve a clearly conceived and well-organized hemispheric movement of African-descendants in Latino/America. The fact that both organizers and participants included Afro-Latinos from across the Americas (including the United States and Canada) gave this effort a particularly diasporic, Afroamerican character.

The political terrain concerning Afro-Latinos in the era of neoliberal globalization is not only composed of social movements from African-descendant communities and networks but also of national states and transnational institutions. Thus, the World Bank and Interamerican Development Bank recently issued reports on the status of Afro-Latinos that declared them among the poorest people in the Americas, at the same time that it suggested policy initiatives to remedy these kinds of inequalities. The United Nations has a longer track record of promoting research and exploring policies for Afro-Latinos that dates back to the UNESCO programs of the 1950s. Also, ecclesiastical institutions like the Catholic Church issued pastoral letters and developed programs for Afro-Latinos.

In the national scenarios, there also are some important developments in the current period, most of which result from the advocacy work of Afro-

Latino social movements. In Colombia, the 1991 constitution stipulated cultural and social rights of ethnic groups, especially for black and indigenous groups. There are similar developments in Guatemala, where the 1994 constitution for the first time placed Garifunas on the national ethnic map, and in Ecuador, Panama, and Uruguay. In Cuba, Afro-Cubans were strategically placed on the central committee of the governing Communist Party in the early 1990s. In Brazil, the Movimento Negro Unificado, organized in the 1980s, prompted state policies adopted in the 1990s against discrimination in employment and public accommodations, along with efforts to promote the increase of Afro-Brazilians in public employment and in the ranks of university students that resemble U.S. affirmative-action measures. Currently, there is a heated public debate in Brazil about whether affirmative-action policies are appropriate and/or desirable in Brazil. There is also a debate about the land and governance rights of *Quilombistas* (a name for Afro-Brazilians who reside in former maroon societies called *quilombos*).[13] The debate on *Quilombismo* also reveals a significant ecological strand in the new Afro-Latino social movements, at the same time raising important political questions about historical continuities and the claim for reparations that are now widespread across the African Diaspora in the Americas.

The relative growth of Afro-Latino middle classes, and particularly of the intelligentsia and the politicians, can be attributed to the long-term effects of the struggles for racial democracy and justice. Nonetheless, at the present moment of neoliberal globalization, there has been a considerable increase in Afro-Latino inequality, marginalization, and poverty, as well as the rise of a new racism against lower-class African-descendants. A growing common sense of fear feeds a politics of vilification and criminalization of socially marginal sectors, especially in urban centers. In cities in Brazil, Cuba, Colombia, Venezuela, and the United States, many of these so-called dangerous classes are Afro-Latinos. An important form of self-affirmation of these youth cultures is hip-hop culture, originally a product of African-descendant urban areas in the United States, which now signifies a global youth movement. For instance, in Brazil and Cuba, many hip-hop musicians define themselves as an African-diasporic movement and as chroniclers of daily life on the margins of society.

African-diasporic consciousness and organization is also manifest in sub-regional and hemispheric groupings of Afro-Latino women. Several meetings of Afro-Latino and Afro-Caribbean women's organizations reunited activists from grassroots groups with feminist intellectuals from across the Americas to address the specific needs and interests of black women in Latino/America. Afro-Latino women participate in larger African-diasporic groupings at the same time that they keep their own organization to address the forms of domination they need to confront (including Afro-Latino patriarchy) and the corresponding struggles for empowerment.

Another key initiative for Afro-Latinos is negotiation for their inclusion in the developing African Diaspora programs whose mappings of the Black Atlantic tend to be centered on the Anglophone world. Likewise, the increasing habit in the U.S. media and even in academic discussions simply to oppose "blacks" to "Latinos" as competing ethnic and/or racial groups is cultivating a tendency to erase Afro-Latinos or to render them invisible. In contrast, an African-diasporic perspective by which Afro-Latinos can be conceptualized in their complexity and diversity on local, regional, national, hemispheric, and global scales will shed light on their historical significance as the largest portion of the African Diaspora in the Americas, whose history and culture provide a creative bridge with the potential of linking different worlds.

· ·

NOTES

1. George Reid Andrews, *Afro-Latin America, 1800–2000* (Oxford: Oxford University Press, 2004); Pedro Perez Sarduy and Jean Stubbs, "Introduction," *No Longer Invisible: Afro-Latin Americans Today* (London: Minority Rights Publication, 1995).
2. The expression Latino/America, instead of Latin America, is intended to signify a region that is circumscribed neither by the north/south imperial borders, in which the Rio Grande is taken as a the divide, nor merely by a juxtaposition of the states created in the aftermath of the Spanish and Portuguese empires. Latino/America is rather defined as a region that is primarily composed of a diversity of peoples who inhabit both the continental and insular territories formerly colonized by the Spaniards and Portuguese, as well as people of Latin American descent in North America.
3. Andrews, *Afro-Latin America*.

4. Laurent Dubois, *Avengers of the New World: The Story of the Haitian Revolution* (Cambridge, Mass.: Harvard University Press, 2004); Sibylle Fischer, *Modernity Disavowed: Haiti and the Cultures of Slavery in the Age of Revolution* (Durham, N.C.: Duke University Press, 1999); Carolyn E. Fisk, *The Making of Haiti: The Saint Domingue Revolution from Below* (Knoxville: University of Tennessee Press, 1990); C. L. R. James, *The Black Jacobins: Toussaint L'Ouverture and the San Domingo Revolution* (London: Secker & Warburg, 1938); Michel-Rolph Trouillot, *Silencing the Past: Power and the Production of History* (Boston: Beacon Press, 1995).

5. Dale Tomich, *Through the Prism of Slavery: Labor, Capital, and World Economy* (Lanham, Md.: Rowman & Littlefield. 2004).

6. In this essay I use a variety of designations for geohistorical and identitarian categories, including Afroamerica, Afro-descendants, Afro-Latino/America, Afro-Iberian, Afro-Hispanic, Black Atlantic, Black North Americas. Even though it may seem confusing, the purpose is not only to acknowledge the plurality of names and their relative value insofar as they express choices of self-naming, but also to demonstrate analytically how they intersect and overlap in complex ways with the intention of conceptualizing African diasporas from various angles and at different levels.

7. I deliberately use the expression *Afroamerica* as coined by the publisher of a journal with the same title in Mexico in the 1940s. The purpose of this usage is to reclaim the idea of African-America and African Americans from the imperial reduction of the Americas to the United States, a reduction that not only excludes Afro-Latino/Americans but also Afro-Canadians from its range of meanings.

8. Aline Helg, *Our Rightful Share: The Afro-Cuban Struggle for Equality, 1886–1912* (Chapel Hill: University of North Carolina Press, 1995), 3.

9. Anibal Quijano, "Coloniality of Power, Eurocentrism, and Latin America," *Nepantla: Views from the South* 1 (2000): 139–55.

10. Fernando Ortiz, *Hampa afro-cubana: Los negros brujos* (Madrid: Librería de Fernando Fé, 1906); José Luciano Franco, *Afroamerica* (La Habana, Cuba: Junta Nacional de Arqueología y Antropología, 1961).

11. There is a strategic inconsistency in the differential way in which intellectuals are introduced. The intention is to show the diverse composition of the group, not simply in terms of nationality but in terms of ethno-racial (and in the case of Herskovits, intellectual) identities.

12. Robin Moore, *Nationalizing Blackness: Afrocubanismo and Artistic Revolution in Havana, 1920–1940* (Pittsburgh, Pa.: University of Pittsburgh Press, 1997).

13. In the Spanish-speaking territories, the most common name used for maroon societies was *palenque*.

BIBLIOGRAPHY

Abu-Lughod, Janet. *Before European Hegemony: The World-System A.D. 1250–1350.* New York: Oxford University Press, 1989.

AfroCubaWeb. Http://www.afrocubaweb.com (accessed May 3, 2006).

Andrews, George Reid. *Afro-Latin America, 1800–2000*. Oxford: Oxford University Press, 2004.

Arroyo, Jossianna. *Travestismos culturales: Literatura y etnografía en Cuba y Brasil*. Pittsburgh: Universidad de Pittsburgh, Instituto Internacional de Literatura Iberoamericana, 2003.

Betancur, John J. "Framing the Discussion of African American-Latino Relations: A Review and Analysis." In *Neither Enemies Nor Friends: Latinos, Blacks, Afro-Latinos*, edited by Anani Dzidzienyo and Suzanne Oboler. New York: Palgrave, 2005.

Blanchard, Peter. "The Language of Liberation: Slave Voices in the Wars of Independence." *Hispanic American Historical Review* 82 (2002): 499–523.

Buscaglia-Salgado, José. *Undoing Empire: Race and Nation in the Mulatto Caribbean*. Minneapolis: University of Minnesota Press, 2003.

Césaire, Aimé. *Discourse on Colonialism*. Translated by Joan Pinkham. New York: Monthly Review Press, 1972.

Clifford, James. "Diasporas." *Routes: Travel and Translation in the Late Twentieth Century*. Cambridge, Mass.: Harvard University Press, 1997.

Daniel, Yvonne. "Embodied Knowledge in African American Dance Performance." In *African Roots/American Cultures: Africa in the Creation of the Americas*, edited by Sheila S. Walker. New York: Rowman & Littlefield, 2001.

DeCosta-Willis, Miriam, ed. *Daughters of the Diaspora: Afra-Hispanic Writers*. Miami: Ian Randle Publishers, 2003.

Dubois, Laurent. *Avengers of the New World: The Story of the Haitian Revolution*. Cambridge, Mass.: Harvard University Press, 2004.

Dussel, Enrique. *1492: El encubrimiento del Otro: Hacia el origen del "Mito de la Modernidad": Conferencias de Frankfurt, Octubre de 1992*. Santafé de Bogotá: Antropos, 1992.

Dzidzienyo, Anani. "Activity and Inactivity in the Politics of Afro-Latin America." *SECOLAS Annals* 9 (March 1978): 48–61.

———. "Coming to Terms with the African Connection in Latino Studies." *Latino Studies* 1 (March 2003): 160–67.

Edwards, Brent Hayes. *The Practice of Diaspora: Literature, Translation, and the Rise of Black Internationalism*. Cambridge, Mass.: Harvard University Press, 2003.

———. "The Uses of Diaspora." *Social Text* 19 (2001): 45–73.

Fanon, Frantz. *Black Skin, White Masks*. New York: Grove Press, 1967.

Feal, Rosemary Geisdorfer. "The Afro-Latin American Woman Writer: Drumming with a Difference." *Afro-Hispanic Review* 14 (1995): 10–12.

Ferrer, Ada. *Insurgent Cuba: Race, Nation, and Revolution, 1868–1898*. Chapel Hill: University of North Carolina Press, 1999.

Fischer, Sibylle. *Modernity Disavowed: Haiti and the Cultures of Slavery in the Age of Revolution*. Durham, N.C.: Duke University Press, 1999.

Fisk, Carolyn E. *The Making of Haiti: The Saint Domingue Revolution from Below*. Knoxville: University of Tennessee Press, 1990.

Fontaine, Pierre-Michel. "The Political Economy of Afro-Latin America." *Latin American Research Review* 15 (1980): 111–41.

Franco, José Luciano. *Afroamerica*. La Habana, Cuba: Junta Nacional de Arqueología y Antropología, 1961.

Freyre, Gilberto. *The Masters and the Slaves: A Study in the Development of Brazilian Civilization*. Translated by Samuel Putnam. New York: Knopf, 1946.

Gilroy, Paul. *The Black Atlantic: Double Consciousness and Modernity*. Cambridge, Mass.: Harvard University Press, 1993.

Gordon, Lewis R. *Fanon and the Crisis of European Man: An Essay on Philosophy and the Human Sciences*. New York: Routledge, 1995.

Hanchard, Michael. "Identity, Meaning, and the African-American." *Social Text* 24, no. 8 (1990): 31–42.

Helg, Aline. *Our Rightful Share: The Afro-Cuban Struggle for Equality, 1886–1912*. Chapel Hill: University of North Carolina Press, 1995.

Hernández, Tanya K. "'Too Black to Be Latino/a': Blackness and Blacks as *Foreigners* in Latino Studies." *Latino Studies* 1 (2003): 152–59.

James, C. L. R. *The Black Jacobins: Toussaint L'Ouverture and the San Domingo Revolution*. London: Secker & Warburg, 1938.

James, Winston. *Holding Aloft the Banner of Ethiopia: Caribbean Radicalism in Early Twentieth-Century America*. New York: Verso, 1998.

Jordan, June. *Some of Us Did Not Die: New and Selected Essays of June Jordan*. New York: Basic Books, 2002.

Laó-Montes, Agustín, and Arlene Dávila, eds. *Mambo Montage: The Latinization of New York*. New York: Columbia University Press, 2001.

Márquez, Roberto. "Raza, Racismo, e Historia: Are All of My Bones from There?" *Latino Research Review* 4 (2000): 8–22.

Martí, José. *Nuestra América*. Buenos Aires: Editorial Losada, 1939.

Martinez-Echazábal, Lourdes. *Para una semiótica de la mulatez*. Madrid: J. Porrúa Turanzas, 1990.

Mercer, Kobena. "Black Art and the Burden of Representation." *Third Text* 10 (1990): 61–78.

———. "Diaspora, Culture, and the Dialogic Imagination: The Aesthetics of Black Independent Film in Britain." In *Blackframes: Critical Perspectives on Black Independent Cinema*, edited by Mbye Cham and Claire Andrade-Watkins. Cambridge, Mass.: MIT Press, 1988.

Moore, Robin. *Nationalizing Blackness: Afrocubanismo and Artistic Revolution in Havana, 1920–1940*. Pittsburgh, Pa.: University of Pittsburgh Press, 1997.

Mosquera, Claudia, Mauricio Pardo, and Odile Hoffman, eds. *Afrodescendientes en las Americas: Trayectorias sociales e identitarias: 150 años de la abolición de la esclavitud en Colombia*. Bogotá: Universidad Nacional de Colombia, 2002.

Mudimbe, V. Y. *The Invention of Africa: Gnosis, Philosophy, and the Order of Knowledge*. Bloomington: Indiana University Press, 1988.

Mullen, Edward J. "Langston Hughes and the Development of Afro-Hispanic Literature: Diasporan Connections." *The Black Scholar* 26 (1996): 10–16.

MundoAfroLatino. Http://www.mundoafrolatino.com (accessed May 3, 2006).

O'Gorman, Edmundo. *The Invention of America: An Inquiry into the Historical Nature of the New World and the Meaning of Its History*. Bloomington: Indiana University Press, 1961.

——. *La idea del descubrimiento de America: Historia de esa interpretación y crítica de sus fundamentos*. Mexico: Centro de Estudios Filosóficos, 1951.

Ortiz, Fernando. *Hampa afro-cubana: Los negros brujos*. Madrid: Librería de Fernando Fé, 1906.

Patterson, Tiffany Ruby, and Robin D. G. Kelley. "Unfinished Migrations: Reflections on the African Diaspora and the Making of the Modern World." *African Studies Review* 43 (2000): 11–45.

Pérez, Emma. *The Decolonial Imaginary: Writing Chicanas into History*. Bloomington: Indiana University Press, 1999.

Piedra, José. "Literary Whiteness and the Afro-Hispanic Difference." In *The Bounds of Race: Perspectives on Hegemony and Resistance*, edited by Dominick LaCapra. Ithaca, N.Y.: Cornell University Press, 1991.

Pratt, Mary Louise. *Imperial Eyes: Travel Writing and Transculturation*. London: Routledge, 1992.

Quijano, Anibal. "Coloniality of Power, Eurocentrism, and Latin America." *Nepantla: Views from the South* 1 (2000): 139–55.

Rabasa, José. *Inventing America: Spanish Historiography and the Formation of Eurocentrism*. Norman: Oklahoma University Press, 1993.

Ribando, Clare. "Afro-Latinos in Latin America and Considerations for U.S. Policy" (4 January). Washington, D.C.: Congressional Research Service, 2005.

Rivera, Raquel Z. "Hip-Hop, Puerto Ricans, and Ethnoracial Identities in New York." In *Mambo Montage: The Latinization of New York*, edited by Agustín Laó-Montes and Arlene Dávila. New York: Columbia University Press, 2001.

Rout, Leslie B. *The African Experience in Spanish America, 1502 to the Present Day*. Cambridge, England: Cambridge University Press, 1976.

Sagás, Ernesto. *Race and Politics in the Dominican Republic*. Gainesville: University Press of Florida, 2000.

Saldívar, José David. *The Dialectics of Our America: Genealogy, Cultural Critique, and Literary History*. Durham, N.C.: Duke University Press, 1991.

Sánchez González, Lisa. "Arturo Alfonso Schomburg: A Transamerican Intellectual." In *African Roots/American Cultures: Africa in the Creation of the Americas*, edited by Sheila S. Walker. New York: Rowman & Littlefield, 2001.

——. *Boricua Literature: A Literary History of the Puerto Rican Diaspora*. New York: New York University Press, 2001.

Sarduy, Pedro Perez, and Jean Stubbs. "Introduction." *No Longer Invisible: Afro-Latin Americans Today*. London: Minority Rights Publication, 1995.

Scott, Rebecca J. "Defining the Boundaries of Freedom in the World of Cane: Cuba, Brazil, and Louisiana after Emancipation." *American Historical Review* 99 (1994): 70–102.

——. "Fault Lines, Color Lines, and Party Lines: Race, Labor, and Collective Action in Louisiana and Cuba, 1862–1912." In *Beyond Slavery: Explorations of Race, Labor, and*

Citizenship in Postemancipation Societies, edited by Frederick Cooper et al. Chapel Hill: University of North Carolina Press, 2000.

Singh, Nikhil Pal. *Black is a Country: Race and the Unfinished Struggle for Democracy*. Cambridge, Mass.: Harvard University Press, 2004.

Sinnette, Elinor Des Verney. *Arthur Alfonso Schomburg: Black Bibliophile and Collector*. Detroit: Wayne State University Press and New York Public Library, 1989.

Stepan, Nancy. *The Hour of Eugenics: Race, Gender, and Nation in Latin America*. Ithaca, N.Y.: Cornell University Press, 1991.

Thomas, Piri. *Down These Mean Streets*. New York: Knopf, 1967.

Thompson, Robert Farris. *Flash of the Spirit: African and Afro-American Art and Philosophy*. New York: Random House, 1983.

Tomich, Dale. *Through the Prism of Slavery: Labor, Capital, and World Economy*. Lanham, Md.: Rowman & Littlefield. 2004.

Torres, Arlene, and Norman E. Whitten, Jr. "General Introduction." *Blackness in Latin America and the Caribbean: Social Dynamics and Cultural Transformations* 1 (1998): 3–33.

Torres-Saillant, Silvio. "Inventing the Race: Latinos and the Ethnoracial Pentagon." *Latino Studies* 1 (2003): 123–51.

———. "Racism in the Americas and the Latino Scholar." In *Neither Enemies Nor Friends: Latinos, Blacks, Afro-Latinos*, edited by Anani Dzidzienyo and Suzanne Oboler. New York: Palgrave, 2005.

Trouillot, Michel-Rolph. *Silencing the Past: Power and the Production of History*. Boston: Beacon Press, 1995.

Vaca, Nicolas C. *The Presumed Alliance: The Unspoken Conflict between Latinos and Blacks and What It Means for America*. New York: Rayo, 2004.

Vasconcelos, José. *La Raza Cósmica: Misión de la raza iberoamericana: Notas de viaje a America del Sur*. Paris: Agencia Mundial de Librería, 1920.

Wright, Michelle M. *Becoming Black: Creating Identity in the African Diaspora*. Durham, N.C.: Duke University Press, 2004.

Yelvington, Kevin A. "The Anthropology of Afro-Latin America and the Caribbean: Diasporic Dimensions." *Annual Review of Anthropology* 30 (2001): 227–60.

CHRONOLOGY

711	Moors invade southern Spain from North Africa and begin establishing a highly sophisticated Arab Islamic culture that endured until 1492, when the last Moorish stronghold in Granada was ceded to King Ferdinand.
1441	European slave trade with Africa begins, with slaves being shipped to Portugal.
1479	Spain signs treaty with Portugal giving Portugal the right to supply Spain with African slaves.
1492	Columbus makes his first voyage to the New World. His navigator is Pedro Alonso Niño, a black man.
1500	Portuguese explorer Pedro Cabral arrives in Brazil. Thirty-two years later the first Portuguese settlement is established, and the Portuguese begin shipping slaves there.

1512	Diego Velásquez executes Chief Hatuey, leader of the indigenous resistance to the Spanish occupation of Cuba, and the Spanish begin their colonization.
1518	The first slaves arrive in the Spanish colonies directly from Africa (not having been shipped to Europe first), beginning the three-and-a-half-century Middle Passage, during which more than twelve million African slaves were shipped across the Atlantic to the Americas.
1562	England begins slave trade with Africa and begins supplying colonies in the Americas.
1789	Garifunas are expelled from the island of Saint Vincent.
1791–1804	Haitian Revolution, when blacks, led initially by Toussaint L'Ouverture, fought for and won freedom from French colonists.
1807	Great Britain outlaws slave trade.
1808	The United States outlaws slave trade.
1810	Creoles establish ruling juntas in Caracas, Venezuela; Santiago, Chile; and Buenos Aires, Argentina.
1811–25	Venezuela, Paraguay, Argentina, Chile, and Bolivia declare independence.
1815	End of the Napoleonic Wars marks the disintegration of the Spanish Empire in the New World.
1817	Slave trade is outlawed in France, to take effect in 1826; Spain signs treaty agreeing to end slave trade north of the equator immediately, and to end slavery south of the equator in 1820.
1823	The Monroe Doctrine warns Europe against attempts to recolonize the New World.
1834	British abolish slavery in the West Indies.
1836	Texas declares independence from Mexico.
1865	Slavery is abolished in the United States.
1886	Slavery is abolished in Cuba.
1888	Slavery is abolished in Brazil.
1898	In the Spanish-Cuban-American War, Cuba gains independence from Spain, and the United States takes control of Puerto Rico, Guam, and the Philippines.
1908	Partido Independiente de Color is formed in Havana, Cuba; it is the first independent black political party in the region. It is outlawed the next year.
1910	The Mexican Revolution begins. It ends in 1917 with the adoption of a new constitution.
1930–61	Rafael Trujillo is brutal dictator of the Dominican Republic, presiding over a government supported, reluctantly at the end, by the United States.
1931	Frente Negra Brasileira, Brazil's first civil rights organization, is formed in São Paulo.
1937	Rafael Trujillo's policy of "Dominicanness" leads to the massacre of some 25,000 Haitians on the border of the Dominican Republic.
1948	Twenty-one nations sign the Organization of American States charter, replacing the Pan-American Union.

1957–86	François "Papa Doc" Duvalier and his son Jean-Claude, known as "Baby Doc," conduct reign of terror in Haiti.
1959	The Inter-American Commission on Human Rights is created.
1959	Fidel Castro overthrows Fulgencio Batista and declares himself dictator of Cuba.
1977	First Afro-Latino Conference is held in Colombia.
1993	The Institute of Caribbean Studies is founded in Washington, D.C., and hosts the first annual Caribbean American Heritage Awards.
1998	The Organization of Africans in the Americas is a leader in organizing Afroamerica XXI, a foundation that encourages Spanish-speaking Afro-Latin Americans to organize themselves and address their common concerns.
2001	World Conference against Racism is held in Durban, South Africa.
2003	The first conference of African-descendant legislators of the Americas and the Caribbean is held in Brasília, Brazil.
2004	The Afro-Latino Development Alliance declares Afro-Colombian cultural week in Washington, D.C.

GLOSSARY

Afroamerica. Journal published in Mexico from 1945–1946 in which prominent scholars of African Diaspora studies collaborated, insisting on the use of the term to designate people from the African Diaspora throughout the Americas, not simply the United States.

Black Atlantic. A concept first coined by Robert Farris Thompson and Peter Linebaugh and coming into more general use after Paul Gilroy's book with that title (Gilroy, 1993), Black Atlantic signifies the intertwined histories, movements, and cultural expressions of African peoples in the Atlantic system.

Caste System. Within the context of Afro-Latino culture, caste, or more precisely the Castillian *casta*, refers to the system of racial classification first developed in the Spanish colonies in the Americas during the sixteenth century. *Casta* was clearly expressed in the seventeenth- and eighteenth-century art genre *pinturas de castas* that depicted such common Latin American racial categories as *indio, mestizo, negro, mulatto, sambo*. These caste designations were included in state policies and legal codes until the first part of the twentieth century.

Cocolos. A name given to people of West Indian descent in the Dominican Republic, most of whom live in the city of San Pedro de Macoris. Puerto Ricans in New York City used the term Cocolo to designate Afro-North Americans.

Coloniality of Power. This key concept coined by Anibal Quijano (Quijano, 2000) signifies a global pattern of power that emerged in the sixteenth century with the conquest of the Americas and the rise of capitalism as the dominant economic system in the world. It includes racial and cultural ideologies that regard Europe and so-called white civilization (and its Western knowledge, politics, and aesthetics) as superior to the culture of nonwhite peoples.

Culture Industries. A concept originally formulated by philosophers Theodor Adorno and Max Horkheimer and recently developed by various scholars in Latin America and the United States, referring to commercial exploitation of cultural production.

Developmentalism. A critical name for the modernizing discourse that became dominant after World War II and that was intended to induce Third World societies to follow Western forms of modernity in order to catch up economically and politically with Europe and the United States.

Eurocentric. An ideology that regards all matters from a narrowly European perspective.

Garifuna. Vernacular name of an Afro-Indian ethnoracial group who primarily emerged from a mixture of black maroons and Carib Indians in the Lesser Antilles. After their expulsion by British forces from the island of Saint Vincent in 1789, they settled in the Caribbean basin of Central America.

Geohistorical Categories. Cartographic classifications that divide the world into distinct spatial units (continents, nations, regions, locales) as keystones of colonial discourse.

Hegemony. The ability to have not only political and economic dominance but also intellectual and ideological supremacy in either a nation-state or in the world system.

Ibero-America. The world-region that resulted from the conquest and colonialization of the Iberian empires in the Americas.

Imperialism. A transnational formation of geopolitical, economic, and cultural power presided over by some modern states.

Latino/Americanism. Ideologies born in the nineteenth century that define Latin America and Latin Americans in terms of the nation-states resulting from independence struggles in Ibero-America.

Mestizaje. The complex process of racial and cultural mixing that began with the conquest and colonization of the Americas. It also designates the hegemonic nationalist ideologies, based on a myth of racial democracy, that are constitutive of each of the Latin American nation-states.

Moors. The name given by the Spanish to the North Africans who occupied the southern part of the Iberian Peninsula from the eighth to the thirteenth century.

Mulataje. The specific process of mestizaje among people of European and African descent, primarily as it occurs in Brazil and the Caribbean.

Négritude. An early to mid-twentieth-century cultural and political movement for decolonization led by intellectuals from the Francophone colonial world (especially continental Africa and the Caribbean), driven by an insistence on the distinct essence or soul of peoples of African descent.

Oligarchic State. The paradigmatic form of the liberal state in late nineteenth- and early twentieth-century Latin America as characterized by an authoritarian rule exerted by a coalition of commercial and military elites.

Islam and African Americans

Richard Brent Turner

Abstract

The first Muslims in the New World traveled with Christopher Columbus in 1492 and brought the religion of Islam to the Americas. Thereafter, African-descended Muslims were enslaved in Latin America from 1502. The larger story of Islam and African Americans began with Atlantic slavery, as thousands of West African Muslims were enslaved in the Caribbean and North America in the sixteenth and seventeenth centuries, respectively. These early Muslims— literate in Arabic and stolen from the ruling elite in West Africa—left a powerful legacy of spiritual resistance and transnational identities that influenced the religion and politics of successive twentieth-century and contemporary African American Muslim communities. The following essay traces the complex and fascinating history of Islam and African Americans in the United States.

Pre-Twentieth-Century Sources

West African Muslim Slaves in the United States

The history of Islam and African Americans began with the institution of slavery, which forcibly transported thousands of West African Muslims to the

United States before the Civil War. Allan D. Austin's 1997 article "'There Are Good Men in America, but All Are Very Ignorant of Africa'—and its Muslims" estimates that 10 to 15 percent of all African slave importations to the United States were Muslims, but Michael A. Gomez's book *Exchanging Our Country Marks: The Transformation of African Identities in the Colonial and Antebellum South* concludes that there is not enough quantitative evidence for such a precise estimate. However, consistent qualitative data supports the following summary of Gomez's assessment of Muslim slave communities in the United States. Enslaved Muslims continued to practice Islam in their family networks and might have converted other slaves. Their religion significantly influenced African American identity, culture, religion, ethnicity, and class stratification in pre-twentieth-century black America. Also, there were important interactions and tensions between enslaved Muslims and non-Muslims. The former were often assigned leadership positions in slave communities and were noteworthy for their expressed superiority to Christians, based on their literacy in Arabic and their continuation of a corporate Islamic identity that transcended hegemonic constructions of race in America.

In her 1998 article "The Muslim Community," Sylviane A. Diouf emphasizes the significance of religious continuities between West Africa and the Americas for understanding the community values of Muslim slaves and how and why they continued to practice orthodox Islam in the United States. The fragmentation of the Jolof empire (in contemporary Senegal) in the 1500s, and later religious and political warfare between Muslims and non-Muslims in Senegambia, the Gold Coast, Sierra Leone, and the Bight of Benin, resulted in Mandingo, Wolof, Yoruba, Tukolor, Fulani, Vai, and Hausa Muslim prisoners of war who were sold to European slave ships and enslaved in the Americas. Many of these captives were part of a vibrant and literate urban ruling elite—traveling scholars, teachers, merchants, statesmen, and religious leaders—who resisted European influences, struggled to preserve the purity of their faith in West Africa, and continued to do so in the New World. The belief in one God and Muhammad as the final Prophet, efforts to dress modestly and to practice the Five Pillars of Islam (*shahada*, profession of faith; *salat*, prayer five times a day; *zakat*, alms for the poor; *sawm*, fasting during Ramadan; and *hajj*, pilgrimage to Mecca) sustained the spirituality of Muslim slaves in the hostile Christian environment of the United States.

Allan D. Austin's 1997 book *African Muslims in Antebellum America: Transatlantic Stories and Spiritual Struggles* (a condensed version of his 1984 book *African Muslims in Antebellum America: A Sourcebook*) cites evidence of seventy-five West African Muslim slaves in North America whose stories contribute significantly to our knowledge of American history and black America's first generation of African religious folk. Detailed information about eight of these individuals is available in the historical literature and is summarized below, with an emphasis on their dynamic communities in the Georgia and South Carolina coastal areas. These practicing Muslims are remembered in history because of their extraordinary contacts with white Americans who recorded and/or disseminated their narratives for posterity.

Salih Bilali and Bilali were the leaders of the most important Muslim community in the United States during the antebellum period, on Sapelo and St. Simons islands. The South Carolina and Georgia Sea islands were significant locations for Islamic continuities because of their isolation from Christian influences and their proximity to the slave port cities of Charleston and Savannah, which brought in a constant influx of first-generation West African slaves. Both Salih Bilali and Bilali were noteworthy for their Sunni Islamic identities in the United States, Muslim names and clothing, and devotion to their faith, and Bilali was known for his literacy in Arabic, which he taught to his nineteen children.

Bilali (d. 1859), who was also known as "Ben Ali" and "Bilali Mahomet," was a slave driver and manager on Thomas Spaulding's Sapelo Island plantation in Georgia in the first half of the nineteenth century. There is little information about Bilali's life before his enslavement in the United States. His first name reflects African Muslims' great respect for Bilal ibn Rabah, the Prophet Muhammad's Ethiopian convert and the first muezzin (one who calls Muslims to prayer) in the seventh century CE. Born in Timbo, Futa Jallon, Bilali, as many other Fulbe Muslims in the New World, was most likely a member of an elite scholarly family in West Africa. Although he probably read and wrote Arabic at an advanced level in his youth, Ronald A. T. Judy's 1993 book *(Dis)Forming the American Canon: African-Arabic Slave Narratives and the Vernacular* analyzes problems in the translation and deconstruction of the Arabic manuscript that Bilali composed on Sapelo Island and suggests that his language skills and knowledge of the Qur'an and Sunnah (traditions of Muhammad) deteriorated over time. The "Ben-Ali Diary" utilized passages from the Malikite legal text, Ibn Abi Zayd's *Risala,* to discuss Islamic sources for a wholesome daily life, and suggests that Bilali struggled to maintain his faith in the United States and resisted Christian religious hegemony.

Bilali's Islamic legacy continued in the memories and narratives of his twentieth-century descendants on Sapelo Island, who were interviewed by the Savannah unit of the Georgia Writers' Project in the 1930s. Although scholars have critiqued these interviews for contextual problems and inaccurate recording of information, they provide valuable evidence of a nineteenth-century community of African-descended people who continued to practice Islam on the Georgia Sea Islands. Bilali's great-grandson Shadrack Hall remembered that his great-grandfather and his wife, Phoebe, were transported to Georgia from the Bahamas and passed on Islamic traditions among the men, women, and children in their family for at least three generations. Bilali's daughters, Yaruba, Hestah, Beentoo, Chaalut, Margret, Medina, and Fatima, were noted for their adherence to Islamic prayer ritual at sunrise and their utilization of prayer beads. Another great-grandchild, Katie Brown, remembered her grandmother Margret, who wore a veil when praying and made saraka-rice cakes to end a day of fast. Another Bilali descendant, Cornelia Bailey, discussed her great-grandmother, Harriet Hall Grovner, who continued to practice Islam until she joined the First African Baptist Church on Sapelo Island in 1866.

Salih Bilali was born into an important Mandigo Fulbe clerical family in 1765. He was enslaved in his teenage years on his way home from the city of Jenne, an important West African Islamic intellectual center, and was purchased by the Couper family in the Bahamas in the early nineteenth century. He became the overseer of their St. Simons Island plantation from 1816 to 1846. According to Salih Bilali's grandson Ben Sullivan, his father, Belali Sullivan, who was a butler on another Couper plantation until the mid-1860s, also made rice cakes on special days, and practiced Islam. Ben Sullivan, who was eighty-eight years old when he told his family history to the Georgia Writers' Project in the 1930s, remembered other devout Muslims in his plantation community—Ole Israel and Daphne who prayed utilizing a book (the Qur'an?), prayer mats, and headdresses. Ed Thorpe, Rosa Grant, and Alec Anderson were other Georgia Sea Island residents who were interviewed by the WPA in the 1930s and remembered their nineteenth-century Muslim relatives' discipline of daily and special Friday prayers.

Biographical information about influential West African Muslim slaves in other U.S. locations includes the following: Job Ben Solomon or Ayuba B. Sulayman (c. 1700–1773), the son of a Fulbe Muslim clerical family who was born in Bondu and enslaved in 1730 while traveling to buy paper and to sell his family's slaves. While he was in a Maryland prison in 1731, he impressed an English minister with his ability to read and write Arabic. In 1733 Job was freed from slavery, sent to England, and returned to West Africa in 1734.

Yarrow Mamout, probably of Fulbe origin, was reportedly more than one hundred years old when his portrait was painted by the white American artist Charles Willson Peale in 1819. Mamout was a devout Muslim and a former slave who owned his own home in Georgetown, Washington, D.C.

Terry Alford's 1977 book *Prince among Slaves* tells the story of Ibrahim Abd ar-Rahman (1762–1829), a Fulbe Muslim prince and military hero from Futa Jallon who was enslaved as a captive of war by Mandinka merchants in 1788 and worked on a Natchez, Mississippi, plantation until 1828. His freedom from slavery was due to a quirk of fate, as he met in the American South an influential white man whose life he had saved in West Africa. Because of his literacy in Arabic, Abd ar-Rahman convinced the United States government officials that he was a Moor who had been illegally captured in Morocco; he promised the American Colonization Society that he would promote Christianity if he were allowed to return to Africa. The former Muslim prince and his wife arrived in Liberia on February 7, 1829; he resumed his practice of Islam and died on July 6, 1829.

Lamine Kaba, a Jakhanke Muslim scholar and teacher from Futa Jallon, was enslaved on South Carolina, Georgia, and Alabama plantations for almost thirty years. Like Abd ar-Rahaman, his literacy in Arabic and his deceptive conversion to Christianity enabled Kaba's freedom and passage back to Africa in 1835. He convinced the Yale linguist Theodore Dwight Woolsey, Jr., that he would circulate Arabic Bibles in Liberia.

This oil-on-canvas portrait of Yarrow Mamout (1819, Historical Society of Pennsylvania) was the work of the prolific painter Charles Willson Peale (1741–1827), who heard about the former slave while in Washington, D.C. and instantly became intrigued with his story. Mamout was reportedly 134 years old and a practicing Muslim. He had been captured in Africa and sold into slavery in Maryland. Mamout had earned his freedom after he aided in the construction of his master's family estate. (Peale consulted with the wife of Mamout's former owner to verify his story.) He owned property and a house in Georgetown, Maryland, where he gained a reputation for "sobriety & a cheerful conduct," two attributes Peale believed contributed significantly to his longevity.

Umar Ibn Said, a Fulbe Muslim scholar, trader, and teacher from Futa, Toro, who ended up as a slave in Fayetteville, North Carolina, convinced his second owner, James Owen, of his conversion to Christianity around 1825 and was exempted from hard labor for the rest of his life. Stereotyped as the Arabian "Prince Moro," the real Umar ibn Said was a complicated man. He was enslaved when he was thirty-one, wrote his Arabic autobiography in a letter to his Muslim compatriot Lamine Kaba, corresponded in Arabic with a Muslim in China in 1858, and may have practiced Islam secretly while he publicly professed Christianity.

Mahommah Gardo Baquaqua was born a Muslim in Benin in 1830; enslaved in West Africa and Brazil, he escaped from his owner's ship in New York and found his way to Boston in 1847. A two-year sojourn in Haiti resulted in his questionable conversion to Christianity by a white minister in the abolitionist American Baptist Free Mission Society. Baquaqua returned to the United States to attend Central College in McGrawville, New York, for three years and then emigrated to Canada. His *Biography of Mahommah Gardo* was published by G. E. Pomeroy in Detroit in 1854. Baquaqua arrived in England in 1857 and tried to raise money to return to West Africa. However, historical evidence does not verify his return to Africa or his reversion to Islam.

Finally, Mohammed Ali Ben Said was born in Bornu to a prominent Muslim military family. Said, an educated man, was caught by Tuareg enslavers in 1849 and served masters in Tripoli, Mecca, Turkey, Russia, and Europe. In his travels, he reported that he was regretfully baptized in Russia and given the Christian name "Nicholas." Liberated from slavery in Russia in 1860 by Prince Nicholas, Said traveled to England and Canada and was a schoolteacher in Detroit in 1861. He served as a soldier in the 55th Regiment of Massachusetts Colored Volunteers from 1863 to 1865. His autobiography, "A Native of Bornoo," was published in the *Atlantic Monthly* in October 1867.

Richard Brent Turner's 1997 book *Islam in the African-American Experience* is the first historical study to integrate the biographical sketches of West African Muslim slaves that were compiled by Austin into a comprehensive history of Islam and African Americans. Samory Rashid's 1999 article "Islamic Influence in America: Struggle, Flight, Community" evaluates the significance of Austin, Turner, and Diouf's research on antebellum Islamic continuities in the Americas. He concludes that their work corrects shortcomings in the scholarship on Islam in the United States—such as C. Eric Lincoln's article "Reaching for the Masses," which focuses exclusively on the twentieth-century Nation of Islam and ignores the significance of an earlier African Muslim presence in America; and Yvonne Y. Haddad and Adair T.

Lummis's 1987 book *Islamic Values in the United States*, which minimizes the long-range contributions of African-descended Muslims to the establishment of Islam in the West by overemphasizing the late-twentieth-century influence of Muslim immigrants.

Michael A. Gomez's *Black Crescent: The Experience and Legacy of African Muslims in the Americas* brings to light the powerful presence of African Muslims in Christopher Columbus's Atlantic voyage to the New World in 1492, and in numerous pre-twentieth-century slave communities in Brazil, Latin America, and the Caribbean. Although the history and experiences of African-descended Muslims varied significantly in different places in the Americas before the twentieth century, he explores African Muslim continuities in the United States by considering them on a broad spectrum with Brazilian, Latin American, and Caribbean Muslim cultures. This dynamic approach resonates with the comparative study of African American and African Diaspora religions, first proposed by the anthropologist Melville J. Herskovits's book *The Myth of the Negro Past* in 1941 and reconsidered in Albert J. Raboteau's 1982 article "African Religions in America: Theoretical Perspectives." Gomez concludes that African Muslim communities in the Caribbean and Brazil were highly visible, organized, and exclusionary, and sometimes threatened the dominant order in the eighteenth and nineteenth centuries. They were therefore repressed by the state and unable to thrive in the twentieth century. On the other hand, African Muslim slaves in the United States were secretive in their religious practices and compliant to the mainstream order, which enabled their religious legacy to "re-emerge" in the early twentieth century in the context of new black nationalist movements.

By the Civil War era, the Sunni Islam of the West African Muslim slaves and their immediate descendants was obsolete in the United States because their communities were overwhelmed by the widespread Christianization of black America, and they were unable to develop Islamic institutions in the nineteenth century. Although the visible practice of Islam among black Americans declined in this period and did not "re-emerge" until the early twentieth century, Rashid's "Divergent Perspectives on Islam in America" argues convincingly that the religion was not destroyed by slavery.

There is some contemporary scholarly speculation about the connections between the early-twentieth-century Moorish Science Temple and the descendants of African Muslim slaves in the United States. Although little evidence is available to prove direct continuities between these two aspects of American Islamic history, Gomez's *Black Crescent: The Experience and Legacy of African Muslims in the Americas* utilizes a diasporic perspective to suggest continuities across generations in the following mixed-race ethnic groups that probably had a degree of eighteenth-century African Muslim ancestry. Twentieth-century descendants probably joined Noble Drew Ali's community: the Melungeons of Virginia, Tennessee, and Kentucky and the Ishmaelites of Indiana, Illinois, and Kentucky. Finally, McCloud's "A Challenging Intellectual Heritage: A Look at the Social and Political Space of African-American Muslims" suggests evidence only for the retention of memories of Islam in the family oral histories about slavery that were collected from black Americans in South Carolina and Georgia in the 1930s by the Works Projects Administration. According to McCloud, these memories influenced the construction of African American "esoteric knowledge" about Islam in the early twentieth century.

Edward Wilmot Blyden and Pan-Africanism

Edward Wilmot Blyden (1832–1912), the Caribbean clergyman, scholar, and statesman from St. Thomas, Virgin Islands, who was based in Liberia, developed important linkages between Islam and Pan-Africanism in the late nineteenth century that contributed to the religion's political and spiritual appeal for black Americans in the twentieth century. Although Blyden was a Presbyterian minister, he argued in his 1888 article "Mohammedanism and the Negro Race" that Islam was a more preferable religion for black community and political development than Christianity because of the positive, autonomous models of monotheism, education, and social organization that he observed among West African Muslims in Liberia and Sierra Leone. In his Pan-African critique of European Christian racism, Blyden, a professor of classics and Arabic at Liberia College and an ambassador and secretary of state for Liberia, viewed Islam's emphasis on racial tolerance, justice, and

African self-determination as the keys to a global Pan-African theory for the redemption of Africa and the black race and the construction of a black nationalist identity. Blyden's work connected the African American freedom struggle to the religious and political heritage of Africa and its anticolonial movements.

Widely acknowledged as the father of Pan-Africanism, Edward Blyden wrote about the positive influence of the Qur'an on the literacy and spirituality of African peoples and envisioned a possible reconciliation between Islam and Christianity in Africa. His ideas about Islam and self-determination influenced the Pan-Africanism of Marcus Garvey's Universal Negro Improvement Association in the early twentieth century, and Garveyism, in turn, influenced many early African American converts to the Moorish Science Temple of America, the Ahmadiyya Movement in Islam, and the Nation of Islam.

It is not known whether Blyden converted to Islam at the end of his life in Sierra Leone. The second edition of Turner's book *Islam in the African American Experience* analyzes Blyden's letters and speculates about such a conversion, while Curtis's book *Islam in Black America: Identity, Liberation, and Difference in African-American Islamic Thought* denies a conversion experience and focuses on the tension between universality and racial particularism in Blyden's understanding of Islam and African peoples. Although more research is needed on Islam and African Americans from 1870 to 1913, McCloud's "A Challenging Intellectual Heritage: A Look at the Social and Political Space of African-American Muslims" provides evidence that alternative global readings of African history and culture, such as Edward Wilmot Blyden's, profoundly influenced the political and religious awareness of "re-emergent" African American Islam in the early twentieth century.

Early-Twentieth-Century Communities

Noble Drew Ali and the Moorish Science Temple

In 1913 Noble Drew Ali established the Canaanite Temple in Newark, New Jersey, which was later known as the Moorish Science Temple of America. By

the 1920s this first mass African American Muslim community in the twentieth century had a membership of thirty thousand, with national headquarters
in Chicago and temples in several southern, northeastern, and midwestern
cities in the United States. Ali's constituency of Moorish Americans came
primarily from the Great Migration of more than one million black southerners to the northern industrial cities from 1916 to 1930. His construction
of a heterodox proto-Islamic identity drew on an awareness of the Muslim
heritage in slavery, the Prophet Muhammad, the Qur'an, and the intellectual
significance of Morocco for pre-modern Islam, according to McCloud's "A
Challenging Intellectual Heritage: A Look at the Social and Political Space
of African-American Muslims." Moorish American women wore turbans,
and the men wore red fezzes; men and women adhered to an Islamic dress
code and gender segregation during prayer. Noble Drew Ali's followers also
abstained from the consumption of meat, pork, and alcohol; said three daily
prayers facing in the direction of the East; and designated Friday as their
Sabbath day. Peace, social justice, freedom, love, and truth were the Islamic
values that the Moorish American community promoted through their spirituality and economic programs of self-help.

Turner's book *Islam in the African-American Experience* emphasizes that
the Moorish Science Temple was inspired and influenced by the internationalist perspective and self-determination of Marcus Garvey's Universal
Negro Improvement Association, the largest Pan-African organization in the
world in the 1920s. Turner argues that Noble Drew Ali's message "The name
means everything" is the key to understanding the religious and political
significance of his organization. World War I was an era of violent legal racial
segregation, and slavery was still fresh in the collective memory of America.
Ali, who was born Timothy Drew in North Carolina and claimed Cherokee
as well as African descent, constructed a viable religious and ethnic alternative to the European-American Christian racial identities of Negro, colored,
and white. His new alternative identity, Moorish American, was of an Asiatic
olive-skinned people who were the New World descendants of Moroccan
Muslims and were genealogically linked to Jesus Christ, a descendant of the
ancient Africans, Moabites, and Canaanites, according to his ideas. "Asiatic"
is a historical term that was in vogue in Noble Drew Ali's time, and he used it

to construct his genealogy of ancient religious connections between Africans and Asians.

Noble Drew Ali designated himself a new prophet of Islam and wrote his own *Circle Seven Koran* or *Holy Koran* in 1927 (circulated privately after Ali's death by his followers) to uplift the "Asiatic nation of North America" with knowledge of its true nationality, genealogy, and religion. He preached that Western civilization was linked to the destiny of the descendants of the first "Asiatic" nations, which included the Moorish Americans, Arabs, Egyptians, Turks, Indians, Southern and Central Americans, Japanese, and Chinese. Here we can discern the articulation of a powerful political and religious discourse that deconstructed American racial categories and unified people of color in the Americas, Africa, and Asia around a Pan-African identity that echoed the geography of the ummah—the global Muslim community. At the same time, the emphasis on signification, naming, and identity can also be discerned in the transformations of the Moorish community's names: Canaanite Temple (1913); Holy Moabite Temple of the World (a splinter group, 1916); Moorish Holy Temple of Science (1923); Moorish Science Temple of America (1928); and Moorish Divine and National Movement of North America, Inc. (1929). Moorish Americans were given identity cards, and the Arabic suffixes Bey or El were added to their surnames when they joined Noble Drew Ali's religious community.

Moorish American women had significant leadership roles in Chicago and Detroit in the 1920s. Sister C. Alsop Bey was a Governess in the national headquarters in Chicago; Sister Whitehead-El was a Grand Sheikess in a Chicago temple; Sister Juanita Mayo Richardson Bey was the editor of the *Moorish Guide* and the secretary-treasurer of the Moorish youth organization; and Sister Pearl Drew Ali was the president of the youth organization. Sister Lomax Bey was the Grand Governess in Detroit.

The Sudanese scholar and missionary Satti Majid Muhammad Al-Qadi Suwar Al-Dahub (1883–1963) guided a small Sunni Muslim community in New York City in the early twentieth century. He established several benevolent groups in the city: the Islamic Missionary Society, the Muslim Unity Society, the Islamic Benevolent Society, and the Red Crescent Society. When Satti Majid learned about Noble Drew Ali's *Circle Seven Koran* and self-proclaimed prophethood, he unsuccessfully tried to sue Ali in the United States for defaming Islam. In 1929, Satti Majid appealed to Muslim scholars in Egypt and Sudan, who issued fatwas condemning Noble Drew Ali's theology. However, these judgments never affected Ali's following in the United States, and this episode underlines the enduring power of his community in the 1920s, despite the tensions with the immigrant community. Ahmed I. Abu Shouk, J. O. Hunwick, and R. S. O'Fahey's 1997 article "A Sudanese Missionary to the United States: Satti Majid, 'Shaykh al-Islam in North America,' and His Encounter with Noble Drew Ali, Prophet of the Moorish Science Temple Movement" analyzes this controversy.

The late 1920s was the high point of the Moorish Science Temple's power in the United States. Noble Drew Ali's followers boldly flashed their nationality cards identifying themselves as Moorish Americans to white people in the streets of Chicago, and clashes with the police developed. The Moorish Manufacturing Corporation, which sold newspapers, pamphlets, and "Asiatic" pictures, charms, and herbal healing preparations, made a fortune for Noble Drew Ali and some of his leaders. Warring factions developed in the Chicago community as a result. On March 15, 1929, Sheik Claude Greene, one of Ali's opponents, was murdered at the Unity Club in Chicago, and the prophet was arrested and jailed by the Chicago Police Department. While free on bail and awaiting his trial, Noble Drew Ali died from tuberculosis on July 20, 1929, and his grave is at Burr Oak Cemetery in Chicago.

After Noble Drew Ali's death, several of his followers attempted to claim leadership of the Moorish Science Temple of America by insisting that they were his reincarnation. In the early 1940s, R. German Ali led a faction that emphasized only the prophethood of Noble Drew Ali, while Steven Gibbons established a new temple in Chicago and claimed to be the Grand Sheik of the organization. Numerous reincarnated "Brother Prophets" also claimed leadership.

Ernest Allen, Jr.'s 1994 article "When Japan Was Champion of the Darker Races: Satokata Takahashi and the Development of Our Own, 1933–1942" traces the FBI's campaign of persecution and incarceration of African American Muslim men for Selective Service violations and alleged seditious links to Japanese national organizers in the United States during World War II.

Although the accusations of sedition were never proven, many Moorish men went to jail. In their absence, women, such as Sister S. Bradley El, Sister A. Moses Bey, and Sister A. Moss Bey in Flint, Michigan; Sister M. Groom El, Sister H. Holden Bey, and Sister E. Cook Bey in New York; Sister B. Stroyer Bey in Milwaukee; Sister M. A. Walker Bey in Louisville; Sister L. Donald El in Toledo; and Sister E. Jones Bey in Trenton, New Jersey, published the monthly magazine *The Moorish Voice*, and served as governors of temples in several cities and as national officers of the Moorish Science Temple.

In the 1980s the organization had missionary programs in several federal penitentiaries in the United States and published a newspaper, *The Moorish Guide*; there were important communities of Moorish Americans in Chicago, Baltimore, and Newark. Finally, in 1986, Maati Jorco, the ambassador of Morocco to the United States, officially recognized and encouraged the connections between the Moorish American community and Morocco in an official message to the Moorish Science Temple. New Moorish American groups established since the 1980s include the United Moorish Republic, the Moorish Great Seal, the Moorish Natural and Divine Movement, and the Moorish Circle of Fulfillment.

Early-twentieth-century research on the Moorish Science Temple perpetuated stereotypes of exotica and cult about African American Muslims. The first study in this genre was that of the anthropologist Arthur Huff Fauset, whose book *Black Gods of the Metropolis: Negro Religious Cults of the Urban North* appeared in 1944. Fauset conducted fieldwork and case-study analysis of five African American storefront religious communities in Philadelphia that were established during the Great Migration. His work was the first serious academic evaluation of the Moorish Science Temple. In addition to studying the origin, organization, membership, beliefs, and rituals of Noble Drew Ali's Moorish Science Temple of America, Fauset framed his theoretical questions around important debates on Africanisms in African American religions. Utilizing Raymond Julius Jones's "cult" categories of Faith Healing, Holiness, Islamic, Pentecostal, and Spiritualist to analyze storefront religious communities, Fauset explored the rationale for their separatism and heterodoxy. Were the Moorish Science Temple's unique beliefs and practices related to African survivals? This was one of Fauset's central questions. He disagreed with E. Franklin Frazier's negative assessment of the African heritage in contemporary African American religions, but also questioned the evidence for Melville Herskovits's comprehensive theory for the reinterpretation of African culture in the United States. Herskovits's groundbreaking anthropological study *The Myth of the Negro Past* focused on vibrant West African cultural evidence in the Caribbean and South America, which he attributed to African continuities in the United States. In Fauset's conclusion, the growth of new urban religious communities, such as the Moorish Science Temple, African American Jewish groups, Father Divine's Peace Mission, and Daddy Grace's United House of Prayer for All People, was the result of American cultural and racial tensions and the new psychological, social, political, and economic needs of the black masses in the cities.

Two classic social-scientific studies of the Nation of Islam in the 1960s also discussed the Moorish Science Temple of America. E. U. Essien-Udom's *Black Nationalism: A Search for an Identity in America*, and C. Eric Lincoln's *The Black Muslims in America* continued to analyze Noble Drew Ali and his followers in the exotic realm of cult that was emphasized in Fauset's earlier ethnographic research. Lincoln and Essien-Udom's emphasis on the social and political implications of black nationalism identified the Moorish Science Temple as an early paradigm for "religious nationalism" among African Americans and as a forerunner to the Nation of Islam. The basic historical information about Noble Drew Ali in these two influential texts was repeated in books and articles for several decades until the publication of the Islamicist Aminah Beverly McCloud's *African American Islam.*

African American Islam explores the interaction between the key themes of *ummah* (the global Muslim community) and *'asabiya* (nationalism in twentieth-century black American Muslim communities) and removes the study of the Moorish Science Temple from the realm of exotica and cult by analyzing its spiritual, racial, and political themes in the context of a variety of early-twentieth-century African American Islamic spiritual philosophies that include both heterodox and orthodox groups, such as the Islamic Mission of America. According to Samory Rashid's article "Islamic Influence in America: Struggle, Flight, Community," McCloud's groundbreaking research and Steven Barboza's *American Jihad: Islam after Malcolm X*, with their focus on the complex historical continuities, worldviews, and race and class tensions in African American Islam, also provide corrective counterpoint to some of the new scholarship on the immigrant community. This scholarship sometimes exoticizes African American Islam in comparison to immigrant Islam. The Islamicists Yvonne Y. Haddad and Adair T. Lummis's influential "assimilationist" paradigm of "immigrant" and "indigenous" Muslims in their sociological study *Islamic Values in the United States: A Comparative Study* is typical of this trend. Their book emphasizes a dichotomy between the authority and experiences of immigrant Muslims who represent orthodoxy in the shaping and future development of American Islam, in contrast to so-called indigenous African American Muslims, who are associated with heterodoxy, and sectarian groups such as the Moorish Science Temple.

Several of the key points in Samory Rashid's critique of Haddad and Lummis's immigration paradigm are important because they emphasize that the study of African American Islam requires comprehensive analysis of African American history. With this perspective in mind, Rashid argues against the "waves of immigration" paradigm because it ignores the significant influence of pre-twentieth-century African and African American Muslims in American Islamic communities, and this oversight leads to errors in historical analysis, such as attributing the establishment of Islam in the United States to twentieth-century immigrant Muslims in Ross, North Dakota, and Cedar Rapids, Iowa. Finally, Rashid discusses the complex "special group interests and political agendas" (p. 10) based on race and class differences among Islamicists that have influenced an exaggerated emphasis on twentieth-century communities in their corpus of research on African-descended Muslims in the United States.

In *Islam and the Blackamerican: Looking toward the Third Resurrection*, the Islamicist Sherman A. Jackson develops a provocative thesis that links Noble Drew Ali's early-twentieth-century appropriation of Islam into the realm of "Black Religion" to the later-twentieth-century ascendancy of Sunni Islam in black America. According to Jackson, despite the Moorish Science Temple's proto-Islamic orientation, its autonomous religious authority and mass conversions of African Americans established for black people "a sense of ownership of Islam" in the United States. It follows that whatever claim contemporary African American Sunni Muslims have to the ownership of Islam in the twenty-first century can be traced back to Noble Drew Ali's reconstruction of blackness in the context of "Black Religion"—"a God-centered holy protest against anti-black racism that emerged out of the experience of slavery." In Jackson's analysis, "Black Religion," a twentieth-century orientation that defines the political and social struggles of both African American Christians and Muslims, accounts for Islam's unique appeal to black Americans, and it is a major ideological divide between contemporary African American and immigrant Muslims. Despite the important and innovative aspects of his thesis about the tensions between African American and immigrant Muslims, Jackson builds his case for "Black Religion" around a retrogressive historical framework that focuses almost exclusively on the twentieth century and denies the significance of pre-twentieth-century sources for African American Islam, such as the resistance strategies of West African Muslim slaves and possible continuities between nineteenth- and early-twentieth-century Islam in black America. Finally, in his zeal to discount "an African connection" in black American Islam, Jackson claims, with weak evidence, that African slaves in the United States were "godless."

Samory Rashid's article "Divergent Perspectives on Islam in America" emphasizes the significance of Richard Brent Turner's *Islam in the African-American Experience* (1997) for the revision of the prevailing assumption among Islamicists that early-twentieth-century African American and immigrant Muslims never interacted with one another. Turner develops a comprehensive historical model for Islam in the United States that synthesizes analysis of pre-twentieth-century African diaspora influences, global theories about hegemony and resistance, FBI records, and oral-history interviews with both African American and immigrant Muslims. These new source materials for research provide evidence that there were complex interactions between black Americans and immigrants in the Ahmadiyya Movement in Islam, Marcus Garvey's Universal Negro Improvement Association, and the dissident factions of the Moorish Science Temple that created a pathway to orthodoxy for African American Muslims in the twentieth century.

The most recent research on Noble Drew Ali and the Moorish Science Temple continues to expand our knowledge about the influence of this important community on African American Sunni Muslims and the continuities between nineteenth- and twentieth-century Islamic culture in black America. The ethnohistorian Robert Dannin, in *Black Pilgrimage to Islam*, theorizes that the Moorish Science Temple's roots in nineteenth-century African American lodges and secret societies and early-twentieth-century storefront religious institutions are an important step in "unchurched" black Americans' spiritual journeys to Sunni Islam. Dannin's interpretation of Noble Drew Ali's teachings builds on Peter Lamborn Wilson's *Sacred Drift: Essays on the Margins of Islam*, which also analyzes the Moorish Americans' esoteric linkages to Freemasonry. Susan Nance's "Mystery of the Moorish Science Temple: Southern Blacks and American Alternative Spirituality in 1920s Chicago" also develops interpretation of the above mystical Freemasonic theme, but discredits Noble Drew Ali's linkages to African American Islam to build a case for his connections to Spiritualism, Gnosticism, New Thought, and Christian Science in African American urban communities during the Great Migration. However, Nance's argument about the Moorish Science Temple's linkages to Black Spiritualist churches in Chicago in the 1920s is provocative but flawed, because it discounts completely the heterodox Islamic identity that Noble Drew Ali explicitly articulated in his writings and speeches to his followers.

The historian Edward E. Curtis IV presents a convincing evaluation of the Moorish Science Temple's significance for African American Islamic history in his 2005 article "African-American Islamization Reconsidered: Black History Narratives and Muslim Identity." Curtis examines how Noble Drew Ali utilized "a black Islamic history narrative as a sacred text" for the construction of a unique African American Islamic identity, and he cautions against scholarly readings of the Moorish Science Temple that are guided primarily by evaluations of Islamic orthodoxy, while ignoring "historical understandings of what it meant to be black" and Muslim in the twentieth-century United States. Herbert Berg's 2005 article "Mythmaking in the African American Muslim Context: The Moorish Science Temple, the Nation of Islam, and the American Society of Muslims" explores the role of mythmaking in the construction of historical narratives and racial identities in the Moorish Science Temple.

Michael Nash's M.A. thesis "History of the Islamic Influence in Newark, New Jersey 1913–Present: An Introductory Study" provides important historical documentation about the Moorish Science Temple's influence on independent African American Islamic religious and social activism in Newark, New Jersey, in the twentieth century. Nash demonstrates that Noble Drew Ali's community work in Newark, which was inspired by the social-justice values of Islam and accomplished since 1913 without help from immigrant Muslims, established a powerful model of self-determination for more than twelve African American Muslim groups in northern New Jersey in the twentieth century, such as Muhammad Ezaldeen's Sunni organization, the Adenu Allahe Universal Arabic Association (established in Newark in 1941). Akel Ismail Kahera's 2002 article "Urban Enclaves, Muslim Identity, and the Urban Mosque in America" builds on Nash's research to evaluate how African American "enclaves of 'urban Islam,'" such as the Moorish Science Temple in Newark, have developed an activist mission similar to that of black churches to reconstruct religion, education, and economics in ghetto communities in the United States.

Finally, Michael A. Gomez's "Breaking Away: Noble Drew Ali and the Foundations of Contemporary Islam in African America" traces the "reemergence" of Islam in early-twentieth-century black America to "the terrain of the nineteenth century" and the triracial communities of the Ishmaelites. Gomez successfully challenges the prevailing assumption that there were no viable connections between nineteenth- and twentieth-century African American Islam. He argues not only for a vibrant pre-twentieth-century West African Muslim community in North America with "organic, cross-generational" continuities in the twentieth century but also for smaller groups of West and North African Muslims who came to North America before the twentieth century and intermarried with Europeans and Native Americans to develop "transracial, polycultural formations in the hinterlands." The Ishmaelites are the most important community in the later category. First noted as a community in the late 1700s in Noble County, Kentucky, they are said to be the descendants of runaway slaves and fugitives from Indian warfare in North and South Carolina, Tennessee, Maryland, and Virginia. Ben Ishmael and his wife Jennie established the community, and in the early nineteenth century their son John Ishmael led the Ishmaelites out of Kentucky into the area of Indianapolis, Indiana. For the next one hundred years, this community was noted for its clans that abstained from alcohol and engaged in a yearly migration from Indianapolis to Illinois and returning to Indianapolis, stopping along the way in towns such as Morocco and Mecca, Indiana, and Mahomet, Illinois. Gomez notes that one-tenth of the recorded names in Mahomet were derived from Muslim names such as "Fard . . . Hassan . . . Mansur . . . Abu Bakr . . . Umar . . . Uthman . . . Sharif . . . Tumane . . . and . . . Turk."

The Ishmaelites became known for their participation in independent forms of unskilled labor, and by the end of the 1800s their clans included ten thousand members who experienced persecution in small towns in Indiana—some of their children were seized as wards of the state, and many adults were institutionalized in hospital wards for the mentally ill. In the early twentieth century their persecution escalated because of state laws that classified them as criminals and permitted their sterilization. Thereafter, the Ishmaelites left the state of Indiana.

Gomez analyzes persuasive evidence from early-twentieth-century oral history interviews to prove a linkage between this nineteenth-century group with obscure Islamic origins and the establishment of the national base of the Moorish Science Temple in the Midwest. Apparently, several of the Ishmaelites who had migrated from Indiana to Michigan were involved in the organization of the Moorish Science Temple in Detroit in the 1920s. Additionally, Gomez tells the story of Sambo Swift, a West African Muslim slave in Darien, Georgia, in the early nineteenth century who migrated in the late nineteenth century to Mecca, Indiana, where his Islamic grave faces the East and is distinguished by "the symbol of tawhid, the oneness of God." He argues that the history of the Ishmaelites and Sambo Swift suggests an important continuity between early-twentieth-century black American Muslims in the Midwest and "a multifaceted African Muslim" heritage from the nineteenth century. Certainly, scholars need to do more research to uncover more of these linkages and their influences on the seminal communities of the Moorish Science Temple and the Nation of Islam. In his "The Islamic Origins of Spanish Florida's Ft. Musa," Samory Rashid speculates that the proto-Islamic foundations of both of the latter groups may have been influenced by the fact that Noble Drew Ali and Elijah Muhammad were born in North Carolina and Georgia—two states where there was a rich and documented pre-twentieth-century presence of West African Muslim slaves, some of whom escaped to Native American communities that "may have also incorporated Islamic beliefs and practices."

The Ahmadiyya Movement in Islam

In February 1920 the Indian missionary Mufti Muhammad Sadiq arrived in New York to begin missionary work for the Ahmadiyya Movement in Islam, an important multiracial community in the early-twentieth-century history of African American Islam. Ghulam Ahmad established the Ahmadiyya Movement in 1889 in British India, and aspects of its heterodox theology departed significantly from the teachings of Sunni Islam. Yohanan Friedmann's *Prophecy Continuous: Aspects of Ahmadi Religious Thought and Its Medieval Background* analyzes the Ahmadi belief in prophecy after Muhammad as follows: Ghulam Ahmad was a Mahdi and modern Prophet of Islam, the Promised Messiah of Muslims and Christians, and an avatar of Krishna for Hinduism; and Jesus survived the crucifixion and traveled to India, where he died and physically ascended to heaven. Despite the aforementioned theological difference with mainstream Islam in the United States, the Ahmadiyya's successful international missionary activities and its translation of the Qur'an into English influenced many African American Muslims in both orthodox and heterodox communities who received their first Qur'ans from the Indian missionaries.

By the end of 1920, Mufti Muhammad Sadiq moved the headquarters of his community to Chicago and Detroit and began extensive missionary work with African American converts to Islam. Eventually, numerous Ahmadi mission houses, established in major northeastern and midwestern cities in the United States, were influenced by the work of African American shaykhs and converts, such as Shaykh Ahmad Din (P. Nathaniel Johnson), Brother Omar (William M. Patton), Brother Hakim (J. H. Humphries), and Sister Noor (Ophelia Avant) in St. Louis, Missouri. Their pictures and conversion narratives were often highlighted in the first Islamic newspaper in the United States, *The Moslem Sunrise*, which was published by Sadiq in 1921 to correct misrepresentations of Islam in the American media. African American teachers of Islam were trained in courses in the Arabic language and Islamic studies, which involved a commitment of several years to earn the title of shaykh.

Richard Brent Turner's 2003 article "The Ahmadiyya Mission to America: A Multi-racial Model for American Islam" analyzes the Ahmadiyya Movement's support for internationalist, anticolonialist, and Pan-Islamic political perspectives in its American and international publications. Mufti Muhammad Sadiq was attracted to the internationalist Pan-African agenda of Marcus Garvey's Universal Negro Improvement Association and recruited at least forty African American converts to Islam from UNIA chapters in Chicago and Detroit in the early 1920s. The new Indian missionaries Maulvi Muhammad Din and Sufi Mutiur Rahman Bengalee continued to promote Ahmadi missionary activities among African Americans in the 1920s and 1930s after Sadiq's departure to India in 1923.

In the 1930s and 1940s, as the membership of the Moorish Science Temple and the Nation of Islam dwindled because of factionalism and persecution by the American government, the multiracial and predominantly black American membership of the Ahmadiyya Movement in Islam grew to several thousand followers. In the World War II era, African American bebop jazz musicians such as Yusef Abdul Lateef, Art Blakey, McCoy Tyner, and Ahmad Jamal joined the community and influenced black converts to Islam in jazz communities in New York City and Philadelphia.

However, by the late 1940s the Ahmadiyya began to lose its edge of popularity among African American Muslims for several reasons. First, some important African American members left the group because early followers were not given leadership positions as missionaries and disagreed with foreign missionaries' insistence on the centrality of Indian rather than African American culture in American Islamic communities. Other African American members left the Ahmadiyya community to join budding African American Sunni groups such as the Islamic Mission to America in New York and the First Cleveland Mosque. Finally, the establishment of the Islamic nation of Pakistan in 1947 was the beginning of a long period of the legal persecution of the Ahmadis in that country because of their sectarianism. In this context, some African American Muslims decided that they did not have a real stake in the Indian missionaries' struggle to defend their people in this expensive and complicated international controversy.

Although the Ahmadiyya Movement does not attract as many black followers as it did in its early years in the United States, it continues to maintain a modest influence among African American Muslims in the twenty-first century, and its national headquarters are located in the Washington, D.C., area.

The Nation of Islam

W. D. Fard Muhammad, an immigrant Muslim missionary, established the Allah Temple of Islam (which was renamed the Nation of Islam) in Detroit, Michigan, in 1930. He espoused a proto-Islamic message of African American self-determination, racial separatism, and community development, advocating this to lower-class black Southern immigrants from Georgia, Alabama, and Mississippi as he peddled exotic goods from door to door in the Paradise Valley section of the city. Fard preached that Islam was the preslavery religion of African Americans, and that the American and European dominance of the world would eventually terminate in warfare between black and white people. He built the following community institutions as the nucleus of a black nation for his new followers, whom he called the lost tribe of Shabazz, to separate African American Muslims from Euro-American Christian culture in the United States—the Muslim Girl Training and General Civilization classes, the University of Islam (an elementary and secondary school), and the Fruit of Islam (a martial-arts and self-defense organization for men).

Building on the Pan-African political and religious legacies of Marcus Garvey's Universal Negro Improvement Association and Noble Drew Ali's Moorish Science Temple, the Nation of Islam selectively utilized aspects of the Qur'an and the Bible to teach white moral inferiority and black spiritual supremacy and economic success. W. D. Fard Muhammad established a close-knit community of approximately eight thousand followers. However, his stringent critique of racism in the United States made him a victim of police harassment and brutality in Detroit, and he disappeared mysteriously in 1934.

His closest disciple, the Honorable Elijah Muhammad (1897–1975), who was born Elijah Poole in Sandersville, Georgia, and was a former Garveyite, led this religious community from 1934 to 1975 and established its national headquarters in Chicago. The members of the Nation of Islam believe that W. D. Fard Muhammad is divine, Elijah Muhammad is the Messenger of Allah, and their ancestors—the "Asiatics"—were the original people of the earth and the first Muslims.

In the World War II era, the membership of the organization dwindled because of internal factions and external political pressures as Elijah Muhammad struggled to establish new temples in Milwaukee and Washington, D.C. He and his son Herbert were friendly with the Japanese national organizer in the United States, Satokata Takahashi, which led to charges of sedition, and they were incarcerated for Selective Service violations from 1942 to 1946 in Milan, Michigan. Elijah Muhammad's wife, Clara Evans Muhammad (1899–1972), kept the Nation of Islam on track during this period of FBI harassment. She visited her husband in prison, brought back his orders to the Chicago headquarters, and in effect functioned as the national leader in her capacity as the Supreme Secretary. Sister Clara Muhammad also established and guided the Nation of Islam's schools, which eventually became known for instruction in the Arabic language and black history and civilization.

The post–World War II years marked the conversion of Malcolm X to the Nation of Islam while he was in prison in Massachusetts. His conversion experience was a family affair, as several of his siblings had joined the organization in the 1940s and proselytized him. Malcolm X was released from prison in 1952, and his relentless missionary work in the 1950s and 1960s to establish new temples and to organize young black men in urban settings produced important communities of the Nation of Islam in the United States. As people of African descent attacked white supremacy in America and Africa, the Nation of Islam under the Honorable Elijah Muhammad's leadership developed a powerful community-based religious and economic model for black nationalism and self-determination. By the 1960s Muhammad's economic plans made his religious community the richest African American organization in U.S. history. The newspaper *Muhammad Speaks* published excellent stories about anticolonial struggles across the globe, Malcolm X's

Hulton Archive / Getty Images

Elijah Muhammad was one of the major figures in the development of the Nation of Islam. Born on October 7, 1897, to a family of sharecroppers and former slaves in Sandersville, Georgia, Poole witnessed three lynchings before the age of twenty. He married Clara Evans in 1917, moved to Detroit in 1923, and worked in an automobile factory. Sometime around 1930 he became acquainted with Wallace D. Fard, founder of the Nation of Islam, who was impressed with the younger man and renamed him Elijah Muhammad. Fard appointed him his assistant at Temple No. 1, and when the "Minister of Islam" disappeared in 1934, Muhammad took over control of the movement. Internal strife led him to move to Chicago and establish Temple No. 2. Between 1942 and 1946 Muhammad was incarcerated because of his opposition to the Selective Service Act. Following World War II he attracted members to the Nation of Islam by advocating the establishment of a separate nation for African Americans and the belief that blacks are the chosen people of Allah. He frequently referred to white people as "blue-eyed devils." In later years he toned down the separatist rhetoric and emphasized the need for self-help in the black community. During the Civil Rights Movement in the 1960s his most prominent pupil was Malcolm X. However, they developed philosophical differences, and Malcolm X decided to break with Muhammad, especially after discovering his mentor's proclivity for extramarital affairs. The Nation of Islam was heavily implicated in the assassination of Malcolm X in 1965, and its membership declined thereafter. When Muhammad died on February 25, 1975, in Chicago, his son Warith Deen, or Wallace, took over leadership of the movement.

internationalist perspective, and his critiques of the integrationist strategy of the Civil Rights Movement that provided political inspiration for the emergence of Black Power in the United States.

However, Elijah Muhammad's single-minded focus on the religious and economic development of his community produced a conservative attitude about political activism, and this became one of the important factors that forced Malcolm X's split with the Nation of Islam. In the aftermath of President John F. Kennedy's murder in 1963, Malcolm X's harsh public remarks about the assassination developed into a public controversy with Elijah Muhammad, whom Malcolm further alienated by accusing him of extramarital sexual affairs that produced children with his secretaries.

Eventually, Malcolm X established a new religious and political identity as he denounced the heterodox spiritual philosophy of the Nation of Islam and embraced Sunni Islam in the last year of his life. In spring 1964 he established the Sunni Muslim Mosque, Inc., in Harlem and traveled to Mecca, Saudi Arabia, to make the Hajj, where he adopted the new name El Hajj Malik El-Shabazz, which signified his new connection to orthodox Islam. Malcolm's Pan-Africanist ideas deepened as he traveled internationally to establish diplomatic connections with North and West African nations. He returned to the United States in the summer of 1964 to establish the Organization of Afro-American Unity, which resonated with his international human-rights agenda that critiqued capitalism, racism, and classism and connected social-justice struggles in black America, Africa, the Caribbean, Latin America, and Asia.

Michael Gomez in *Black Crescent: The Experience and Legacy of African Muslims in the Americas* theorizes that if Malcolm X had lived, he could have united many people of African descent in the United States and abroad in a liberation struggle that could have brought the United States government before the United Nations for crimes against humanity. Therefore, in his view, there is no question that the intelligence community had the incentive to be involved in Malcolm's assassination, which occurred in the presence of his wife, Betty Shabazz, and his children in the Audubon Ballroom in Harlem on February 21, 1965.

Louis Farrakhan's (1933–) leadership of the revived Nation of Islam began in 1978 and originated in his dissatisfaction with the orthodox direction of the

Malcolm X at a Black Muslim rally in Washington, D.C., in 1962. Born Malcolm Little on May 19, 1925, in Omaha, Nebraska, this militant black leader had a traumatic childhood. He grew up in Lansing, Michigan, and saw his house burned down by the Ku Klux Klan. His father was murdered soon thereafter, and his mother was committed to a mental ward. As a young man Little lived with his sister in Boston, where he became a street hustler and pimp. In 1946, while incarcerated for burglary, he converted to the Black Muslim faith. Upon his release six years later he met the Nation of Islam leader Elijah Muhammad and changed his surname to "X," a common practice among Black Muslims who wish to reject any association with white slaveholders. Malcolm X drummed up support for the movement by going on a speaking tour, and was rewarded for his efforts by being appointed minister of Temple No. 7 in Harlem. He called for black pride and rejected integration. He did not believe in the nonviolent approach of Martin Luther King Jr., and advocated instead the use of "any means necessary" (including violence) to achieve racial justice. Nevertheless, Elijah Muhammad reprimanded Malcolm X after the latter described the assassination of President John F. Kennedy as a "case of chickens coming home to roost." By this time Malcolm X's popularity caused much jealousy among some leaders of the Nation of Islam, and in March 1964 he left to establish his own religious movement. Following a pilgrimage to Mecca, he converted to orthodox Islam and changed his name to el-Hajj Malik el-Shabazz. On February 21, 1965, rival Black Muslims assassinated Malcolm X at a rally in Harlem.

religious community under Warith Deen Muhammad's leadership, which commenced in 1975, the year Elijah Muhammad died. Farrakhan has been successful with the publication of the *Final Call* newspaper, the construction of 120 mosques, and a $5 million interest-free loan from Libya in 1985 for black economic development. His connections with the Congressional Black Caucus and other mainstream African American organizations and community businesses for health, nutrition, cosmetics, food, clothing, pharmaceuticals, media, and security guards have ushered the Nation of Islam into a new period of national prominence. Since the 1980s the programs and rhetoric of the Nation of Islam have been a beacon of hope for self-determination for black America, and Farrakhan has questioned the U.S. government's oppressive economic and political policies in the late-twentieth century. His greatest success was the Million Man March in 1995, the largest political rally of black Americans in American history.

On Savior's Day in Chicago in February 2000, Farrakhan announced changes in the Nation of Islam's theology and ritual practices that bring his community closer to mainstream Islam in the United States. Although the Nation of Islam's theology still regards the Honorable Elijah Muhammad as the Messenger of Allah and emphasizes a stringent critique of institutional racism in the American government, there are now peaceful and significant social and political interactions between African American Muslims in Sunni communities and the Nation of Islam. On October 15, 2005, Farrakhan launched the Millions More Movement in the National Mall in front of the U.S. Capitol in Washington, D.C. This is an ecumenical movement of black Christian and Muslim organizations united in their plans to revive the Civil Rights Movement and to eliminate poverty in black America.

Major factions of the Nation of Islam are led by John Muhammad in Highland Park, Michigan; Silis Muhammad in Atlanta, Georgia; and Emmanuel Muhammad in Baltimore, Maryland. Clarence 13X founded the Five Percent Nation in New York City in 1984. Also called the Nation of Gods and Earths, the Five Percenters are popular among rap musicians and the hip-hop community. The scholarship on the Nation of Islam is voluminous. However, much of the research is repetitive, based on the groundbreaking insights in the selected articles and books discussed below, which focus primarily on W.

Louis Farrakhan during a celebration in Washington, D.C., in 1992. Born Louis Eugene Walcott in the Bronx, New York, on May 11, 1933, he was a calypso guitarist and singer before converting to the Nation of Islam in 1955. Later renamed Farrakhan, he quickly rose to prominence in the movement. When Malcolm X converted to Sunni Islam, Farrakhan replaced him as the minister of Temple No. 7 in Harlem. He stayed in that position for a decade, and left after falling out with the new iman of the movement, Wallace D. Muhammad, son of Elijah Muhammad. In 1978 Farrakhan formed his own sect of the Nation of Islam which emphasizes the family, unity, and economic self-sufficiency. His followers lead a structured lifestyle, abstaining from certain foods and sexual promiscuity and dressing in distinctive, somber clothes. Farrakhan's fiery rhetoric has led some critics to label him a racist and anti-Semite. He organized the Million Man March in 1995 and the Million Family March in 2000. His charisma has been a contributing factor in the Nation of Islam being a powerful force in contemporary African American life. The Nation of Islam currently has mosques and study groups in more than 120 cities throughout the United States, the Caribbean, and Europe.

D. Fard Muhammad, Elijah Muhammad, Malcolm X, Warith Deen Muhammad, and Louis Farrakhan. The white American sociologist Erdmann D. Benyon initiated scholarship on the Nation of Islam in his 1938 article "The Voodoo Cult among Negro Migrants in Detroit." This case study of the religion provides valuable information about the social conditions and religious experiences of the first Southern migrants who converted to the organization, and about the mysterious identity of W. D. Fard Muhammad. Benyon interviewed more than two hundred families in the Nation of Islam in the 1930s. Most of the early members had been Baptists and Methodists in the South and were alienated by the poverty of ghetto life in the first years of the Great Depression. However, as the title of his article suggests, Benyon also introduced exotic stereotypes about human sacrifice among the early converts. These rumors were never validated and may have been influenced by his documented conferences with an officer in the Detroit Police Department who was investigating the Nation of Islam.

The true identity of W. D. Fard Muhammad was initially discussed in Benyon's research and remains an unresolved issue in the academic literature on the Nation of Islam. Zafar Ishaq Ansari's manuscript "The Religious Doctrines of the Black Muslims of America, 1930–1980" posited that Fard was Muhammad Abdullah, an Indian imam for the Lahore faction of the Ahmadiyya Movement who lived in the San Francisco Bay area in the 1980s. Abdullah was friendly with Elijah Muhammad and tutored his son, Warith Deen Muhammad, in Arabic, but denied in an interview with the author that he was the true W. D. Fard, who he claims was a real missionary from the Middle East, fluent in several languages and incarcerated in the United States. Turner's *Islam in the African-American Experience* provides the analysis of the voluminous FBI documents on W. D. Fard Muhammad. According to FBI sources, Fard had many aliases and was born either in Mecca, Saudi Arabia; New Zealand; or Portland, Oregon. He may have lived in Seattle and then in Los Angeles, where he was arrested and incarcerated for selling drugs. However, Turner's evaluation of the evidence on W. D. Fard Muhammad's identity points to the statement by Elijah Muhammad's son, Akbar Muhammad, that the founder of the Nation of Islam was "Turko-Persian culturally." Gomez's *Black Crescent: The Experience and Legacy of African Muslims in the Americas* suggests that W. D. Fard was born in 1891 in New Zealand as Wali Dodd Fard, of East Indian and English parentage. He may have changed his name to George Farr in San Francisco, where he joined the Theosophical Society and Marcus Garvey's Universal Negro Improvement Association in the early 1920s, and to Wallace D. Fard in Chicago, where he became a member of the Moorish Science Temple and participated in the activities of the Ahmadiyya mission in 1929.

C. Eric Lincoln and E. U. Essien-Udom published two social-scientific studies on the Nation of Islam in the early 1960s that are classic monographs because of their comprehensive and insightful analyses, but both works also have major conceptual flaws. Sociologist of religion C. Eric Lincoln, in his *The Black Muslims in America*, established the direction of twentieth-century scholarship on African American Islam. His is the most brilliant case study ever published on a Muslim community in the United States. However, the weaknesses of the work are his single-minded focus on its male membership and his interpretation of the Nation of Islam as a lower-social-class social-protest movement, instead of as a religious community. Lincoln's term the "Black Muslims" was constructed specifically for his book and does not reflect the religious identity of the members of the Nation of Islam who call themselves "Muslims." Political scientist Essien-Udom's *Black Nationalism: A Search for Identity in America* also deemphasized the Nation of Islam as a religious community and discussed the organization as an expression of political behavior, derived from the psychological pathology of African American subculture. In the same period, the paranoid ideas of African American journalist Louis E. Lomax led to the television program "The Hate That Hate Produced," which stereotyped the Nation of Islam as a hate organization and at the same time introduced the religion to the American public. Ironically, Lomax's book *When The Word is Given: A Report on Elijah Muhammad, Malcolm X, and the Black Muslim World* was one of the first studies to recognize the Nation of Islam as a religious community with connections to the ummah.

Recent studies of Elijah Muhammad shed new light on his pivotal status not only as an important religious leader but also as one of the major black nationalist figures in the twentieth century. Claude Andrew Clegg III's "Messenger of Allah" comes from his important biography of Muhammad that illuminates the intersection of religious and conservative economic agenda in his programs for the Nation of Islam in the twentieth century. Clifton E. Marsh's "The Nation of Islam, 1930–1959" provides important social-scientific analysis of Elijah Muhammad's legacy and the growing influence of the

Nation of Islam in the context of other nineteenth- and twentieth-century black nationalist social and religious movements. Ernest Allen, Jr., analyzes the factors that influenced the ascendancy of Elijah Muhammad as the Messenger of Allah in the Nation of Islam from 1958 to 1975, in "Religious Heterodoxy and Nationalist Tradition: The Continuing Evolution of the Nation of Islam." These factors included the mainstream spiritual influence of Jamil Diab, a Palestinian Arabic teacher at the Nation of Islam's parochial school; the conversion of middle-class African Americans to the religion; the dissemination of Elijah Muhammad's teachings in the *Muhammad Speaks* newspaper, books such as *Message to the Black Man in America*, and on radio; and the development of a multimillion-dollar economic empire in Chicago. Moreover, Michael A. Gomez speculates that Muhammad was the author of the Nation of Islam's earliest instructional literature from the 1930s, *Teaching for the Lost-Found Nation of Islam in a Mathematical Way* and *Secret Ritual of the Nation of Islam*, in his *Black Crescent: The Experience and Legacy of African American Muslims in the Americas*.

Elijah Muhammad's profound religious and economic agenda for the Nation of Islam was inseparable from the educational and community programs for women and children established by his wife, Clara Muhammad, the "cofounder" of the organization, according to Rosetta E. Ross in *Witnessing and Testifying: Black Women, Religion, and Civil Rights*. Cynthia S'Thembile West develops an analytical framework for understanding Clara Muhammad's foundational influence on African American women as "agents of change" in the religion, in her article "Revisiting Female Activism in the 1960s: The Newark Branch Nation of Islam." Her interviews with Muslim women from the 1960s demonstrate how women and men together, participating in the programs of the Nation of Islam, transformed the economic, educational, and family values of Black Newark with the same dedication to family and community as "Southern civil rights activists."

In "Savior," Alex Haley and Malcolm X chronicle the beginning of Malcolm X's religious transformation in the Detroit Nation of Islam community after his release from prison in 1952. Although *The Autobiography of Malcolm X* is still the best source of information on this important figure, we now know that Alex Haley's published account of Malcolm X's life is incomplete and was influenced by his conservative political motives. Manning Marable's "Rediscovering Malcolm's Life: A Historian's Adventures in Living History" sheds light on these issues, analyzes the significant gaps of information in *The Autobiography of Malcolm X*, and suggests new source materials to reconstruct a more complex international political picture of Malcolm's life. Apparently, Haley, an advocate of integration and civil rights, did not agree with the separatist politics of the Nation of Islam and Malcolm X, and was persuaded by his publisher, Doubleday, to omit three chapters from the final version of *The Autobiography* that detailed Malcolm's political plans in 1963 and 1964. The missing chapters, which are owned by a lawyer in Detroit, may have discussed Malcolm X's plans to create a comprehensive national coalition of African American political and community organizations involving both black nationalist and civil rights advocates.

Marable, editor of the Malcolm X Project at Columbia University, notes that until recently, most of the literature on Malcolm X has been based on the same secondary source materials. However, in the near future, substantial new primary sources will be available to scholars, as the Malcolm X Project publishes new FBI files on Malcolm that go far beyond those published in Claybourne Carson's book *Malcolm X: The FBI File*. Also, the Schomburg Center for Research in Black Culture in Harlem will soon make available to scholars a new collection of primary materials "lent for 75 years" by the Shabazz family.

Collections of Malcolm X's speeches, interviews, and accounts written by people who worked with him provide important primary sources for scholarship. George Breitman's *By Any Means Necessary: Speeches, Interviews, and a Letter by Malcolm X* and Steve Clark's *Malcolm X—February 1965: Final Speeches* document Malcolm X's profound religious and political work in 1964 and 1965, as his internationalist Pan-African perspective blossomed and he established the Organization of Afro-American Unity. Herman Ferguson, one of the original members of the Organization of Afro-American Unity, provides a fascinating first-hand account of Malcolm X's leadership of the OAAU and the Muslim Mosque, Inc., in Harlem in his "The Price of Freedom: Herman Ferguson." Ossie Davis, the late African American actor who was a personal friend of Malcolm X, foreshadows black America's contemporary veneration of Malcolm as a black hero in his article "'Our Shining Black Prince' Eulogy Delivered by Ossie Davis at the Funeral of Malcolm X, Faith Temple Church of God." Malcolm's nephew, Rodnell P. Collins, discusses the enduring influence of Malcolm's sister, Ella Little Collins, on his uncle's religious and political ideas, in his book with A. Peter Bailey, *Seventh Child: A Family Memoir of Malcolm X.*

On the scholarly order, there are several important books on Malcolm X. Peter Goldman's *The Death and Life of Malcolm X* is the most thoroughly researched and well-argued biography. Louis A. DeCaro, Jr.'s article "Religious Revolutionist," in his *On the Side of My People: A Religious Life of Malcolm X*, provides the most detailed analysis of Malcolm's religious transformation after his Hajj to Mecca. William W. Sales, Jr.'s 1994 article "The OAAU and the Politics of the Black United Front," collected in his *From Civil Rights to Black Liberation: Malcolm X and the Organization of Afro-American Unity,* is an excellent study of the Pan-Africanist organization that Malcolm X established in Harlem in 1964. Michael Eric Dyson's *Making Malcolm: The Myth and Meaning of Malcolm X* reflects renewed interest in Malcolm X in American popular culture after Spike Lee's influential 1992 film *Malcolm X.* Historian Russell J. Rickford's *Betty Shabazz: A Remarkable Story of Survival and Faith Before and After Malcolm X* is the most thorough biographical account of the life and work of Malcolm's wife, Betty Shabazz (1934–1997). Thomas Hauser's biography *Muhammad Ali: His Life and Times* provides interviews about Ali's deep friendship with Malcolm X that ended abruptly when Malcolm left the Nation of Islam in 1964.

Karl Evanzz, an investigative journalist, analyzes the possibility that U.S. intelligence agencies influenced Malcolm X's murder, in his intriguing book *The Judas Factor: The Plot to Kill Malcolm X.* His evidence for the complicity of the CIA and FBI is based on Evanzz's evaluation of voluminous interviews and documents from the COINTELPRO program, which wiretapped and infiltrated civil rights and black nationalist groups in the 1960s. However, Michael Gomez has developed the most persuasive analysis of the political rationale for Malcolm X's assassination in *Black Crescent: The Experience and Legacy of African Muslims in the Americas.* His argument focuses on Malcolm's plan to utilize his international contacts to support a program to charge the United States government with genocide against African Americans in the United Nations forum. Gomez writes with great insight about possible motives of U.S. intelligence agencies for involvement in Malcolm X's death: "Had Malcolm been able to garner the backing of independent African nations for which he lobbied, it would have meant the dawn of a new era . . . There in New York City, a conflict largely framed as a domestic issue would have been incorporated into a much larger struggle on a global scale, and the African in America would have perhaps understood for the first time the efficacy of waging concomitant war against Jim Crow and apartheid."

Lawrence H. Mamiya utilizes the model of Malcolm X in the Nation of Islam phase of his career—the "old Malcolm"—to analyze Louis Farrakhan's message and programs in the revived Nation of Islam, in "Minister Louis Farrakhan and the Final Call: Schism in the Muslim Movement." He notes the striking similarities between the "old Malcolm" and Louis Farrakhan in personal appearance, oratory, and charisma and argues that the growth of the revived Nation of Islam is based on its particularistic appeal to the African American lower class, and its stringent black nationalist critique of racism in the United States. Mattias Gardell's *In the Name of Elijah Muhammad: Louis Farrakhan and the Nation of Islam* moves beyond the controversies in Farrakhan's leadership of the Nation of Islam that began with the accusations of anti-Semitism during Jesse Jackson's 1984 presidential campaign, to provide a comprehensive understanding of his ideas. Gardell's viewpoint is that Farrakhan incorporates orthodox Islamic rituals in Mosque Maryam in Chicago and at the same time engages in a critique of racism against black people in the Islamic world that maintains institutional separatism from orthodox Islam for his followers. The latter idea is in line with the late Elijah Muhammad's thinking, as are Farrakhan's strong critique of racism in the U.S. government and his conservative economic and community uplift programs.

Louis Farrakhan's speech at the 1995 Million Man March is the subject of Ernest Allen, Jr.'s incisive analysis in "Toward A 'More Perfect Union': A Commingling of Constitutional Ideals and Christian Precepts." According to Allen, Farrakhan's speech presented a new dynamic program for black redemption in America despite the March's nonprogressive elements, such as its exclusion of women and its failure to articulate "concrete social issues."

Farrakhan's emphasis on public reconciliation and atonement for black men, and his deemphasis on Nation of Islam theology positioned him as an important leader of both black Christians and Muslims. The final recommendations in his speech—to join black community and religious organizations, to register to vote, to adopt African American inmates and foster children, and to develop an economic fund for black business and civil rights organizations—signaled a new phase of the Nation of Islam's movement to the center of the American public square. Finally, historian and former Nation of Islam member Vibert L. White, Jr., presents a mixed evaluation of Louis Farrakhan's leadership and motives in the Million Man March in *Inside the Nation of Islam: A Historical and Personal Testimony by a Black Muslim.*

Sunni Islam and African Americans

African Americans who are Sunni Muslim can trace their origins to several twentieth-century communities in which there were important interactions between black American and immigrant Muslims in the United States. They include the Islamic Mission of America, Jabul Arabiyya, the First Cleveland Mosque, Darul Islam, the American Society of Muslims, and The Mosque Cares. These organizations were initially influenced by proto-Islamic groups such as the Ahmadiyya Movement in Islam, the Moorish Science Temple of America, and the Nation of Islam, in addition to anticolonial revivalist organizations in Egypt and Pakistan such as Ikwan Al-Muslimum and Jamaat-e-Islami.

The Islamic Mission to America in New York City was influenced by the Arab Muslim immigrant community; Muslim sailors from Somalia, Yemen, and Madagascar; the Ahmadiyya Movement's English translation of the Qur'an; and dynamic black community values. Daoud, who was born in Morocco and emigrated to the United States from Trinidad, established this community in 1924, which was also later known as the State Street Mosque. His wife, "Mother" Sayeda Khadija, who was of Pakistani Muslim and Barbadian descent, was the leader of the Muslim Ladies Cultural Society. The Islamic Mission to America produced its own literature about orthodox Islam. Shaykh Daoud advised black American Muslims to transform themselves not only spiritually but also culturally, to link themselves to Islamic societies in Africa and Asia. He mediated the significant interactions and differences between Muslim immigrants and African American converts to Islam in Brooklyn and Manhattan from the 1920s to the 1960s.

The English teacher Muhammad Ezaldeen was a member of the Moorish Science Temple of America in Newark, New Jersey, in the 1920s. He studied Arabic and Islam in Egypt and returned to New York to develop the Islamic connections between African American and Arab American culture in the Adenu Allahe Universal Arabic Association. Ezaldeen and his followers founded an African American Muslim community ruled by Islamic law, called Jabul Arabiyya, in West Valley, New York, in 1938. Branches of this organization were established in New Jersey (Ezaldeen Village); Jacksonville, Florida; Rochester, New York; Philadelphia; and Detroit from the 1930s to the 1990s. Each community focused on the Sunni Muslim concept *hijra*—the movement of early Arabian Muslims from Mecca to Medina, Saudi Arabia, in 622 CE—as the centerpiece of their spiritual ideas.

The orthodox First Cleveland Mosque, founded by Wali Akram in 1936, and the First Muslim Mosque, founded in Pittsburgh by Nasir Ahmad and Saeed Akmal, were the result of tensions between black American and immigrant leaders in the Ahmadiyya Movement. Akram severed all connections with foreign Muslims to establish his African American Sunni community. He and his wife Kareema taught Arabic and the Qur'an to African American converts. Akram also developed the Muslim Ten-Year Plan to utilize the discipline and values of Islam to get black people off welfare, and to ensure economic and social self-determination in black American Muslim communities.

In the World War II era and the 1950s, bebop—a new genre of jazz popularized by Dizzy Gillespie's band that utilized jazz musicians and sounds from the Caribbean and Africa—produced a fascinating culture for the conversion of jazz musicians to orthodox Islam. Rudy Powell, Liaqat Ali Salaam (Kenny Clarke), Mustafa Dalil (Oliver Mesheux), Yusef Abdul Lateef (William Evans), Talib Dawud (Alfonso Barrymore, born in Antigua), Hajj Rashid (Lyn Hope), and Yusef Muzafaruddin Hamid (born in Dominica) were jazz musicians who accepted Islam.

Wali Akram founded the Uniting Islamic Society of America in Philadelphia in 1943 to unify the following black American Sunni groups: Shaykh Omar Ali's Harlem Academy of Islam, the Adenu Allahe Universal Arabic Association, Moslems of America, the Muslim Ten-Year Plan, and A. I. Malik's Wa-Hid Al-Samad Society against the leadership of immigrant Muslims. The organization disbanded in the late 1940s because of internal conflicts. The tensions between black American Sunni Muslims and the immigrant community reached a high point in the late 1950s and 1960s.

The former jazz musician Dawud opened the Islamic and African Institute in Philadelphia in 1957. He worked with the Egyptian Muslim Mahmoud Alwan, a teacher of Arabic, and the black historian J. A. Rogers at the institute. He believed that unity with the political agenda of the international community of Islam was the answer for the African American Sunni identity quest. Dawud linked his institute with mosques in Washington, D.C., Providence, and Boston, and with Abdul Raheem's International Muslim Brotherhood in New York City.

The Philadelphia Police Department's harassment of, and attacks on, African American Muslims influenced Sulaiman al-Hadi to move to New York City and join Shaykh Daoud Faisal's mission to black American converts. In 1962 Daoud's mosque in Brooklyn on State Street attempted to unite African American Muslim converts and Arab immigrants in the Islamic Mission to America. However, cultural and racial tensions between these different communities resulted in a new African American Sunni group—Darul Islam—when the African American converts, Rijab Mahmud and Abdul Karim, decided to found Yasin Mosque in Brownsville, Brooklyn, in 1959.

Darul Islam (House of Peace) has mosques in Philadelphia, Boston, Washington, D.C., Cleveland, Columbus, Raleigh, Dallas, San Antonio, Atlanta, Los Angeles, San Diego, and Sacramento. The Dar Prison Committee established Masjid Sankore in Green Haven State Prison in New York, which was the paradigm for Darul Islam's prison missions in the 1960s and 1970s. Darul Islam's commitment to orthodox Islam, on the one hand, and to community work in poor black communities and prisons, on the other, is an important activist paradigm for black American Sunni Muslims in the United States.

In the same period, Shaykh K. Ahmad Tawfiq, a former member of Malcolm X's Muslim Mosque, Inc., who had studied at al-Azhar University in Cairo, Egypt, established the Sunni Mosque of Islamic Brotherhood in Harlem in 1967. He was inspired by the political and religious revivalism of the Islamic movements he had encountered in Cairo. Tawfiq's community included Muslim stores, schools, clubs, a newsletter, housing, drug rehabilitation, and a missionary program for inmates at Rikers Island.

Hamid, a black musician who had spent time in Africa, Asia, and the Middle East and had worked for the Islamic Center, which serves the embassies in Washington, D.C., established the Islamic Party in North America in Washington, D.C., in 1972. This Sunni community's mosque included African American professionals, college students, and previous Black Panther Party members. The Islamic Party was also influenced by anticolonial movements in the Islamic world and the emphasis on orthodox Islam in the last year of Malcolm X's life. In the 1970s it established a journal, *Al Islam*, a taxicab company, bookstore, dormitory, restaurant, school, grocery store, bakery, cultural center, and a Department of Oppressed Peoples Affairs in the District of Columbia. In the 1980s, emphasis by the Islamic Party in North America on internationalism and its religious work in Trinidad and Tobago resulted in the termination of its headquarters in Washington, D.C., and the establishment of new sites on St. Croix in the Virgin Islands, Grenada, Dominica, Belize, Honduras, and Tate, Georgia. Hamid died in Honduras in 1991.

Warith Deen Muhammad, Elijah Muhammad's son, is an important figure in Sunni Islam in black America. He assumed leadership of the Nation of Islam after his father's death in 1975. In the 1970s he created significant changes, which are known as the "Second Reconstruction" of black Americans, in order to facilitate the transition of his community to Sunni Islam. Muhammad abandoned the racial-separatist ideas of the Nation of Islam and emphasized his father's role in creating the "First Reconstruction" of African Americans by reintroducing them to Islam. However, the community's new mission focused not only on African Americans but also on American society. Warith Deen Muhammad initiated the following name changes for his organization: the Bilalians in 1976, the World Community of Al-Islam in the West in 1976, the

American Muslim Mission in 1980, and the American Society of Muslims in the 1990s. Ministers became "imams," and temples became "mosques" and "masjids." The Nation of Islam's material wealth was liquidated, and orthodox rituals and customs were mandated. Although Warith Deen Muhammad's positive connections with the immigrant community, the Islamic world, and the U.S. government are significant developments, his organization's membership has diminished since the 1980s, and he stepped down as the leader of the American Society of Muslims in 2003. He now guides the spirit and consciousness of his community through his organization The Mosque Cares.

The nationally known African American speaker Siraj Wahhaj is the leader of a large and influential black Sunni community in Bedford Stuyvesant in Brooklyn, New York. There are small Sufi communities in other American cities. Currently, Islam is the second largest religion in the United States (after Christianity), and there are significant race, class, cultural, and ethnic tensions between black Americans and the immigrant community in Sunni Islam. African American Muslims, spiritually and politically inspired by Malcolm X's conversion to orthodoxy in 1964, continue to view Islamic values through the lens of powerful social-justice struggles in poor and middle-class black communities, while immigrant Muslims, primarily middle- and upper-class and politically conservative, see Islam as "a colour- and race-blind" religion, as they pursue the American dream in the post-9/11 world of the American Patriot Act (which has been questioned for its limitations on civil liberties) and racial and religious profiling in the United States. The scholarship on African Americans and Sunni Islam reflects the above interactions, tensions, and boundaries between these two communities of Muslims.

Robert Dannin's *Black Pilgrimage to Islam* provides the most comprehensive and detailed portrait of black American conversions to Sunni Islam in a variety of orthodox communities in the twentieth century. Dannin's basic premise is that there is too much scholarship on proto-Islamic communities such as the Nation of Islam, in light of the fact that mainstream Islam has been the theological norm for twentieth-century African American Muslims and is now numerically dominant in black America. His fascinating chapter "Be-bop to Brotherhood and Beyond" examines the influences of post–World War II revivalism from Egypt and Caribbean Pan-African culture on a new generation of African American converts from the jazz community. Dannin's chapter "Island in a Sea of Ignorance" is the best account of Darul Islam's Prison Committee in the New York State Department of Corrections. His work helps to explain the contemporary significance of Islam in American prisons and complements Aminah McCloud and Frederick Thaufeer al-Deen's *A Question of Faith for Muslim Inmates.*

McCloud's "A Challenging Intellectual Heritage: A Look at the Social and Political Space of African-American Muslims" analyzes how black American Sunni communities have utilized esoteric knowledge and po-litical strategies from proto-Islamic and African American cultural sources to construct the contemporary social and political path of Islam in the United States. In "Wallace D. Muhammad (b. 1933), Sunni Islamic Reform, and the Continuing Problems of Particularism," Edward E. Curtis IV traces Warith Deen Muhammad's orthodox transformation of the Nation of Islam after the death of his father, Elijah Muhammad, to a long history of universalist and particularistic tensions in black American Islamic thought that began with Edward Wilmot Blyden in the nineteenth century. Clifton E. Marsh's book *The Lost Found Nation of Islam in America* provides an important 1979 interview with Warith Deen Muhammad that discusses the aforementioned religious transitions in his community.

Sherman A. Jackson's "Islam and Black Religion" is the most thorough and convincing analysis of the struggle between African American and im-migrant Muslims to define Islam's agenda in the United States after the re-scission of the National Origins Quota system in 1965, which resulted in the arrival of several million Muslim immigrants in America in the late-twentieth and twenty-first centuries. There is now a major and blossoming scholarly discourse about the contemporary contours of the interactions and tensions between African American and immigrant Sunni Muslims that underlines the recent phenomenal growth of the Muslim community in the United States to an estimated six to seven million people. It has been highlighted in the following articles, books, and reports.

Melissa D'Agostino's "Muslim Personhood: Translation, Transnational-ism and Islamic Religious Education among Muslims in New York City" charts the religious, racial, and ethnic complexity of New York City's contemporary

Muslim community—with more than six hundred thousand people and one hundred Islamic institutions. Ihsan Bagby's A *Portrait of Detroit Mosques: Muslim Views on Policy, Politics, and Religion* discusses the ethnic and racial complexities of Islamic institutions in Detroit, which is the home of the oldest African American and Arab American Muslim communities in the United States. Richard Brent Turner's *Islam in the African-American Experience*, and Lori A. Peek's "Reactions and Response: Muslim Students' Experiences on New York City Campuses Post 9/11" discuss the urgency in both the African American and the immigrant communities to educate the American public and to construct positive images of Islam after September 11, 2001. Analysis of the influence of both immigrant Muslims and the Nation of Islam on the identities of young African American Sunni Muslims is the subject of Jamillah Karim's "Between Immigrant Islam and Black Liberation: Young Muslims Inherit Global Muslim and African American Legacies."

Two important studies on the demography and institutions of the American Muslim Community were sponsored by the Council on American-Islamic Relations in Washington, D.C.: Mohamed Nimer's *The North American Muslim Resource Guide: Muslim Community Life in the United States and Canada*; and Ihsan Bagby, Paul M. Perl, and Bryon T. Froehle's *The Mosque in America: A National Portrait; A Report from the Mosque Study Project* provide incomplete information about the numerical dominance of African American Muslims in U.S. Islamic communities, because neither study includes proto-Islamic groups such as the Nation of Islam for theological reasons. Despite the shortcoming of these studies in terms of counting the Muslim population, clearly, African Americans are the largest community of Muslims in the United States, and young black men make up a significant percentage of the new converts to Islam in this country in the early twenty-first century.

Hip-hop, created in New York City in the 1970s by African American, Caribbean, and Latino crews, rappers, disc jockeys, graffiti artists, and break dancers as a youth culture of resistance to the postindustrial devastation of American cities in the early years of the Reagan-Bush era, is an important voice of African American Muslim youth and will influence new conversions to Islam in the twenty-first century. Chuck D and Yusuf Jah's *Fight the Power: Rap, Race, and Reality*; Joseph D. Eure and James G. Spady's *Nation Conscious Rap*; and Jim Fricke and Charles Ahern's book *Yes Yes Y'all: The Experience Music Project Oral History of Hip-Hop's First Decade* trace the significant influence of Islam on Afrika Bambaataa and the Zulu Nation, Daddy-O, Poor Righteous Teachers, Defiant Giants, Paris, Chuck D, and Public Enemy in the early years of hip-hop. The introduction to the second edition of Richard Brent Turner's book *Islam in the African-American Experience* analyzes the "Islamic messages" and the impact of 9/11 on rappers such as Mos Def, Nas, the DPZ, and Busta Rhymes. Hisham Aidi's "Let Us Be Moors: Islam, Race, and Connected Histories," and Hesham Samy Abdel-Alim's work on "Hip Hop Islam" document the global influence of African American hip-hop culture on the resistance strategies of marginalized Arab and African-descended Muslim youth in France, and on French Islamic hip-hop artists such as Al Malik and the New African Poets, La Fonky Family, Yazid, and Eeme Oeil (Third Eye). This research underlines the fact that Islam's influence as the iconic religion of hip-hop culture in the late-twentieth century is related to urban mapping. New York City and the northern New Jersey area, the birthplace of rap, is also home to the largest and most ethnically and racially diverse communities of Muslims in North America. Finally, it is noteworthy that Rami Nashashibi, the immigrant Muslim leader of the Inner City Muslim Action Network (IMAN) in Chicago, utilizes hip-hop poetry to bridge the communication gap between African American and immigrant Muslim youth in Chicago neighborhoods.

We know little about the history of African American women in Sunni Islam. Carolyn Moxley Rouse's book *Engaged Surrender: African American Women and Islam*, an ethnographic study of select African American women converts to Sunni Islam in Los Angeles, provides modest historical analysis to map these women's experiences. Aminah Beverly McCloud's chapter "Women in Islam," in her book *African American Islam*, is still the best resource on this important topic. Finally, there are fascinating stories of contemporary African American Muslim women's lives in Saleemah Abdul-Ghafur's book *Living Islam Out Loud: American Muslim Women Speak*.

Conclusion

The study of Islam and African Americans is a blossoming field, with an extensive literature published since the 1990s that charts the complex history and spiritual philosophies of important African American Muslim communities and their leaders. However, several areas of research are still relatively unexplored and warrant further study. There is a great need for a comprehensive historical study of African American Muslim women that begins with analysis of African-descended Muslim women in slave communities in the United States and follows the significant influences of black women in Islamic communities, cultures, and institutions in the twentieth- and twenty-first century United States. Aminah McCloud, Jamillah Karim, Carolyn Moxley Rouse, and Cynthia S'Thembile West have written on the topic, but we still do not know enough about the history of African American women in Islam. A comprehensive sociological study of gender and class in African American Muslim communities will reveal whether African American Muslims are primarily male or female, working-class or middle-class, and will explain the spiritual, social, political, and economic rationale for the growing popularity of Islam in black America.

Robert Dannin's research on Islam and World War II–era jazz musicians in *Black Pilgrimage to Islam* has initiated conversations among scholars about the need for a comprehensive study of Islam and African American music. The author is planning to write a book in the near future which will map the influence of Islam on diverse black musical genres in the United States: blues, jazz, rhythm and blues, and rap.

Malcolm X is a pivotal figure in the history of the Nation of Islam and Sunni Islam in the United States. Yet, research on this important American Muslim has been on a treadmill since the 1960s because of the limited primary sources that have been available, until recently, to scholars. There is a critical need for a skilled and careful scholar of African American history to write a new biography of Malcolm X that provides a fuller understanding of the religious and political transformations in the last year of his life. Indeed, the treasure trove of new materials on Malcolm X in Columbia University's Malcolm X Project and the Schomburg Center for Research in

Black Culture may provide the primary documents for the aforementioned biography.

The historical significance of Malcolm's conversion to the Nation of Islam in prison in the 1940s, and the contemporary significance of the exemplary prison work of African American Muslim imams underline the urgent need for a comprehensive study of Islam and African Americans behind bars (given the fact that one-third of black men in their twenties in the United States are currently in jail, on probation, or on parole). Dannin's work on Darul Islam's Prison Committee in New York State in the 1960s and 1970s has given scholars a head start in research on this significant topic.

Finally, Michael Gomez's brilliant research on the historical threads and connections between pre-twentieth-century communities of African-descended Muslims in the Americas and those of twentieth-century African American Muslims, in *Black Crescent: The Experience and Legacy of African Muslims in the Americas*, shines a bright light on how little we know about Islam in African American slave communities, and how crucial that knowledge is for understanding the contemporary history and transnational ramifications of Islam and African Americans.

· ·

BIBLIOGRAPHY

Abdel-Alim, Hesham Samy. "Hip Hop Islam: Hesham Samy Abdel-Alim Follows the Rise of Hip Hop as a Global Phenomenon, Paying Particular Attention to Its Connection with the Current Rise of Islam." *Al-Ahram Weekly* (2005). Http://weekly.ahram.org.eg/2005/750/feature.htm (accessed June 12, 2006).

Abdul-Ghafur, Saleemah, ed. *Living Islam Out Loud: American Muslim Women Speak*. Boston: Beacon, 2005.

Aidi, Hisham. "Let Us Be Moors: Islam, Race, and 'Connected Histories.'" *Souls: A Critical Journal of Black Politics, Culture, and Society* 7 (2005): 36–51.

Alford, Terry. *Prince among Slaves*. New York: Harcourt Brace Jovanovich, 1977.

Allen, Ernest, Jr. "The Farrakhan Speech—Toward a 'More Perfect Union': A Commingling of Constitutional Ideals and Christian Precepts." *The Black Scholar: Journal of Black Studies and Research* 25 (1995): 27–34.

———. "Religious Heterodoxy and Nationalist Tradition: The Continuing Evolution of the Nation of Islam." *The Black Scholar: Journal of Black Studies and Research* 26 (1996): 2–34.

——. "When Japan Was Champion of the Darker Races: Satokata Takahashi and the Development of Our Own, 1933–1942." *The Black Scholar: Journal of Black Studies and Research* 24 (1994): 23–46.

Ansari, Zafar Ishaq. "Aspects of Black Muslim Theology." *Studia Islamica* 53 (1981): 137–76.

——. "W. D. Mohammad: The Making of a 'Black Muslim' Leader (1933–1961)." *American Journal of Islamic Social Sciences* 2 (1985): 245–62.

Austin, Allan D. *African Muslims in Antebellum America: A Sourcebook.* New York: Garland, 1984.

——. "'There Are Good Men in America, but All Are Very Ignorant of Africa'—and Its Muslims." *African Muslims in Antebellum America: Transatlantic Stories and Spiritual Struggles.* New York: Routledge, 1997.

Bagby, Ihsan. *A Portrait of Detroit Mosques: Muslim Views on Policy, Politics and Religion.* Clinton Township, Mich.: Institute for Social Policy and Understanding, 2004.

Bagby, Ihsan, Paul M. Perl, and Bryan T. Froehle. *The Mosque in America: A National Portrait; A Report from the Mosque Study Project.* Washington, D.C.: Council on American-Islamic Relations, 2001.

Baldwin, Lewis V., and Amiri YaSin Al-Hadid. *Between Cross and Crescent: Christian and Muslim Perspectives on Malcolm and Martin.* Gainesville: University Press of Florida, 2002.

Barboza, Steven. *American Jihad: Islam after Malcolm X.* New York: Doubleday, 1994.

Benyon, Erdmann D. "The Voodoo Cult among Negro Migrants in Detroit." *American Journal of Sociology* 43 (1937–38): 894–907.

Berg, Herbert. "Mythmaking in the African American Muslim Context: The Moorish Science Temple, the Nation of Islam, and the Muslim Society of America." *Journal of the American Academy of Religion* 73 (2005): 685–703.

Blyden, Edward W. "Mohammedanism and the Negro Race." *Christianity, Islam and the Negro Race.* London: Whittingham, 1887; Baltimore, Md.: Black Classic Press, 1994.

Carew, Jan R., and Malcolm X. *Ghosts in Our Blood: With Malcolm X in Africa, England, and the Caribbean.* Chicago: Lawrence Hill Books, 1994.

Carson, Claybourne. *Malcolm X: The FBI File.* New York: Carroll and Graf, 1991.

Chuck D and Yusuf Jah. *Fight the Power: Rap, Race, and Reality.* New York: Delacorte, 1997.

Clark, Steve, ed. *Malcolm X—February 1965: Final Speeches.* New York: Pathfinder, 1992.

Clarke, John Henrik, ed. *Malcolm X: The Man and His Times.* Toronto, Ontario: Collier Books, 1969.

Clegg, Claude Andrew, III. "Messenger of Allah." *An Original Man: The Life and Times of Elijah Muhammad.* New York: St. Martin's Press, 1997.

Collins, Rodnell P., and Peter A. Bailey. *Seventh Child: A Family Memoir of Malcolm X.* Secaucus, N.J.: Carol Publishing Group, 1998.

Cone, James H. *Martin and Malcolm and America: A Dream or a Nightmare.* Maryknoll, N.Y.: Orbis Books, 1991.

Cuba, Prince A., ed. *Our Mecca Is Harlem: Clarence 13X (Allah) and the Five Percent.* Hampton, Va.: UB and US Communications Systems, 1994.

Curtis, Edward E., IV. "African-American Islamization Reconsidered: Black History Narratives and Muslim Identity." *Journal of the American Academy of Religion* 73 (2005): 659–84.

———. "Wallace D. Muhammad (b. 1933), Sunni Islamic Reform, and the Continuing Problem of Particularism." *Islam in Black America: Identity, Liberation, and Difference in African-American Islamic Thought.* Albany: State University of New York Press, 2002.

D'Agostino, Melissa. "Muslim Personhood: Translation, Transnationalism, and Islamic Religious Education among Muslims in New York City." *Journal of Muslim Minority Affairs* 23 (2003): 285–94.

Dannin, Robert. "Be-bop to Brotherhood and Beyond." *Black Pilgrimage to Islam.* Oxford: Oxford University Press, 2002.

———. "Island in a Sea of Ignorance." *Black Pilgrimage to Islam.* Oxford: Oxford University Press, 2002.

Davis, Ossie. "'Our Shining Black Prince' Eulogy Delivered by Ossie Davis at the Funeral of Malcolm X, Faith Temple Church of God." *Malcolm X: The Man and His Times.* Compiled by John Henrik Clarke. Toronto, Ontario: Collier Books, 1969.

DeCaro, Louis A., Jr. "Religious Revolutionist." *On the Side of My People: A Religious Life of Malcolm X.* New York: New York University Press, 1996.

Diouf, Sylviane A. "The Muslim Community." *Servants of Allah: African Muslims Enslaved in the Americas.* New York: New York University Press, 1998.

Dyson, Michael Eric. *Making Malcolm: The Myth and Meaning of Malcolm X.* New York: Oxford University Press, 1995.

Early, Gerald, ed. *The Muhammad Ali Reader.* Hopewell, N.J.: Ecco Press, 1998.

Epps, Archie C., ed. *Malcolm X Speeches at Harvard.* New York: Morrow, 1968.

Essien-Udom, Essien Udosen. *Black Nationalism: A Search for Identity in America.* Chicago: University of Chicago Press, 1962.

Eure, Joseph D., and James G. Spady, eds. *Nation Conscious Rap.* New York: PC International Press, 1991.

Evanzz, Karl. "Introduction." *The Judas Factor: The Plot to Kill Malcolm X.* New York: Thunder's Mouth Press, 1992.

Farrakhan, Louis. *A Torchlight for America.* Chicago: FCN, 1993.

Fauset, Arthur Huff. *Black Gods of the Metropolis: Negro Religious Cults of the Urban North.* Philadelphia: University of Pennsylvania Press, 1944/1971.

Ferguson, Herman. "The Price of Freedom: Herman Ferguson." *Souls: A Critical Journal of Black Politics, Culture, and Society* 7 (2005): 84–106.

Floyd-Thomas, Juan M. "A Jihad of Words: The Evolution of African American Islam and Contemporary Hip Hop." In *Noise and Spirit: The Religious and Spiritual Sensibilities of Rap Music,* edited by Anthony B. Pinn. New York: New York University Press, 2003.

Fricke, Jim, and Charles Ahearn. *Yes Yes Y'all: The Experience Music Project Oral History of Hip-Hop's First Decade.* Cambridge, Mass.: Da Capo Press, 2002.

Friedmann, Yohanan. *Prophecy Continuous: Aspects of Ahmadi Religious Thought and its Medieval Background.* Berkeley: University of California Press, 1989.

Gardell, Mattias. *In the Name of Elijah Muhammad: Louis Farrakhan and the Nation of Islam.* Durham, N.C.: Duke University Press, 1996.

Goldman, Peter. *The Death and Life of Malcolm X.* 2nd edition. Urbana and Chicago: University of Illinois Press, 1973/1979.

Gomez, Michael A. *Black Crescent: The Experience and Legacy of African Muslims in the Americas.* New York: Cambridge University Press, 2005.

——. "Breaking Away: Noble Drew Ali and the Foundations of Contemporary Islam in African America." *Black Crescent: The Experience and Legacy of African Muslims in the Americas.* New York: Cambridge University Press, 2005.

——. "Caribbean Crescent." *Black Crescent: The Experience and Legacy of African Muslims in the Americas.* New York: Cambridge University Press, 2005.

——. *Exchanging Our Country Marks: The Transformation of African Identities in the Colonial and Antebellum South.* Chapel Hill: University of North Carolina Press, 1998.

Haddad, Yvonne Yazbeck, and Adair T. Lummis. *Islamic Values in the United States: A Comparative Study.* New York: Oxford University Press, 1987.

Haley, Alex, and Malcolm X. "Savior." *The Autobiography of Malcolm X.* New York: Ballantine, 1965.

Hauser, Thomas. *Muhammad Ali: His Life and Times.* New York: Simon & Schuster, 1991.

Herskovits, Melville J. *The Myth of the Negro Past.* New York: Harper, 1941.

Jackson, Sherman A. "Islam and Black Religion." *Islam and the Blackamerican: Looking toward the Third Resurrection.* Oxford: Oxford University Press, 2005.

Judy, Ronald A. T. *(Dis)Forming the American Canon: African-Arabic Slave Narratives and the Vernacular.* Minneapolis: University of Minnesota Press, 1993.

Kahera, Akel Ismail. "Urban Enclaves, Muslim Identity, and the Urban Mosque in America." *Journal of Muslim Minority Affairs* 22 (2002): 369–80.

Karim, Benjamin, Peter Skutches, and David Gallen. *Remembering Malcolm.* New York: Carroll & Graf, 1992.

Karim, Jamillah. "Between Immigrant Islam and Black Liberation: Young Muslims Inherit Global Muslim and African American Legacies." *The Muslim World* 95 (2005): 497–513.

Lee, Spike, with Ralph Wiley. *By Any Means Necessary: The Trials and Tribulations of the Making of Malcolm X.* New York: Hyperion, 1992.

Lincoln, C. Eric. "The American Muslim Mission in the Context of American Social History." In *The Muslim Community in North America,* edited by Earle H. Waugh, Baha Abu-Laban, and Regula B. Qureshi. Edmonton: University of Alberta Press, 1983.

——. "Reaching for the Masses." *The Black Muslims in America.* Boston: Beacon, 1961; Grand Rapids, Mich.: William B. Eerdmans, 1994.

Lomax, Louis E. *When the Word Is Given: A Report on Elijah Muhammad, Malcolm X, and the Black Muslim World.* Cleveland: World, 1963.

Madhubuti, Haki R., and Maulana Karenga. *Million Man March/Day of Absence: A Commemorative Anthology: Speeches, Commentary, Photography, Poetry, Illustrations, Documents.* Chicago: Third World Press, 1996.

Maglangbayan, Shawna. *Garvey, Lumumba, and Malcolm: Black National–Separatists.* Chicago: Third World Press, 1972.

Malcolm X. *By Any Means Necessary: Speeches, Interviews, and a Letter by Malcolm X.* Edited by George Breitman. New York: Pathfinder Press, 1970.

Mamiya, Lawrence H. "From Black Muslim to Bilalian: The Evolution of a Movement." *Journal for the Scientific Study of Religion* 21 (1982): 138–52.

———. "Minister Louis Farrakhan and the Final Call: Schism in the Muslim Movement." In *The Muslim Community in North America,* edited by Earle H. Waugh, Baha Abu-Laban, and Regula B. Qureshi. Edmonton: University of Alberta Press, 1983.

Marable, Manning. "Rediscovering Malcolm's Life: A Historian's Adventures in Living History." *Souls: A Critical Journal of Black Politics, Culture, and Society* 7 (2005): 20–35.

Marsh, Clifton E. "The Nation of Islam, 1930–1959." *The Lost Found Nation of Islam in America.* Lanham, Md.: Scarecrow Press, 1996.

McCloud, Aminah Beverly. "A Challenging Intellectual Heritage: A Look at the Social and Political Space of African-American Muslims." In *Muslims in the United States: Demography, Beliefs, Institutions,* edited by Philippa Strum and Danielle Tarantolo. Washington, D.C.: Woodrow Wilson International Center for Scholars, 2003.

———. "Women in Islam." *African American Islam.* New York: Routledge, 1995.

McCloud, Aminah, and Frederick Thaufeer al-Deen. *A Question of Faith for Muslim Inmates.* Chicago: ABC International, 1999.

Miyakawa, Felicia M. *Five Percenter Rap: God Hop's Music, Message, and Black Muslim Mission.* Bloomington: Indiana University Press, 2005.

Muhammad, Elijah. *Message to the Blackman in America.* Chicago: Muhammad Mosque of Islam no. 2, 1965.

Muhammad, Warith D. *As the Light Shineth from the East.* Chicago: WDM, 1980.

Muhammad, Zakiyyah. "Islamic Schools in the United States: Perspectives of Identity, Relevance and Governance." In *Muslims in the United States: Demography, Beliefs, Institutions,* edited by Philippa Strum and Danielle Tarantolo. Washington, D.C.: Woodrow Wilson International Center for Scholars, 2003.

Nash, Michael. "History of the Islamic Influence in Newark, New Jersey, 1913–Present: An Introductory Study." M.A. thesis, Fairleigh Dickinson University, 1999.

Nance, Susan. "Mystery of the Moorish Science Temple: Southern Blacks and American Alternative Spirituality in 1920s Chicago." *Religion and American Culture: A Journal of Interpretation* 12 (2002): 123–66.

Nimer, Mohamed. *The North American Muslim Resource Guide: Muslim Community Life in the United States and Canada.* New York: Routledge, 2002.

Nuruddin, Yusuf. "The Five Percenters: A Teenage Nation of Gods and Earths." In *Muslim Communities in North America,* edited by Yvonne Y. Haddad and Jane I. Smith. Albany: State University of New York Press, 1994.

Nyang, Sulayman S. "Continental African Muslim Immigrants in the United States: A Historical and Sociological Perspective." In *Muslims in the West: From Sojourners to Citizens,* edited by Yvonne Y. Haddad. Oxford: Oxford University Press, 2002.

———. *Islam in the United States of America*. Chicago: ABC International, 1999.

Peek, Lori A. "Reactions and Response: Muslim Students' Experiences on New York City Campuses Post 9/11." *Journal of Muslim Minority Affairs* 23 (2003): 271–83.

Perry, Bruce. *Malcolm: The Life of a Man Who Changed Black America*. Barrytown, N.Y.: Station Hill, 1991.

Pinn, Anthony B. *Varieties of African American Religious Experience*. Minneapolis: Fortress Press, 1998.

Raboteau, Albert J. "African Religions in America: Theoretical Perspectives." In *Global Dimensions of the African Diaspora*, edited by Joseph E. Harris. Washington, D.C.: Howard University Press, 1982/1993.

Rashid, Samory. "Divergent Perspectives on Islam in America." *Journal of Muslim Minority Affairs* 20 (2000): 75–90.

———. "Islamic Influence in America: Struggle, Flight, Community." *Journal of Muslim Minority Affairs* 19 (1999): 7–31.

———. "The Islamic Origins of Spanish Florida's Ft. Musa." *Journal of Muslim Minority Affairs* 21 (2001): 209–26.

Rickford, Russell J. *Betty Shabazz: A Remarkable Story of Survival and Faith before and after Malcolm X*. Naperville, Ill.: Sourcebooks, 2003.

Ross, Rosetta E. *Witnessing and Testifying: Black Women, Religion, and Civil Rights*. Minneapolis: Fortress Press, 2003.

Rouse, Carolyn Moxley. "Conversion." *Engaged Surrender: African American Women and Islam*. Berkeley: University of California Press, 2004.

Sales, William W., Jr. "The OAAU and the Politics of the Black United Front." *From Civil Rights to Black Liberation: Malcolm X and the Organization of Afro-American Unity*. Boston: South End Press, 1994.

Schmidt, Garbi. *Islam in Urban America: Sunni Muslims in Chicago*. Philadelphia: Temple University Press, 2004.

Shabazz, Ilyasah, and Kim McLarin. *Growing Up X*. New York: Ballantine, 2002.

Shouk, Ahmed I. Abu, J. O. Hunwick, and R. S. O'Fahey. "A Sudanese Missionary to the United States: Satti Majid, 'Shaykh al-Islam in North America,' and His Encounter with Noble Drew Ali, Prophet of the Moorish Science Temple Movement." *Sudanic Africa* 8 (1997): 137–91.

Singleton, Brent. "The *Ummah* Slowly Bled: A Select Bibliography of Enslaved African Muslims in the Americas and the Caribbean." *Journal of Muslim Minority Affairs* 22 (2002): 401–12.

Strickland, William, and the Malcolm X Documentary Production Team. *Malcolm X, Make It Plain*. Edited by Cheryll Greene. New York: Viking, 1994.

Strum, Philippa, and Danielle Tarantolo, eds. *Muslims in the United States: Demography, Beliefs, Institutions*. Washington, D.C.: Woodrow Wilson International Center for Scholars, 2003.

Turner, Richard Brent. "African Muslim Slaves, the Nation of Islam, and the Bible: Identity, Resistance, and Transatlantic Spiritual Struggles." In *African Americans and the Bible: Sacred Texts and Social Textures*, edited by Vincent L. Wimbush. New York: Continuum, 2000.

——. "The Ahmadiyya Mission to America: A Multi-racial Model for American Islam." *Islam in the African-American Experience*. 2nd edition, Bloomington: Indiana University Press, 2003.

——. "The Ahmadiyya Mission to Blacks in America in the 1920s." *Journal of Religious Thought* 44 (1988): 50–66.

——. "Edward Wilmot Blyden and Pan-Africanism: The Ideological Roots of Islam and Black Nationalism in the United States." *The Muslim World* 87 (1997): 169–82.

——. "Introduction to the Second Edition." *Islam in the African-American Experience*. 2nd ed. Bloomington: Indiana University Press, 1997/2003.

——. "Islam in the African-American Experience." In *The Black Studies Reader*, edited by Jacqueline Bobo, Cynthia Hudley, and Claudine Michel. New York: Routledge, 2004.

——. "Islam in the United States in the 1920s: The Quest for a New Vision in Afro-American Religion." Ph.D. dissertation, Princeton University, 1986.

——. "Mainstream Islam in the African-American Experience." *Middle East Affairs Journal* 15 (1999): 35–41.

——. "Pre-Twentieth Century Islam." In *Down by the Riverside: Readings in African American Religion*, edited by Larry G. Murphy. New York: New York University Press, 2000.

——. "What Shall We Call Him? Islam and African American Identity." *Journal of Religious Thought* 51 (1995): 1–28.

Walker, Dennis. *Islam and the Search for African-American Nationhood: Elijah Muhammad, Louis Farrakhan, and the Nation of Islam*. Atlanta: Clarity Press, 2005.

West, Cynthia S'Thembile. "Revisiting Female Activism in the 1960s: The Newark Branch Nation of Islam." *The Black Scholar: Journal of Black Studies and Research* 26 (1996): 41–48.

White, Vibert L., Jr. *Inside the Nation of Islam: A Historical and Personal Testimony by a Black Muslim*. Gainesville: University Press of Florida, 2001.

Wilson, Peter Lamborn. *Sacred Drift: Essays on the Margins of Islam*. San Francisco: City Lights Books, 1993.

Wolfenstein, E. Victor. *The Victims of Democracy: Malcolm X and the Black Revolution*. Berkeley: University of California Press, 1981.

Wood, Joe, ed. *Malcolm X in Our Own Image*. New York: St. Martin's Press, 1992.

CHRONOLOGY

1492   The first Muslims arrive in the Americas on Christopher Columbus's voyage.

1859   The death of Bilali Mohammed, the leader of a vibrant community of West African Muslim slaves in Sapelo Island, Georgia, marks the end of the era of West African Muslim slaves in the United States.

1887   Edward Wilmot Blyden's *Christianity, Islam, and the Negro Race* (Blyden, 1887/1994) is the first book to make the case for Islam as the iconic religion of Pan-African thought.

1913   Noble Drew Ali establishes the Moorish Science Temple of America, the first mass-based Islamic community in the United States.

1920   Mufti Muhammad Sadiq, Indian missionary for the Ahimadiyya Movement in Islam, arrives in the United States and establishes a mission for African Americans in Chicago.

1924   Shaykh Daoud Ahmed Faisal establishes the Islamic Mission to America in New York City, one of the first Sunni communities to focus on missionary work among African Americans.

1930   W. D. Fard Muhammad founds Allah's Temple of Islam (later called the Nation of Islam) in Detroit, Michigan.

1934   Elijah Muhammad becomes the leader of the Nation of Islam, and his leadership continues until 1975.

1936   Imam Wali Akram establishes the First Cleveland Mosque, one of the first African American Sunni communities in the United States.

1959   The television documentary "The Hate That Hate Produced" introduces the Nation of Islam, Elijah Muhammad, and Malcolm X to the American public.

1963   African American Sunni Muslims found Yasin Mosque in Brownsville, Brooklyn, marking the beginning of Darul Islam—one of the most influential African American orthodox communities.

1964   Malcolm X makes the Hajj to Mecca, Saudi Arabia, converts to Sunni Islam, and soon after establishes the Muslim Mosque, Inc., and the Organization of Afro-American Unity in Harlem.

1965   Malcolm X is assassinated in the Audubon Ballroom in Harlem on February 21.

1975   The Honorable Elijah Muhammad dies, and his son Warith Deen Muhammad begins the Nation of Islam's transition to Sunni Islam.

1978   Louis Farrakhan leaves Warith Deen Muhammad's organization and revives the Nation of Islam.

1995   The Million Man March, led by Nation of Islam leader Louis Farrakhan in Washington D.C., is the largest African American political gathering in American history.

2001   Terrorist attacks in New York City, Washington, D.C., and Shanksville, Pennsylvania, on September 11 kill more than three thousand people and result in the American Patriot Act that enables the detention and racial profiling of Arab and Muslim Americans and Muslim immigrants.

2003   Imam Warith Deen Muhammad resigns as the leader of the American Society of Muslims and establishes his organization The Mosque Cares.

GLOSSARY

Darul Islam. Darul Islam, which means "House of Peace," was established as an African American Sunni community by Rijab Mahmud and Abdul Karim in Brownsville, Brooklyn, in

1963. Darul Islam initially excluded immigrant Muslims (from its midst) in order to meet the particular spiritual and cultural needs of black Americans in mainstream Islam. With branches in numerous American cities and the establishment of one of the first Muslim prison programs in Green Haven State Prison in New York, Darul Islam is one of the most influential African American Sunni communities in the United States.

Islamic Mission to America. In 1924 Shaykh Daoud Ahmed Faisal established the Islamic Mission to America in New York City, which was eventually called the State Street Mosque. Daoud was born in Morocco and emigrated to the United States from Trinidad. From the 1920s to 1960s he and his wife, "Mother" Sayeda Khadija, led this vibrant Sunni community, which included African American Muslims, Arab immigrants, and Muslim sailors from Somalia, Madagascar, and Yemen. Daoud taught African American Sunni Muslims to change their spirituality and customs to connect black Americans to Islamic revivalism in Asia and Africa.

About the Authors

Howard Dodson is Chief of the Schomburg Center for Research in Black Culture of the New York Public Library. A specialist in African- American history and a noted lecturer, educator, and consultant, he has taught extensively around the country, at institutions including Emory University, Shaw University, and Columbia University. He is a former consultant in the Office of the Chairman of the NEH, served as the executive director of the Institute of the Black World, and worked in the Peace Corps. He has also been a consultant for the Congressional Black Caucus, Atlanta University; the Library of Congress; and the U.S. Department of Education.

Michael A. Gomez (Ph.D., University of Chicago, 1985) is Professor of History and Middle Eastern Studies at New York University. His research projects include African Muslims in the Americas, African repatriation, illegal slave trade to North America, and conversion in the Islamic, Christian, and Judaic traditions. He has been involved with the launching of a new academic organization, the Association for the Study of the Worldwide African Diaspora (ASWAD) and has published extensively. *Exchanging Our Country Marks: The Transformation of African Identities in the Colonial and Antebellum South* was published in 1998 by the University of North Carolina

Press, and *Pragmatism in the Age of Jihad: The Pre-colonial State of Bundu* was published in 1992 by Cambridge University Press.

Barbara Krauthamer is an Assistant Professor of History at New York University. Her primary research interests include slavery and the transition to freedom, and African American women's labor and political activism. Her current work focuses on Black/Indian relations in the nineteenth-century United States. She has published a number of articles on slavery and emancipation in the Choctaw and Chickasaw nations, black women in the Creek nation, and runaway slaves in the southeast. She is currently completing a book manuscript that examines the history of African Americans' slavery, emancipation, and struggles for citizenship in the Choctaw and Chickasaw nations. It explores the makings and meanings of race and citizenship within these Indian nations and also in the United States in the second half of the nineteenth century, an era in which federal efforts to establish Black people's freedom coincided with policies to erode Indian peoples' tribal autonomy and land claims.

Agustín Laó-Montes teaches in the sociology department of the University of Massachusetts at Amherst, and is affiliated with its Center for Latino/American and Caribbean Studies, and with the Afro-American Studies Department. He co-edited the book *Mambo Montage: The Latinization of New York* and is completing a manuscript titled "Afro-Latin@s: Black Cultures and Racial Politics in the Americas." His new co-edited book "Techno-Futuros: Critical Interventions in Latino Studies" will be published next spring. He has published articles in fields such as world-historical sociology, cultural studies, political sociology, decolonial critique, American studies, Latino/American studies, and African Diaspora studies.

Paul E. Lovejoy is Distinguished Research Professor in the Department of History, York University, Toronto, and holds the Canada Research Chair in African Diaspora History. He received his Ph.D. from the University of Wisconsin in 1973, and has conducted extensive research in West Africa, the Caribbean, North America, and Latin America. He has published more than twenty books and 120 articles and papers on African history and the African Diaspora, including *Transformations in Slavery: A History of Slavery in Africa* (1983), which was awarded the Certificate of Merit by the Social Sciences Federation of Canada; and with J. S. Hogendorn, *Slow Death for Slavery: The Course of Abolition in Northern Nigeria, 1897–1935* (1993), which was awarded the Howard K. Ferguson Prize by the Canadian Historical Association. He has edited or coedited several books on ethnicity and the African Diaspora, and has been a member of the International Scientific Committee of the UNESCO "Slave Route" Project, Secteur du Culture. Currently he is Director of the Harriet Tubman Resource Centre on the African Diaspora (www.yorku.ca/nhp). He is also a Fellow of the Royal Society of Canada and Research Professor at the Wilberforce Institute for the Study of Slavery and Emancipation, University of Hull, U.K. He is on the editorial boards of *Slavery and Abolition* and *Atlantic Studies*, and is coeditor of *African Economic History*. He is currently compiling a biographical database of enslaved Africans and their descendants.

Colin A. Palmer is Managing Editor of the Schomburg Studies on the Black Experience Series and Dodge Professor of History at Princeton University. His interests include African-American Studies, the African Diaspora, Colonial Latin America, and the Caribbean. He is the author of a number of books on slavery.

Richard Brent Turner (Ph.D., Religion, Princeton University) is Associate Professor in the Department of Religious Studies and Coordinator of the African American Studies Program at the University of Iowa. Professor Turner's publications include *Islam in the African-American Experience* (Indiana University Press, 1997/2003) and articles published in *The Muslim World, Middle East Affairs Journal, Religion Today*, the *Journal of Haitian Studies*, the *International Institute for the Study of Islam in the Modern World Newsletter, The Black Perspective in Music*, and the *Journal of Religious Thought*.